LEW FREEDMAN

THE INDIANAPOLIS 500

A CENTURY OF HIGH SPEED RACING

BLUE RIVER PRESS
Indianapolis, Indiana

The Indianapolis 500: A Century of High Speed Racing

Published by Blue River Press
Indianapolis, Indiana
www.brpressbooks.com

Distributed by Cardinal Publishers Group
Tom Doherty Company, Inc.
www.cardinalpub.com

ISBN: 978-1-68157-016-7
Publication Date: May 2016

Author: Lew Freedman
Editor: Morgan Sears
Book Design: Dave Reed
Cover Design: Phillip Velikan
Cover Photo: Courtesy of the Indianapolis Motor Speedway
Interior Photos: Courtesy of the Indianapolis Motor Speedway unless otherwise noted
Race Car Illustrations: Ian Friday & James Keuning via www.thenounproject.com

Contents

The Indianapolis 500:
A Century of High Speed Racing

Introduction

The first Indianapolis 500 took place in 1911 when the average Joe in the United States did not even own a car for private transportation, or at least one that had an enclosed body and could take him very far.

Compared to the cars on the road these days, passenger cars moved at the speed of golf carts, so right from the beginning, just being able to watch a race car speed around an oval at more than ninety mph was breathtaking.

Initially construction of the Indianapolis Motor Speedway was not aimed at auto racing, but automobile development. Indianapolis was vying to become the nation's motor vehicle center, competing against Detroit for the soul of the industry. Detroit had Henry Ford. Indianapolis wanted to lure manufacturers with a splendiferous testing facility.

The world's most famous automobile race was begun as a tenant for the Speedway, which opened its doors in 1909 and successfully attracted crowds well into the thousands for motorcycle racing and other events.

It was not long before the track's reason for being changed from catering to the fledgling auto industry to catering to the agog spectator so enthralled with speed in the beginning he didn't care who won the race as long as everybody kept adding mph to their maximum capacity.

The Speedway itself was a showplace from the start and it took almost no time before the Indianapolis 500 race added more cache to its fundamental reason for being. From its inception – and its reputation only grown and enhanced – the Indy 500 was the longest, most prestigious, most popular and most exciting automobile race in the world.

This new gravel-and-tar track built for $250,000 on 328 acres of what had been farmland six miles west of the city at the (now-famous address) corner of 16th Street and Georgetown Road lured fans fascinated by speed. Man has always been attracted to the notion of who and what could go the fastest. Whether the challenge was on foot, on water, or on horseback, there was always a curiosity about head-to-head competition where the miles per hour were clocked.

The more sophisticated steam engine automobiles became, as they were propelled by petrol, the more the mind wondered about just what was capable to be built and what driver could pilot the fastest car.

Although the creators of the Indianapolis 500 could not know that their race would grow into an internationally renowned event and still be going strong more than a century later with ever-slicker and faster cars, they tapped into this speed gene for Memorial Day entertainment.

Carl G. Fisher and three co-owners, James Allison, Arthur Newby and Frank Wheeler, planned to build the Speedway to benefit the automotive business. They began searching for a site in 1906 and originally looked for property in French Lick, Indiana. The Indianapolis population center proved more attractive.

They were thinking big and as large as the 2.5 mile long track is they originally contemplated making the course five miles in circumference. Even after reducing the plan to three miles long, they scaled down again in order to provide more grandstand seating.

Spectators could not see the entire track at once, even with the use of binoculars. Those who visited for the first time gaped at the sheer scope of the Speedway, even when it lay dormant.

Often referred to as an example of "oval" racing, the *500* actually takes place on somewhat of a rectangular track. The listed capacity of the Indianapolis Motor Speedway is 257,325, the largest stadium in the world. However, when demand far exceeded tickets many times spectators were allowed into the infield, which was later labeled "The Snake Pit". Owners never gave out the *500*'s attendance figures, but for years the crowd was estimated at 400,000. Nearly one hundred years later there were only forty American cities with populations that large as the single-day Indy 500 attendance.

The builders did a good enough job building that Speedway that while it has been spruced up and remodeled in different ways, much of it remains intact and the track was placed on the National Historic Register list.

Despite the car that went into building the track, not eventualities were thought through. It was soon learned that there was a major flaw. The Speedway's surface was not very hospitable for racing. Drivers and mechanics perished in accidents and the track was of a terrible consistency in 1910. Fans were particularly put off that year.

To remedy the problem, drastic change was made to the surface, a change that completely transformed the image of the track before the first Indy 500 took place and has linked the Speedway to a specific nickname ever since.

Fisher and his co-owners repaved the track with 3.2 million bricks at a cost of thirteen cents apiece. Somehow the work was accomplished in only sixty-three days. That action led to the appellation "The Brickyard" as a nickname for the Speedway. That is a moniker that stuck even after most of the track was again refinished with asphalt in 1937 and repaved periodically since. In the modern era of racing only a few foot-wide section of bricks remain on the track, mostly for nostalgia purposes.

From the start, Fisher, whose own company made headlights for cars, stated his goal in building the track was more for the benefit of manufacturers as a testing ground than as an entertainment hub, but he needed to sell tickets to his races to pay the bills. Early on he was open to suggestions – the first event at the Speedway in June of 1909 was a hot-air balloon race.

The early part of the 20th century was an exciting time to be in the automobile business. Henry Ford began mass-producing vehicles at his factories with a price point that made the Model T accessible to more families than ever. Other entrepreneurs and inventors also began making cars. The cars became more efficient and gained the ability to go faster.

Specially designed race cars could always outdo the street vehicles. Whatever the speed typical of a family vehicle, the race cars could cover the same ground almost unimaginably quicker. In some ways the Indianapolis 500 was a laboratory that encouraged experimentation. Things learned in the production of these ultra-fast cars could be applied to those sold to the citizenry.

The *500* was an outgrowth of the early Motor Speedway events. As many as 40,000 people (just 15,000 of them paying customers) turned out for races, but fans seemed to grow bored by the activity and so attendance declined. After the disastrous 1910 season, the track operators huddled and decided to go with a one-race program, a single, signature event. A twenty-four hour race was considered. This was years before the famous

24 Hours of Le Mans was established. Thought was also given to staging a one thousand mile race. Organizers settled on five hundred miles as the best distance to promote. Once the number was committed to that never changed.

The Indianapolis 500 has always been linked to Memorial Day. It has either been conducted on the day of the holiday itself or the weekend of it. Track owners Fisher, Wheeler, Newby and Allison compared the fan turnouts of 1910 racing on Memorial Day, July 4 and Labor Day. Memorial Day was the clear winner. The tradition of when the Indy 500 was scheduled was that simple.

Fisher's ambition for the new race was enunciated firmly when the track introduced its new long race in 1911.

"We're talking about the greatest automobile race ever put on anywhere on the face of the earth," he said. "Everything connected with it is going to have to be bigger and better than ever before – or we'll miss the boat."

The debut race took place on May 30, 1911 and there was enough curiosity that forty cars and drivers were entered. One driver was Ray Harroun, who won the 1910 Memorial Day race at the track before 60,000 and then retired for good. He had already given up driving after the 1910 races. Only the first Indy 500 intrigued him.

While some racers had competed on the track before nobody had actual Indy 500 experience and charts from those days list the entire field as rookies.

From 1911 to 1916, the new race was officially called "International 500 Mile Sweepstakes Race." But from the beginning, people more commonly referred to it as the Indianapolis 500, the Indy 500, or just the *500*.

The 100th anniversary of the Indianapolis Motor Speedway was celebrated in 2009. The 100th anniversary of the first Indianapolis 500 was celebrated in 2011. However, despite being more than a century old there had not been a hundred Indianapolis 500 races contested. That is because there was no racing during United States' participation in the two world wars.

Gasoline was at low supply or rationed during the two conflicts, so the race was skipped in 1917 and 1918, 1942, 1943, 1944 and 1945. After each period the race came back stronger in public consciousness.

Along the way, over one hundred years of racing, numerous traditions took hold, from the one hundred mph and two hundred mph barriers being broken, to the winner drinking milk and kissing the bricks.

Drivers entered from all over the world and reputations were established as oftentimes upwards of 400,000 spectators gathered to listen to the roar of the engines and to view the fastest cars in the world. The race became both the drivers and manufacturers' favorite place to be seen in the auto racing world.

"Indy is where everything happens," said three-time winner Bobby Unser. "It's the trigger for automobile racing. It spurs midgets and dirt cars and modifieds and everyone dreams of coming to Indy. It was so important it took all month to do it."

Unser was right. Indy morphed from being a one-day extravaganza into a month-long show of practice and qualifying, monopolizing attention with speed on display almost every day of May.

Speed made for glamour and danger contributed to the atmosphere. Although nobody wanted to see drivers killed or seriously injured, for many years there was a sort of ghoulish fascination with watching cars crash and burst into flame. Fatalities were a cost of doing business at the Indianapolis 500 and answers on how to make the race safer were elusive for decades. It took a long time, but those problems were virtually solved as well.

Eventually, the Indianapolis 500 became the most famous motorsport competition in the world, far outgrowing its simple Midwestern United States roots. The action riveted hundreds of thousands in person and millions more on television. The Indy 500 transcended disciplines of auto racing and was viewed as the most prestigious race of all to win.

The race captivated racers. They grew up on the lore of the Motor Speedway and the Indy 500 and imagined themselves behind the wheel some Memorial Day.

"I always dreamt that one day I would have the joy of participating in an Indy 500 race, on that wonderful oval track full of tradition, and in its centennial history (which) had some of the best drivers in the world," said Brazilian Helio Castroneves, a three-time champion.

Castroneves was just echoing what Unser said and so many other drivers have recognized through the years.

Fisher's aim from the start was to make the Indianapolis 500 so grand, so exciting that it would live up to the claim of being "The Greatest Spectacle In Racing."

And that is exactly what the Indy 500 became.

The Indianapolis Motor Speedway Hall of Fame.

The Beginnings

1911-1919

The Indianapolis 500 made its debut in 1911, two years after the Indianapolis Speedway was built. The first race was won by a mechanic named Ray Harroun. For his accomplishment, Harroun, and the car he drove, a Marmon Wasp, gained everlasting fame in Indy 500 lore. The winning speed was just over seventy-four mph for the five hundred miles. It was Harroun's only 500 race.

The Indianapolis 500 was quickly morphing into the most famous automobile race in the world and spent the next several years getting itself established. Already it appealed to foreign drivers who crossed the Atlantic Ocean to participate.

The first crisis the Indy 500 face was a shuttered Speedway as the United States participated in World War II and thus no race was held in 1917 nor in 1918.

1911

The grand experiment began on May 30, Memorial Day 1911, with forty of the speediest cars in the universe lined up at the Indianapolis 500 starting line inside the Indianapolis Motor Speedway.

Unlike the modern car, the entries were designed to carry a mechanic along with the driver, so in case of breakdown the man aboard could fix breakage and help the driver resume the race. He also yelled into the driver's ear when traffic was approaching and kept his eye on the oil pressure. This was the pit crew of the time.

Only Ray Harroun's job was as a mechanic for the Marmon Motor Company and he felt he could handle the duties alone. His vehicle was a Marmon Wasp, a yellow, boxy car and it was decorated with the number 32. The car lives on in the Indianapolis Motor Speedway Hall of Fame Museum, spiffy enough that it appears to be ready to take a lap on short notice.

Memorial Day began as a holiday to honor deceased servicemen after the Civil War and was called Decoration Day. It is not precisely clear where the holiday formally originated, but in 1966 the federal government recognized Waterloo, New York as the first community of Memorial Day based on its May 5, 1866 observance. More officially, on May 30, 1868, General James Garfield gave a speech at Arlington National Cemetery and 20,000 graves were decorated with flowers.

Decoration Day gradually morphed into Memorial Day and gained wider attention after World War I.

Ever since 1911, with the birth of the Indianapolis 500, the race has always been associated with Memorial Day.

In a century of racing it has rained numerous times on the day of the race, but for the first one Speedway owners invested $10,000 for $100,000 worth of rain-out insurance coverage. They couldn't afford such an interruption. They lucked out with clear enough weather, anyway.

Instead of transporting a mechanic, Harroun affixed a rear-view mirror to his car to aid his vision. In automobile racing lore this is said to be the first rear-view mirror attached to any car in history, but there are indications some street vehicles had them as early as 1908.

Ray Harroun was the first Indianapolis 500 winner in the inaugural 1911 race.

The announcement of the creation of the Indianapolis 500 provoked considerable excitement in the auto racing world. One reason was the purse offering of $27,550. No race before that had put so much money up as a prize. Forty-six cars sought entry, but two did not show up and four other teams did not qualify in pre-race practice competition leading up to the end of May. The drivers were required to complete laps at minimum speeds of eighty-eight mph or to hit seventy-five mph in a quarter of a mile.

In the future, spots in the starting grid were determined by speeds recorded in qualifying, but in this first race the order was set based on the received date of entry paperwork. Cars were lined up five to a row, though the eventual system called for three cars in each of the eleven rows.

A red flag was dropped to start the race and from the beginning racing in the Indianapolis 500 was risky business. Mechanic Sam Dickson was killed when his driver Arthur Grenier hit the famously unforgiving track wall on the twelfth lap.

The Marmon team's strategy was to drive seventy-five mph at all times, believing steady going would help prevent the car engine from burning up. Harroun was the main driver, but each team also had a relief driver. While Harroun is credited with the victory in the inaugural *500*, co-driver Cyrus Patschke took a turn steering for thirty-five of the two hundred laps. The Marmon Wasp led the race for eighty-eight laps .

The Wasp's average winning speed was 74.602 mph. A total of fourteen of the forty cars broke down and others paused frequently to change flat tires. Just twelve cars completed the full two hundered laps with another fourteen still running, but flagged to a halt at the end with the best of those completing 197 laps.

Fans, who had been wooed by the scope of the race, turned out 80,000 strong, proving immediately that the Motor Speedway was to something.

It took the Marmon Wasp under Harroun's and Patschke's guidance six hours, forty-two minutes and eight seconds to complete the five hundred miles. The first-place prize was $14,250.

The second-place finisher was Ralph Mulford, who finished one minute and forty-three seconds behind. It was said that he protested Harroun's ride because he did not carry a mechanic, but other historical reviews show that Mulford did not do so.

Harroun put his company on the map and promptly retired from racing for a second year in a row.

1912

Rather than learning that riding mechanics were not necessary, in 1912, race officials made them a requirement. However, they also upped the prize money to $50,000, nearly doubling what had already been a world-record purse in 1911.

This time there were twenty-five cars at the starting line. The fastest practice time was 88.45 mph by driver David L. Bruce-Brown.

For the most part, the 1912 event was dominated by Ralph DePalma. DePalma was born in Italy in 1882 and his family migrated to the United States the next year. In the earliest days of auto racing in the U.S. he was a constant championship figure. DePalma won races on dirt tracks and paved ones in all kinds of cars.

DePalma had even raced bicycles and motorcyles. He won national championships in cars wherever he traveled during the first decade of the 20th century and seemed destined to capture the 1912 Indy 500.

So swift that he led 196 of the two hundred laps, DePalma's strength was never in doubt. Nearing the end of the 500 his car led second place by an astonishing eleven minutes and five-and-a-half laps. If ever a car was expected to simply cruise to the finish line it was DePalma's.

Only the unthinkable occurred. A connecting rod broke on the 197th lap. His Mercedes engine began misfiring and as the car rolled on it slowed and slowed. On the 199th lap it came to a halt. DePalma and his companion mechanic Rupert Jeffkins jumped out of the car and as the crowd of 80,000 cheered their gumption, began pushing the car towards the finish line.

Joe Dawson, who had been a distant second, finally overtook DePalma. Dismayingly, car after car shot by under engine power as the twosome sought to bring home their car under human power. Dawson was just twenty-two and he held the record for youngest winner until 1952.

Ultimately, DePalma placed eleventh and was credited with just the 198 laps. Under the rules only the top ten received prize money and only those completing all two hundred laps were eligible. DePalma was out of luck in several ways, although his efforts were greatly admired.

Dawson raced in the first 500, placing fifth, and also ran the race a third time in 1913 when he crashed on the twenty-fifth lap. He retired after that accident. In 2012, ninety-nine years later, an Indy 500 driver gained victory by leading fewer laps than Dawson. The 196 laps led by DePalma set an all-time record for the most laps led without winning the race.

1913

The fastest qualifying time for the 1913 race was clocked by Jack Tower at 88.230 mph as neither the swiftest practice times nor the average finishing time for the five hundred miles changed much over the first few years of Indy 500.

Tower was knocked out of the race when he upended on the 51st lap and broke his leg, and his mechanic, Lee Dunning broke three ribs.

Consistent with Carl Fisher's vision, and a payout of $20,000 for first place, Europeans were attracted to the Indianapolis 500 in numbers for the first time. A half-dozen sought entry in what became a twenty-seven car field.

The winner was a Frenchman named Jules Goux driving a Peugot who led 138 laps and whose winning average time of 75.933 mph did not much differ from Harroun's. Goux's father was the Peugot factory supervisor. The victory made Goux $21,165 and the first non-American winner of the *500*, although he had been challenged for a chunk of the day by first-time racer Bob Evans, whose car blew out.

Goux's car featured a dual cylinder overhead camshaft engine, which was a revolutionary development that became a prototype for other Indy cars for years. Although Spencer Wishart took second, he was a gargantuan thirteen minutes behind Goux. While driving and in his pit stops, Goux and his crew partook of their country's best-known beverage, inhaling bottles of champagne. This could be said to give early meaning to drinking and driving.

Not many eyes were on Wishart as he crossed the finish line because third placer Charlie Merz was coming on strong, about twenty-six minutes back, but driving with his car on fire. Merz was dead-set on taking third and the $5,165 paycheck accompanying it, so he did not bother to brake to put the fire out after it flared on the 199th lap.

Instead, riding mechanic Harry Martin crawled onto the hood of the car and sought to beat back the flames while also releasing straps that held the hood cover on. As crazy and risky as the scene was, they made it to the end without injury.

1914

Qualifying speeds jumped a bit in 1914 with Jules Goux returning and averaging 98.130 mph. He led a contingent of Frenchmen no doubt inspired by his 1913 triumph who crossed the Atlantic Ocean to test the track at the Indianapolis Motor Speedway.

Although Goux was on hand to defend his crown, he did not even post the fastest qualifying time. That honor went to Georges Boillet, another French driver, whose top speed was 99.860 mph, so close to the one hundred mph barrier.

French drivers owned the day. Rene Thomas won, Goux placed fourth, and other Frenchmen took second, third, sixth, fourteenth, fifteenth, and 29th.

Thomas' average speed for the 500 miles was 82.4 mph, a new record, and there was plenty of reason for the visitors to share champagne.

The most notable American performance was turned in by Barney Oldfield, who became the best known U.S. racer of the first two decades of the 20th century. Oldfield took fifth, but he already had a reputation. At the Indiana State Fairgrounds in 1903 he became the first driver to steer a car at 60 mph. Famous for his driving during his lifetime, Oldfield was also safety conscious and is said to be the first driver to wear a harness in his race cars.

Boilett made it through 141 laps, but his car broke down and he did not finish. One racer who did, placing tenth, was Eddie Rickenbacker. That was to become the least of his life's achievements, including later on purchasing the Indianapolis Motor Speedway.

1915

It took a few years, but Ralph DePalma made up for his heartbreak of 1912. He at last became an Indianapolis 500 champion in 1915, leading 132 laps after qualifying at 98.580 mph.

By then, World War I was underway in Europe and the top French drivers were otherwise occupied.

During the intervening years DePalma had been dropped by his sponsoring car company, which gave his ride to Barney Oldfield. But driving a Mercedes he won the 1914 U.S. national driving championship. He also bested Oldfield, who had a faster car. DePalma drove a Mercedes to his 1915 Indy 500 win.

Oldfield was not in that race, but Rickenbacker was back, even if a thrown rod ejected him from the race after 103 laps. Ralph's brother John DePalma raced, finishing twenty-first. Finishing just ahead of him was a man who bore one of the most famous names in the automobile world over the rest of the century – Louis Chevrolet.

Chevrolet was of French descent, but from Switzerland. He co-founded the Chevrolet Motor Company in 1911 which still builds street cars for the public. In 1916 Louis teamed with brothers Gaston, also an Indy car racer, and Arthur to start the Frontenac Motor Corporation, which specialized in manufacturing race cars.

1916

For the only time in the history of the Indianapolis Memorial Day race, the distance was set for less than five hundred miles. The one-year fiddling around by management called for a three hundred mile race because operators thought it might appeal more to spectators. As proof that it probably did not is the fact that the altered distance was never tried again.

There were just 120 laps scheduled instead of the standard two hundred. Also, only twenty-one cars entered in 1916, the fewest ever. There was a very limited contingent from Europe.

Eddie Rickenbacker went after the early lead, but his car seized up and knocked him out of the race after nine laps. That year Rickenbacker and another racer named Pete Henderson drove their cars while wearing steel helmets of the type construction workers used for added protection instead of the normal leather helmet variety.

Barney Oldfield was back and finished fifth, but the winner was Dario Resta, who was runner-up to DePalma in 1915.

Resta was born in Italy, but raced out of England. His nickname was "Dolly." During the early part of the 20th century he and partners competed in a series of events over different distances for time, setting new speed marks as engines became more powerful. He came to the United States for the first time in 1915 and he won the U.S. national championships in 1916, the same year he won the *500*.

There was little auto racing during World War I and Resta was mostly inactive. He returned to the sport in the early 1920s and was killed at age forty-two while trying to set a land speed record at the Brooklands in England. That was the same place where Resta had won the first race ever contested on the course.

1917-1918

The United States entered World War I in 1917 and was in it to the end when an Armistice was declared in November 1918.

Indianapolis Motor Speedway owners voluntarily suspended racing. The track was shuttered for drivers, but it played a role in the U.S. war effort, serving as a landing strip for planes shuttling between air bases in Dayton, Ohio and Rantoul, Illinois.

1919

The Indianapolis 500 was back in business in 1919 after a two-year hiatus because of World War I.

For the first time the field was set for thirty-three cars, which has remained the standard. The set-up is eleven rows of three cars each. The rule requiring riding mechanics remained in place. During the time off some conversation took place about the possibility of expanding the race to a thousand miles in length and to moving it to July 4. In the end neither of those changes was adopted.

A key factor in retaining the May 30, Memorial Day running stemmed from the casualties of World War I. The so-called war to end all wars had just concluded and mourning the losses was still fresh. However, after Speedway manager T.E. "Pop" Myers, a fixture at the track for forty years, announced the old date as a keeper, a minor change was made.

In deference to the loss of so many lives, track management chose to run the race two days earlier than usually scheduled so as not to interfere with the meaning of the holiday.

The United States suffered more than 116,000 military deaths during the war, which was less than the other powers because it had been a latecomer to the conflict, but still of serious magnitude.

It was a rainy month of May and the weather interfered with practice and qualifying. While days were washed out some official dates were added to give cars enough time on the track. This was important because there were nineteen rookie drivers amongst the thirty-three entries.

For that year only the Indianapolis 500 was called the Liberty Sweepstakes. That was also connected to the cessation of hostilities in World War I.

On the Tuesday before the race, Rene Thomas, back at Indianapolis after a break of a few years, qualified the fastest, and to that date, the fastest of all time with a speed of 104.7 mph. As late as the first week in May driver Howard "Howdy" Wilcox was haunting the track looking for a race ride. He got one and qualified second for the day at one hundred mph even.

The next day five others topped one hundred mph, with Louis Chevrolet leading the way at 103.1 mph. Also over one hundred were Louis Wagner, Joe Boyer, Ralph Mulford, who had been a steady competitor since the first race, and Gaston Chevrolet. Nobody hit triple digits on the third day of qualifying.

Fourteen drivers completed the two hundred laps and it was Wilcox in front at the end, besting Eddie Hearne in second and former champ Jules Goux in third. Thomas placed eleventh.

Wilcox was a local, from suburban Crawfordsville, Indiana, and he had six Indy 500s under his belt by the time he claimed victory. Wilcox competed in the first Indianapolis race and every one through 1916 when the race took time off. Wilcox ran four more times, every year through 1923, after his win, but never finished higher than seventeenth again. In all he raced at the Brickyard eleven times.

Wilcox died at age thirty-four in a crash during a race in Pennsylvania in September of 1923. His son, Howard Wilcox Jr., was the founder of the Little 500 bicycle race at Indiana University in 1954, a popular event still contested today.

When the race returned to the sports calendar people were referring to the garage area as Gasoline Alley. Almost concurrent with the revival of the race following the war break the long-running comic strip "Gasoline Alley" made its debut in 1918.

The Race Gains Speed and Drivers Gain Fame

1920-1929

The Indianapolis 500 resumed its stature in the racing world and with fans after World War I.

In 1920, a man whose name remains synonymous with passenger automobiles won the race – Gaston Chevrolet.

The great, early American racer Tommy Milton became the first two-time champion (1921 and 1923).

Manufacturers built swifter and swifter cars and in 1925, driver Peter DePaolo became the first champion to average triple-digit speed for the five hundred miles. DePaolo ran his car at 101.127 mph.

1920

It was a near-ugly instant replay for Ralph DePalma in the 1920 race. He was leading by two laps or five miles, on the 187th lap when his car stalled. DePalma's riding mechanic, his nephew Pete DePaulo, guessed that the car had run out of gas. He jumped out of the race car, ran to the pits, and brought back a can of gasoline.

Meanwhile, DePalma got the car moving again and DePaulo jumped back in and the chase of the new leaders was on. The result was not as demoralizing for DePalma as in 1912, but he did place fifth instead of first. Gaston Chevrolet, whose brother Louis finished eighteenth, captured the championship. Rene Thomas was second.

Gaston nearly faded unexpectedly, as well, running out of gas on lap 197. He was far enough ahead that he could refuel in the pits and hold on for the win. An astonishing aspect of Chevrolet's victory was his not needing a tire change throughout the five hundred miles.

This was only Gaston's second Indy 500 and he was running one of the family's American-built race cars. However, only months later he was killed while racing at the Beverly Hills Speedway in California at age twenty-eight.

Ralph DePalma

His given name when born in Bicarri, Italy was Raffaele, but it was Americanized to Ralph when the DePalma family moved to the United States in 1893 when he was eleven.

Ralph DePalma was one of those boys who always wanted to go faster than his feet alone could carry him. He tried bicycle racing and moved into motorcycle racing. He was twenty-seven in 1909 by the time he gravitated to automobile racing.

Whether it was dirt track racing or on asphalt, DePalma was a brilliant driver. He said – and the International Motorsports Hall of Fame backs him up – that he won more than two thousand races during a career that continued until 1936.

Some estimates put his success rate even higher, at 2,500 wins. DePalma won whatever he tried and he believed he collected $1.5 million in prize money during his career. That would be a remarkable sum for the time period.

Ernie Pyle, the legendary war correspondent who died in World War II, grew up in Indiana. He once said, "I would rather be Ralph DePalma than president."

DePalma was known as a genial man amongst drivers and to fans, but he was a fierce competitor on the track. Nothing better defined that attitude than his effort to capture the 1912 Indianapolis 500. Although it took place more than a century ago, the sight of DePalma and his auto mechanic partner pushing their broken-down vehicle towards the finish-line is one of the most memorable scenes in race history.

After leading for 196 of the two hundred laps, piling up a huge lead, DePalma was desperate to win the race. He could not push his dead car fast enough and placed eleventh. Still, it was a stirring scene, wildly applauded by the 80,000 fans at the Speedway.

When the fans provided a grand ovation DePalma, who was hurting inside, and who had only moments before worn a face of complete disappointment, smiled and waved. He was not going to win either the race or prize money, but acclaim was showered on him nonetheless and reward for a good try was all he was going to get out of this year's race.

DePalma won his coveted Indianapolis 500 title in 1915 and placed second another time. Although he competed at a time when racing was more rudimentary and there was much to be developed in machinery, DePalma somewhat resembled A.J. Foyt and Tony Stewart of the future. Both men are regarded as terrific all-around racers regardless of distance and type of cars. DePalma fit that bill.

In 1923, DePalma started a manufacturing company to build race cars and airplanes. He died of cancer at seventy-three in 1956 in California.

Gaston Chevrolet, who is buried in Indiana, did enough that season to merit the 1920 national driver's championship. In future years, Tommy Milton, the third-place finisher at Indy, was considered the champion in some quarters, but not initially, and some historians believe that Milton was mistakenly given credit.

1921

Tommy Milton did earn the Indianapolis 500 title in 1921. Once again, Ralph DePalma seemed to have the race under control, leading for 109 laps, but when a connecting rod snapped he was forced to the sidelines and could not finish.

Milton was very much a deserving winner, leading ninety laps. Born in 1893 in St. Paul, Minnesota, Milton began racing on dirt in 1914. He competed in eight Indianapolis 500 races, finishing in the top five four times. He won twice, making him the first two-time winner of the classic.

Most extraordinarily, Milton had vision in just one eye, a disability that in the future would have banned him from racing. He was blind in his right eye and had diminished sight in his left eye. Yet he somehow compensated and recorded a sterling career. He also overcame severe burns incurred during a Uniontown, Pennsylvania race in 1919 when his car exploded in flames.

Considered the greatest American driver of his time, Milton compiled an enviable record. Besides his two Indy 500 victories he routinely broke land speed records, conquered fields fifty times in board track races that were common in the early part of the 20th century, and won fifteen times in races longer than one hundred miles.

1922

Jimmy Murphy, both friend and rival of Tommy Milton, was the 1922 champion. He had a pretty easy time of it, leading 153 laps after qualifying at 100.5 mph. Milton was far back that year, forced out by car failure after forty-four laps. Harry Hartz was the runner-up after leading forty-two laps in what was basically a two-car race.

Pete DePaolo, Ralph DePalma's former riding mechanic, was now a driver and although he finished in twentieth he led three laps. The only other lap leader was Leon Duray whose axle failed him after ninety-four laps.

The distinctive aspect of Murphy's triumph was that he was the first Indy 500 winner to take the title after starting on the pole. All of his predecessors had been out-raced or suffered from mechanical failures during the race after recording their top-flight qualifying runs.

Murphy drove a Dusenberg, which could have been termed the flavor of the month since eight of the top ten finishers drove that model car.

The driver, who was born in San Francisco in 1894, won the French Grand Prix in 1921 and was a two-time American champion in 1922 and 1924. After his mother died in the San Francisco Earthquake of 1906, his father gave him to family cousins to raise.

Murphy's early experience at Indianapolis Motor Speedway was as a riding mechanic for several top drivers. He helped DePalma, DePaolo, Milton, Hartz and Eddie Rickenbacker during their races.

Like so many of his contemporaries, however, Murphy died young due to a race-track accident. He was competing on a dirt track in Syracuse, New York when a crash killed him three days after his 30th birthday.

1923

This year Tommy Milton won his second Indianapolis 500 and during qualifying he set a new speed record of 108.170 mph. Harry Hartz placed second and Jimmy Murphy took third.

In a somewhat unusual twist, though legal under the rules, past winner Howdy Wilcox sat in as a relief driver for Milton for laps 103 to 151. Milton, who as a racer normally seemed impervious to physical problems, went to the sidelines for medical attention on his hands and feet. His hands were forming blisters and his feet didn't feel right in his shoes. He added bandages and changed his footwear.

A sixteen year old spectator was killed by driver Tom Alley after his car crashed and went through a wall into the stands.

After retiring from Indy 500 competition after the 1927 race, Milton returned to the Speedway to drive the pace car before the 1936 race. In

1949 he assumed the job of chief steward and kept it until 1957.

Milton died at age sixty-eight in 1962. Several accounts said he killed himself with a gun. Some others say he died after a long illness.

1924

For the first time during an Indianapolis 500 live radio reports were filed from the track for a listening audience. They were carried on WGN and broadcast by A.J. Kaney.

In a peculiar development that seemed only natural at the time, the 1924 race had one winning car, but two winning drivers who equally shared the responsibility of completing the five hundred miles.

Given the rules in effect it seemed bound to happen that a relief driver would someday play such a big part in the results. The No. 15 Dusenberg burst off the starting line with Lora Lawrence Corum at the wheel. After driving 111 laps, he turned the car over to Joe Boyer, who ran it the rest of the way.

Even stranger, Boyer started the race in another car and led the first lap. He drove the first car through 109 laps, then turned it over to relief driver Ernie Antersburg, who then yielded to Corum and finally to Thane Houser. Houser was involved in a crash and the car's journey ended on lap 176. That car finished eighteenth and Boyer was actually given the placing on his record. So he finished both first and eighteenth when race officials declared he and Corum co-winners.

Later that same year Boyer perished at thirty-four in a fatal accident on a track in Pennsylvania. Corum never came closer than the tenth he recorded in 1933 to winning the big race again. He died at fifty in 1949.

Second place went to Earl Cooper, followed by other familiar names of the time. Jimmy Murphy took third, Harry Hartz fourth, and Pete DePaolo sixth.

Previous winners also had relief help, but they were at the wheel when the top car crossed the finish line.

1925

For the first time while getting both drivers and fans revved up for the start of the race a call came over the loudspeaker at Indianapolis Motor Speedway that approximated the routine traditional starting call of the future.

"Gentlemen, start your motors," it was said.

Eventually, that one-liner morphed into, "Gentlemen, start your engines," the popular cry that fans are so familiar with now.

The 1925 race was notable for several reasons. Pete DePaolo, who had worked his way up to the front of the car and pack after first assisting his uncle Ralph DePalma as a riding mechanic, sped his car 113.083 mph in qualifying. While that was only second-fastest as more drivers than ever before recorded one hundred mph plus clockings, it positioned him well to win the championship.

Eighteen of the twenty-two starters exceeded one hundred mph in qualifying, including leader Leon Duray at 113.196 mph. Duray placed fourth.

The most attention-getting achievement of May 30, 1925, however, was DePaolo's ability to sustain high speed for the five hundred miles. His victory represented the first time a winner averaged more than one hundred mph for the entire race. DePaolo, who led 115 of the 2.5 mile laps, posted an average speed of 101.127mph, instigating a new era at the Indianapolis Motor Speedway.

Born in 1898 DePaolo's hometown was Roseland, New Jersey. He saw his first Indy 500 in 1919 and was enraptured by the experience.

During his winning race DePaolo drove a Dusenberg. He built a large lead, but his hands began blistering. Car owner Fred Dusenberg ordered medical attention. DePaolo pulled the car over, turned the driving over to Norm Batten for twenty-one laps, and visited the infield infirmary. DePaolo had his hands bandaged, stepped back into the car on lap 127 after Batten dropped to fifth place, and drove it to victory.

Hand blisters or not, DePaolo tried to resist his driving intermission.

"My heart ached to see my baby rolling away from the pits without me," he said, "and more so when the engine sputtered as though it was dissatisfied with the change. It almost stopped as Batten was leaving the pits."

DePaolo took second in the Indy 500 in 1927 with his own manufactured car and then raced extensively overseas. His driving career ended in 1934 after two major happenings. The first occurred when he was racing in the rain near Berlin, Germany and had his vehicle throw two rods. The rods flew through the air and narrowly missed hitting Adolf Hitler, who was seated near the track. How world history would have been changed if Hitler was struck and incapacitated or killed.

Later that same year DePaolo was in a crash in Spain and spent eleven days in a coma. That convinced him to retire from driving. After he gave up driving DePaolo became a team owner and his car won the *500* in 1935. Not long after retirement DePaolo wrote a biography titled *Wall Smacker*.

Although some people think of the song "Back Home Again in Indiana'' as a much more recent innovation, DePaolo sang it at the Speedway before the 1951 Indy 500. He is the only driver to do so.

Two decades after DePaolo shepherded an Indy car to a *500* crown he became a NASCAR team owner, rather successfully pursing that aspect of motor racing for three seasons. None of his drivers won a stock-car racing title, but they finished in the top three in points three times and captured 109 races.

One of his prominent drivers in 1956 was Joe Weatherly, a fun-loving man who once drove a qualifying trial while wearing a Peter Pan costumer. Weatherly's life was cut short in a track accident in 1964 after winning two season championships in the preceding two years.

DePaolo lived to be eighty-two, passing away in 1980.

1926

At various times Frank Lockhart seemed poised to have a spectacular qualifying performance. Four-lap qualifying runs were being used to determine the placement of vehicles in the thirty-three car field and Lockhart got off to a sizzling start.

His first 2.5 mile lap was clocked at 115.488 mph, a new record, but it did not count because he did not complete the run. A tire problem on the second lap sent him back to the pits. On his next qualifying attempt Lockhart suffered a blown engine. From the high of notable speed to

Eddie Rickenbacker

The man born Edward Vernon Rickenbacker in 1890 in Columbus, Ohio, led a remarkable life.

Rickenbacker's achievements were so extraordinary, yet not everyone knows how integral he was to the Indianapolis 500 and the Indianapolis Motor Speedway because of the variety of his accomplishments.

After an upbringing in Ohio, Rickenbacker began a career as a race car driver and entered the Indy 500 four times before World War I. He picked up the nickname "Fast Eddie." Always fascinated by machines, Rickenbacker seemed to be at least as home piloting an airplane as he was driving a swift car.

"Long practice in driving a racing car at one hundred miles an hour or so gives first-class training in control and judging distances at high speed and helps tremendously in getting motor sense," he said, "which is rather the feel of your engine than the sound of it, a thing you get through your bones and nerves rather than simply your ears."

Rickenbacker became an American hero during the World War I, earning the Congressional Medal of Honor and downing twenty-six enemy planes in combat. The irony was that his parents were Swiss-German and at the same time Rickenbacker was becoming the best-known American fighter pilot, he was trying to elude prejudice. Something else Rickenbacker had to overcome was his lack of education. His formal schooling ended in seventh grade and pilots were normally college-educated.

Rickenbacker was certified as an "ace" by the U.S. military and flew three hundred combat missions, rising in rank from sergeant to captain. He won numerous other medals during the war in addition to the Medal of Honor.

Resuming his connection with automobiles, Rickenbacker founded his own motor company in 1920. He introduced the innovation of four-wheel brakes, but the company failed, going into bankruptcy in 1927. That same year Rickenbacker took charge of the Indianapolis Motor Speedway.

Although Rickenbacker worked for car manufacturers and became founder and president of Eastern Airlines for decades, first as a driver and then as track operator he was linked to the Speedway and the *500*.

Rickenbacker had grown up poor and was not wealthy enough to ante up $700,000 for the Speedway, so he used his name to gain control for investors from Detroit. These silent partners in turn allowed Rickenbacker to run things as he wished.

One of his earliest innovations at the Speedway was the installation of a golf course on the property. Half the holes were inside the track

and half outside. A reason behind what seemed to be Rickenbacker's unusual project was to make the Speedway more accessible to members of the public at other times of the year outside of May.

A difficulty that Rickenbacker faced, even if he seemingly had ultimate authority, was an inability to spend on whatever he wanted. He did not have a personal fortune. Track upkeep was a worrisome challenge and the track that was home to the fastest race was deteriorating a little bit at a time.

Before the 1933 race Rickenbacker was confronted with a driver rebellion. The health of Howdy Wilcox II was the issue. He suffered from diabetes and when a Speedway doctor proclaimed him not fit to drive the five hundred miles, his fellow drivers took up his cause.

They threatened to go on strike within the hour before the race was due to start. A tense meeting took place between Rickenbacker, other track officials, and the drivers. He laid down his own law, saying the race was going to start and if the drivers wanted to be part of it they better show up on time.

"This race is going to start in exactly five minutes," Rickenbacker said, "if there is only one car ready to run at that time and I have to drive it myself."

The race started fifteen minutes late. Wilcox did not ride. His car did, however, guided by another driver.

Once he began competing in the Indianapolis 500, and then became an ace pilot, Rickenbacker was established as one of the most famous Americans. He tried not to let that go to his head, however.

"When I was racing, I had learned that you can't set stock in public adoration or your press clippings," he said. "By the time I was twenty-six, I'd heard crowds of 100,000 scream my name, but a week later they couldn't remember who I was. You're a hero today and a bum tomorrow – hero to zero, I sometimes say."

To some degree that was disingenuous because once he won the Congressional Medal of Honor Rickenbacker never ceased being a hero.

Rickenbacker, who died at eighty-two in 1973, was selected for three different motorsports halls of fame.

That was despite his reign at the Indianapolis Motor Speedway being less-glamorous than he might have liked. Much of what affected that tenure was out of his hands, very much related to World War II.

the low of mechanical failure, the driver ended up making it into the field, but being placed twentieth on the starting line.

Lockhart was from Southern California and he first made his reputation as a sharp driver on dirt tracks. He was also successful on board tracks and he won nine American Automobile Association races. That was the sanctioning body of much racing between 1904 and 1955.

The race itself seemed as snake-bitten for drivers as a group as Lockhart was in his individual endeavors. Rain began falling and caused a delay on lap seventy-two. The goal was to wait it out and more than an hour after cars were parked racing resumed. However, the sky did not clear and rain came down harder later in the event, causing the Indianapolis 500 to be cut short at four hundred miles. This was the first time weather chopped mileage off of the usual distance.

Lockhart was a rookie in the race and he fended off many challenges from more experienced drivers, but when officials stopped the race he was leading by two laps and claimed the championship.

By this time, demonstrating a steady growth in its popularity, attendance at the Speedway for the race topped 140,000 spectators.

One thing those fans might have noticed was a new structure overlooking the track called the pagoda where the timers were headquartered. The pagoda was modeled after Japanese-style buildings. The old pagoda rose three stories off a boxy base. After the 1925 race it was purposely burned to the ground and replaced by new construction. While it did not change much in appearance it was relocated a little bit farther away from the track.

In another development concerning the Speedway, the town of Speedway was incorporated on July 14, 1926. Although sportswriters always place the dateline of Indianapolis on their stories when reporting on the *500*, and the name Indianapolis figures prominently in the race and the track, the track location is technically in Speedway, not Indiana's capital city. As of the 2010 census, the population of Speedway was 11,800.

1927

A rookie won again in 1927, this time George Souders, whose victory was noteworthy for another reason. For the first time since Ray Harroun the winner of the Indianapolis 500 was not aided by a riding mechanic or a relief driver. Souders drove the car the entire distance and won by a huge margin.

At the end Souders led second-place finisher Earl Devore by eight laps. The last time anyone had won by that much was 1913. Souders led the race for fifty-one laps in all, and easily could have found himself behind Frank Lockhart. Lockhart led for 110 laps, but was forced out of the race by a broken rod after 120 laps.

Souders, who was from nearby Lafayette, Indiana, averaged 111.551 mph for the five hundred miles.

One thing Lockhart did was overcome the qualifying blues. He grabbed the pole position with a record time of 120.10 mph.

Among the drivers finishing behind Souders was Wilbur Shaw in fourth, a man who would play a significant role at the Indianapolis Motor Speedway in later years.

1928

Between the end of the 1927 race and the start of the 1928 race the Indianapolis Motor Speedway was sold. The original partners turned over the iconic track to Eddie Rickenbacker, one-time racer and after World War I a full-time war hero.

Rickenbacker took over on November 1, 1927 and was chief operator of the track for eighteen years.

Cars were getting faster by the end of the 1920s. It seemed nearly every May a new pole record was set. In 1928 the pole was won by Leon Duray with a timing of 122.391 mph. But as had been proven many times capturing the pole did not ensure victory over the long haul.

That year the Indianapolis 500 was won by Louis Meyer. Meyer was considered a rookie driver even though he had some experience in 1927 as a relief man. Meyer, who was soon to become a big man at Indy, did not qualify very strongly, placing thirteenth. But two hundred lap stamina beat four-lap speed.

Several other drivers took a shot at Meyer and the lead with Duray actually leading the most laps with sixty-four. His car overheated, however, and he had to drop out. Jimmy Gleason led fifty-five laps, but car problems kept him from completing more than 195 laps. Tony Gulotta led for thirty-five laps, but finished tenth. Meyer led for just nineteen laps. Overall, with the lead changes, the burn-outs and the challenges, it was a crowd-enthralling race.

Louis Meyer's first of three wins in 1928. He became the first three time winner in the history of the Indianapolis 500.

Three of the four top finishers were rookies. Third place went to George Souders.

Although Meyer was not well-known to the public when he won the 1928 race, over the next few years he would become the most famous driver of his era.

One of the most humorous tales about Meyer's triumph was that he never even told his wife June that he entered the race. She was in Pennsylvania and while there stopped by a track in Reading to visit Eddie Meyer, Louis' brother. While she was at the track the announcer introduced Eddie as the brother of new Indy 500 champ Louis Meyer

1929

One of those rookies in the top four in 1928 learned his lessons well. In 1929, Ray Keech, who took fourth the previous year, won the event, averaging 114.905 mph after leading forty-six laps. He edged Meyer, who led sixty-five laps, and placed second.

Keech brought a certain kind of reputation to Indianapolis when he began racing there. On April 22, 1928, Keech set a world land-speed record by being clocked at 207.55 mph. The site of the record was Daytona Beach, which long before becoming a cornerstone site of stock-car racing, had earned fame as a place where drivers could cover considerable flat ground at high speed.

Keech was just 29 when he won Indy, but he never made it to his 30th birthday. Only sixteen days later he died during another race in Pennsylvania, killed in a crash during a two hundred mile race in Tipton.

That had not left his team and car owner much time to celebrate before they went into mourning. The owner was Maude A. Yagle, the first female owner of a championship Indianapolis 500 car. Indianapolis has for the most part been a man's domain, in the cars, in the pits, and throughout its history, with limited exceptions. After a century of racing at the Speedway, Yagle remains the only woman owner to send a car to victory.

Chugging Milk

1930-1941

Louis Meyer forever linked himself to Indianapolis 500 history in two ways. First by claiming victory in 1928, 1933 and 1936. He became the famous race's first three-time champion.

After Meyer's 1933 triumph he gulped down a glass of buttermilk in Victory Lane. This was the first time a *500* championship driver celebrated with the dairy product and eventually swigging milk became an ingrained tradition. There is more of a chance of an eclipse of the sun occurring in Indianapolis in 2016 for the 100th running of the *500* than the winner in the anniversary race not drinking milk.

Soon after Meyer accomplished the feat, Wilbur Shaw tied the three win record with driving championships in 1937, 1939 and 1940.

1930

Billy Arnold ran one of the most sensational races in Indy 500 history in 1930.

Arnold, who was in his third race, captured the pole with a time of 113.268 mph. When the race began he trailed for the first two laps and then shot to the front. Proving he had the fastest car, Arnold held the lead for the rest of the five hundred miles.

His accomplishment of leading 198 laps is the best-ever performance. Arnold won by seven minutes, seventeen seconds over second-place finisher Shorty Cantlon, who had relief help. Arnold completed the five hundred miles in less than five hours and essentially blew away the field.

Although Arnold was a solo driver he was accompanied by a riding mechanic, Spider Matlock. It seemed a star was born and that Arnold, who was just twenty-four, would be a driver to be reckoned with for years to come. However, that did not come to pass.

One of Eddie Rickenbacker's innovations took hold that year. Changes were made in rules that limited some of the speed capacity. Rickenbacker said he was trying to restore a stronger connection between the *500* and the manufacturers of street vehicles. His goal was less the pursuit of seeing cars going faster and faster than to have race cars more closely resemble cars that families or other purchasers could better relate to when they went to a dealership. From a physical standpoint, that idea never took.

1931

There was a fresh face in the winner's circle in 1931 when Louis Schneider cruised across the line ahead of the field, although for quite some time the race appeared to be an instant replay of the 1930 *500*.

Rain fell heavily before the race and it postponed the start for two hours. Once the race began Billy Arnold put the pedal to the metal and sought to reincarnate his brilliant showing of 1930.

Arnold's car was flying along, seemingly unthreatened by fellow drivers. He led for 155 laps and seemed certain to win back-to-back titles. Arnold was ahead by five laps or 12.5 miles, a margin that seemed to be insurmountable.

It might well have been if an accident had not occurred. Holding the lead on lap 162, Arnold's car incurred a broken axle. He was traveling at high speed and could not control the car. In a terrible scene, Arnold spun out in turn four, was bashed by another car catching up, and then had his car hurdle the track wall. The impact broke pieces off his car and one wheel was propelled into the street adjacent to the Speedway. In a surreal result, the wheel careened across Georgetown Road, slammed into an eleven year old boy and killed him.

The accident broke Arnold's pelvis and his riding mechanic, the same Spider Matlock from his winning year, received a broken shoulder. Arnold was averaging 116.08 mph when the calamity occurred and he finished nineteenth.

Schneider, who led for thirty-nine laps, took over and took the championship ahead of Fred Frame in second. Schneider was an Indianapolis resident and worked as a motorcycle policeman.

1932

As it turned out, Fred Frame was just tuning up for victory in 1932 with his runner-up slot in 1931.

He prevailed in one of the most episodic, adventurous, and scrappy of all Indianapolis 500 races. There were forty cars in the field and twenty-six of them were sidelined due to breakdowns, one after another suffering a broken this and a broken that.

Lou Moore had taken the pole position with a 117.363 mph qualifying run, but he was one of the non-finishers. His timing gear failed and he ended up twenty-fifth. While Frame looked good in 1931 he did not look good in qualifying with only the 27th fastest time

Frame was born in Exeter, New Hampshire in 1894, but he moved to California when he began racing cars. Before trying the Indy 500 Frame broke speed records at short distances on dirt tracks.

One of the many cars to flame out belonged to Billy Arnold. Arnold had chosen the perfect strategy in 1930 of going to the front and going hard. He followed it again in 1931 and it was working until his car broke down. Once again in 1932, Arnold was chasing an Indy win. Once again he took off and led fifty-seven laps. But as in 1931 Arnold was involved in an accident, this time on lap fifty-nine.

The crash broke riding mechanic Spider Matlock's pelvis, for the second year in a row sending him to the hospital. Arnold broke his shoulder, for the second year in a row making the acquaintances of doctors himself. That was enough for Arnold's wife, who talked him into retiring from auto racing.

Action of the bad kind disrupted car after car in the first one hundred miles. Once Arnold was ousted, Bob Carey took over and he led from laps fifty-nine to ninety-four. Then Carey crashed on the 94th lap.

Eventually, despite three late crashes that knocked out more cars, the lead fell to Frame, who was able to keep his car in one piece. One of the mishaps involved Tony Gulotta who had a tire rip off and fly into the stands.

Frame gained his only Indy title with the help of riding mechanic Jerry Houck. His average speed for the five hundred miles of 104.144 mph was a new record. Frame could well have been another casualty. His engine was constantly overheating and he made six pit stops to pour water into it.

1933

In many ways the 1933 Indianapolis 500 was 1932 to the extreme. In 1932, cars were demolished at a high rate. In 1933, as the clearest-ever evidence just how dangerous auto racing could be, there were five deaths between qualifying and the race, a stunning rate of carnage.

This was becoming an unfortunate trend. Either during the race, in practice or qualifying, one driver a year was dying at the Indianapolis Motor Speedway. May was particularly devastating this year.

Bill Denver and riding mechanic Bob Hurst were killed on the track in practice. Driver Mark Billman was killed on lap seventy-nine at turn two during the race and driver Lester Spangler and riding mechanic Monk Jordan died in a crash on lap 132 at turn one. It was a somber Memorial Day for more than one reason at the Speedway.

Of the forty-two cars entered, just fourteen were running at the end of the race. It was difficult to be in a partying mood after such a deadly stretch of disasters, but Louis Meyer was happy to earn his second Indy 500 victory.

Rather than refresh himself by gulping water at the finish-line Meyer was handed a glass of milk, actually buttermilk that year. This was the first time the winning driver downed milk after his victory and Meyer's action began a tradition that continued.

The buttermilk was a drink of choice for Meyer, but according to the American Dairy Association, a savvy Milk Foundation official saw a photograph in the next day's newspaper of Meyer imbibing and jumped in as a sponsor so the winner would always drink milk as soon as he parked.

Although there was a hiatus between 1947 and 1955 when the winner did not promptly drink milk, or pour it over his head, as has sometimes been done in celebration, the interrupted tradition resumed and has been in place for the last sixty years without a break.

1934

Mechanical failure was a dominant theme in 1934. Car attrition was remarkably high with twenty-one of the thirty-three entries sidelined before the finish line. Just twelve cars completed the 200 laps and the fastest belonged to Bill Cummings.

Cummings began entering the *500* in 1930 and this was his fifth appearance. He finished fifth as a rookie, but this drive was his best. Cummings qualified at 116.116 mph, not the fastest, but close to the front, although two cars topped 117 mph.

Cars were flaking off so frequently from minor crashes, crankshaft problems, camshaft drives, and thrown rods, that the five hundred miles was more about perseverance than winning. Cummings led fifty-seven laps, but runner-up Mauri Rose (of whom more would be heard from soon) led sixty-eight. Ninth placer Frank Brisko led sixty-nine laps.

Rose was in the hunt until near the end, finishing just over twenty-seven seconds arrears of Cummings.

Cummings competed in four more Indianapolis 500 races, but in February of 1939 he was driving a street car on an Indiana highway when he struck a guard rail. The car plunged through and landed in a creek. Cummings was hauled out of the water by good Samaritans, but he died two days later at age thirty-two.

The Offenhauser Engine Company was founded by Fred Offenhauser and working with Harry Miller, a new front-end engine began showing up in Indy cars. The engine was so efficient everyone wanted one and from the 1930s to the 1970s, cars with Offenhauser engines won the race twenty-seven times.

Between 1950 and 1960 all winners drove cars with Offenhauser engines, as did all second and third place finishers, and ten of the eleven winners of the pole did so as well.

1935

The honorary referee for the 1935 Indy 500 caused a stir with her presence. Famed aviatrix Amelia Earhart was at the Indianapolis Motor Speedway.

Kelly Petillo captured the race in a car owned by Pete DePaolo, the first to triumph as a driver and an owner. It was really only a two-car race. Rex Mays, who had taken the pole with a run of 120.736 mph, led eighty-nine laps, but experienced mechanical failure. Petillo led for 102 laps. Wilbur Shaw was second and Cummings, in his second-best finish, was third.

Louis Meyer was twelfth, the last car to complete two hundred laps.

The atmosphere was gloomy at the Speedway by late May because the track extracted a very high price. Johnny Hannon's car shot over a wall and he died from a fractured skull during practice May 21. On the same day, Stubby Stubblefield also lost control and had his car climb a wall. Stubblefield and riding mechanic Leo Whittaker were thrown from the car and died.

During the race, driver Clay Weatherly was killed in a crash at turn four. That made four deaths in one race.

Aghast over these incidents, race organizers began an indoctrination and testing program for rookies, hoping to weed out drivers too inexperienced for the challenges of driving so fast for so long.

1936

The 1936 race stood out because of the showing of Louis Meyer. Meyer became the Indianapolis 500's first three-time champion, adding this title to his victories in 1928 and 1933. He led for ninety-six laps in 1936.

Meyer continued the tradition he set in 1933 of drinking buttermilk after his victory, but this time he downed nearly the entire bottle. Today, drivers drink plain white milk, not buttermilk.

Former winner Tommy Minton lobbied race officials to make the pace car used to start the race a part of the winner's booty and Meyer was the beneficiary of this prize when the suggestion was adopted. The pace car was a Packard and after the race it belonged to Meyer.

Lawson Harris, Meyer's riding mechanic, had served in the same role in 1933 and this triumph made him the first two-time riding mechanic contributor to victory.

Even more memorable than the pace car prize being added and milk being drunk was the debut of the Indianapolis 500's new trophy.

The trophy has become one of the longest-awarded and best-known trophies in sport, perhaps second to the Stanley Cup in recognition. This is not a trophy that travels, or even comes into possession of the winner, but remains on site at the Speedway, housed in the Hall of Fame Museum.

Meyer, the proud first winner, said, "Winning the Borg-Warner Trophy is like winning an Olympic medal."

Meyer is one of the best-remembered and distinctive of the early Indianapolis 500 races because of his three driving championships, his link to drinking milk, and being the first Borg-Warner recipient.

A three-time U.S. national driving champion, Meyer lived to be ninety-one, passing away in 1995 in Searchlight, Nevada.

1937

One thing the lengthy Indianapolis 500 proved so many times was that the driver and team with the best car did not always win. Luck and stamina are required, as well as a car that can stand up to the rigors of the distance and speeds attained, and can cope with the weather.

This was the twenty-fifth Indianapolis 500, but because of the World War I blackout on racing, not the twenty-fifth annual.

A long-time habitué of the Speedway, it took nine tries for Wilbur Shaw to earn his first Indy 500 title, although he had run fourth as a rookie 1927 and came in second in 1935 and 1938. Arguably, it was simply his turn to reign. But Shaw did more than win. He ran away with the race, leading for 131 laps.

It was a great moment for the native of Shelbyville, Indiana, an Indianapolis suburb. Shaw could have been pardoned for thinking, "At last." But his prime years at the Speedway were just beginning and so was his influential role in track history.

Shaw's riding mechanic was Jigger Johnson, who had already won with Louis Schneider in 1931, making him the second riding mechanic to triumph twice.

Although Shaw was in charge for most of the day he did face a problem at the end, one that he feared might doom him. His car began leaking oil with twenty laps, or fifty miles, remaining. One crankcase was almost empty and a secondary tire with a worn tire also haunted him. Shaw had to slow his pace to make sure the car made it to the finish. Shaw and Johnson both incurred burns from the leaking oil.

These weaknesses allowed trailing cars to get back within striking distance. Ralph Hepburn ground out lap after lap to close the distance. Shaw still held on and on the last straightaway, feeling sure Hepburn would overtake him, he ceased his cautious outlook and stepped on the gas. It was just enough oomph to hold off Hepburn, who made it the closest Indy to date by finishing 2.16 seconds behind.

There was a peculiarity in qualifying. Jimmy Snyder went out near the end of the day on May 22 and scorched the track. His first of ten scheduled laps was turned in 130.492 mph, a new qualifying record. However, Snyder could not complete his ride before darkness fell. The ride was disqualified for starting line positioning, but the record stood.

1938

The 1938 running of the Indy 500 was, as had been the case in certain years, basically a two-car competition.

Jimmy Snyder led for ninety-two laps, but didn't finish the race because of mechanical woes. Floyd Roberts also led for ninety-two laps, but they were the right ones.

Roberts, from North Dakota, was in his fourth Indianapolis 500 and had finished as high as fourth in 1935.

During this race a spectator was killed due to a driver crash. Driver Emil Andres clipped the wall in turn two on lap forty-five. The car rolled over several times and began to break apart. One wheel flew a hundred feet through the air and hit a fan, killing him.

It could not only be risky to your health to race at the Indianapolis Motor Speedway, it was dangerous to sit too close to the action because the unfathomable occurred all-too-often.

The Borg-Warner Trophy

The perpetual Borg-Warner Trophy is won by the champion of the Indianapolis 500 each year. Introduced at a pre-race banquet by Indianapolis Motor Speedway owner Eddie Rickenbacker for the 1936 race, it is one of the most esteemed trophies in sports.

The sterling silver trophy has been measured at five-feet, four inches tall. However, after being placed on a solid base it towers over the men who covet it. With more rings and bigger bases added, anyone standing next to it appears child-like in height and the trophy looms at about eight feet tall. Originally weighed at eighty pounds, the trophy has added poundage over the years. The current weight is listed at 150 pounds. While it may have once been a one-man job to lift the trophy it has become a two-person effort.

Impressive even at a distance, the cup-like trophy topped by an official waving a checkered flag, the prize is not something easily picked up and moved, but it has made it to the winner's circle in victory lane every year since 1936.

However, the trophy does not ever go far from there, its public appearances pretty much limited to activities at the track. Housed in the Hall of Fame Museum on the Speedway grounds, the Borg-Warner Trophy is not presented directly to the owner and driver of the winning vehicle each May. They are given much smaller replicas. That practice has been followed since 1988.

The name of the trophy originated with and was paid for by the Borg-Warner Automotive Company (an automobile supply firm) at a cost of $10,000. The trophy is valued at more than $1.3 million now.

Annually, following each race, the year, the name of the winner and the average speed in completing the five hundred mile course, are engraved onto the big trophy. In a distinctive touch, the face of the winning driver is etched into the silver and is raised perhaps a half-inch in bas-relief from the surface. Under the category of no-one's perfect, 1950 champion Johnnie Parsons' name was misspelled as Johnny in the engraving. No eraser could fix the problem, but years later, when the trophy was restored it was suggested that Parsons' name be corrected. In the end that plan was turned down and it was decided to leave the name just the way it was primarily as a story of trophy lore.

As the years passed, and as space came to be at a greater premium, the trophy was inching towards becoming over-crowded by 1986. Some modifications through the base were made to enable new winners to be added.

After the most recent addition was made to the trophy, it has space for winner engravings through the 2033 race.

1939

Jimmy Snyder was from Chicago, excelled at midget racing, and had a knack for brilliant qualifying driving. In 1939, the Indianapolis 500 modified its procedures, doing away with ten lap qualifying runs and replacing them with four lap runs. That has basically remained the qualifying method ever since.

It didn't matter to Snyder, who had set his previous speed record during a qualifying run that didn't actually count in toto. This time his speed was fully recognized and he set a new track record of 130.138 mph to capture the pole. An Indy 500 title, however, continued to elude him. Snyder finished second in 1939.

The winner once more, for the second time in three years, was Wilbur Shaw. He had found his groove. The contest was an intriguing battle, mostly between Shaw (fifty-one laps led), Snyder (sixty-five laps lead) and Louis Meyer (seventy-nine laps led). Meyer was going for a record fourth title at the Speedway.

However, Meyer crashed near the end of the race, on lap 197. Although he walked away from the accident at one hundred mph with only minimal physical aggravation, his car didn't roll away. Meyer's mishap ended his Indy career on a down note, but even worse was the result of another crash.

Defending champion Floyd Roberts cracked up on lap 109 after his car was struck by driver Bob Swanson. Swanson's car caught fire. Roberts' plowed into a track wall at more than one hundred mph. Roberts was dead at thirty-nine before the race even ended. A third car, driven by Chet Miller, was also involved. Debris from the disintegrating cars harmed two spectators.

A month after the race Jimmy Snyder was killed in a midget race in Cahokia, Illinois. He was thirty.

1940

May 30, 1940 was a rainy day, the Indianapolis 500 was in jeopardy because of the weather, but the thirty-three drivers began as usual.

While Wilbur Shaw became the first driver to win the *500* in consecutive years, and tied Louis Meyer for the most victories with three, it was not a typical day at the Speedway. Shaw averaged 114.277 mph, which was nothing earthshaking, but given the weather circumstances it was surprising he covered the two hundred laps at such a pace.

That is because the last fifty laps, or 125 miles, were run under caution and the drivers could not fully open the throttle. Shaw coped best. Among his prizes, besides cash and the pace car, was a refrigerator.

Although not one of the best-known drivers, Ted Horn, who finished fourth, was one of the most consistent in Indy 500 history. He was one driver who could keep his car going rather than cope with frequent breakdowns. As a teenager Horn was stopped by an officer of the law for speeding, but rather than being given a ticket he was ordered to go to a nearby race track and drive until he was weary of speed. The idea backfired because Horn learned he loved going fast and became a race-car driver.

Wilbur Shaw chugging the victory milk after his third Indy 500 win in 1940.

On this day in 1940, Horn was flagged to a stop in the rain on lap 199, one lap shy of completing the event. This was of particular interest because over nine years of racing the *500* between 1936 and 1948 Horn finished every single other lap, 1,799 out of 1,800. It was not his car that let Horn down this time, either, but the weather.

Horn had his share of driving mishaps, as all drivers do, and he had enough of them to be declared 4-F when he volunteered for U.S. military service when World War II broke out. He was rejected because of lingering physical ailments incurred while racing.

Horn won American national driving championships in 1946, 1947 and 1948, but as easy as he was on car engines there did come a time behind the wheel when an on-track accident caught up to him. Only two laps into a race at the DuQuoin State Fairgrounds Racetrack in Illinois he crashed and was killed at age thirty-eight .

1941

Track owner Eddie Rickenbacker was not at the Indianapolis Motor Speedway for the 1941 race. The daring pilot who had escaped death in World War I despite many battles, had been in a serious plane crash as a passenger in February near Atlanta. He was still recuperating and listened to the race on the radio.

Wilbur Shaw was gunning for a third straight win and a record fourth victory overall and led for 107 laps before a crash in turn four put him out of the race. Shaw lost control of the vehicle and hit a wall. The force of the impact ruptured his gas tank. The gasoline poured all over Shaw and in other circumstances would have likely ignited, perhaps causing his death. However, the fuel did not catch on fire, even though a back injury suffered in the crash prevented Shaw from quickly exiting the car.

Car owner Lou Moore, a past winner, employed Floyd Davis as his driver at the start of the race, but yanked him out of the car during a pit stop in favor of Mauri Rose. Rose steered the car to victory after taking command on lap seventy-three. The result went down in the records as a co-victory for Davis and Rose.

The duo led thirty-nine of the two hundred laps. Second placer Rex Mays led thirty-eight laps.

What no one realized at the time was that this was going to be the last Indianapolis 500 for quite some time.

On December 7, 1941, a little more than six months later, the Japanese bombed Pearl Harbor in a sneak attack and the United States plunged into World War II. At a time of international crisis, when civilians experienced gas rationing and rubber manufactured was used for the war effort, the *500* was shut down.

Without the showcase Memorial Day race, the Indianapolis Motor Speedway was also temporarily out of business. The most famous auto race of them all was cancelled in 1942, 1943, 1944 and 1945. The world's attention was on other things.

Troubled Times

1942-1949

For the second time in barely more than a quarter of a century, the Indianapolis Motor Speedway shut down because of war. There was no Indianapolis 500 in 1942, 1943, 1944, and 1945.

During the war, the Speedway fell into disrepair. Practically nobody performed maintenance. Eddie Rickenbacker, the World War I hero, saw his ownership of the Speedway become a burden because of World War II.

When the war ended he contemplated selling the increasingly valuable land to housing developers and folding the Indianapolis 500. Wilbur Shaw, now retired as a driver, became the key middleman to a new owner Tony Hulman, and took over as president of the track and shepherded the Speedway and *500* into a new era.

It was an era that spawned a third three-time winner in Mauri Rose.

1946

Back in business for the 30th running of the Indianapolis 500, the 1946 race was reawakening after the bleak war years of no racing and the decline of the Indianapolis Motor Speedway.

This was the first Indy 500 conducted on new owner Tony Hulman's watch and under president Wilbur Shaw's leadership.

Just being back in operation was a milestone considering how close to foregoing the entire enterprise former owner Eddie Rickenbacker came to keeping padlocks on the gates forever. Fresh ownership was invigorating and the mood of racing fans starved for speed embraced the excitement of the moment on May 30.

Although they could not know how deeply ingrained the custom would become, a new tradition took hold. Before the start of the race James Melton sang the tune, "Back Home Again in Indiana." Each year since the song has been performed during pre-race ceremonies.

Indianapolis Motor Speedway during World War II

The grass was overgrown. The grandstands were empty. The gigantic, 2.5 mile track was lonely.

During World War I, Carl Fisher, the lead owner of the Speedway, promptly offered the Indianapolis Motor Speedway grounds to the United States government for use for military purposes during the conflict. That resulted in the Speedway becoming an airstrip.

Current owner Eddie Rickenbacker, the hero pilot of World War I, made the same offer immediately after December 7, 1941. But this time the U.S. government had no interest in using the property.

Recognizing there would be no racing during the war, Rickenbacker was quick to shut down the Speedway. His brother Al became a caretaker, but overall the place fell into disuse. The general plant deteriorated. No money was invested in maintenance. The track was a veritable ghost town, although it was said that area children snuck into the structure to actually swim in flooded tunnels after rains.

No attention otherwise was paid to the Speedway while all eyes were on the war fronts in Europe and the South Pacific. Paint began peeling. Seats began disintegrating. Flowers actually grew between some of the famous bricks.

To all intents and purposes, the Speedway was an abandoned house left to fend for itself against snow, cold, wind, rain and extreme heat.

The track was in such a state of disrepair that the scene appalled Wilbur Shaw when he visited in 1944 in the company of some manufacturers who wished to run tire tests. He wondered about the future of a building he loved, a race he loved, and to which he owed the biggest successes of his life.

"To me the track was the world's last great speed shrine, which must be preserved at all costs," Shaw said. "I felt that all I was, or ever hoped to be, I owed to the Indianapolis 500 mile race."

Rickenbacker, who had been imbued with the same passion for the track for more than two decades, had given up on it. When the war ended Rickenbacker did not plan to resurrect the *500*, nor did he foresee the Speedway continuing as a race track. He intended to sell the property for the purpose of constructing a housing subdivision.

A disappointed Shaw then assumed his most critical role at the Speedway. He asked Rickenbacker if he would sell to buyers willing to restore the track to its racing glory and Rickenbacker agreed. Shaw then became a broker, a middle man searching for money men that could save the Speedway and wanted to keep it a speedway.

Shaw met with bankers and businessmen, car manufacturers and other wealthy prospects before he made the acquaintance of Anton "Tony" Hulman Jr., from Terre Haute, Indiana, located just seventy-seven miles from Indianapolis. Hulman's family was involved in the grocery business since 1850 and under his guidance it grew splendidly. A key ingredient in making him wealthier was the care given to promoting Clabber Girl Baking Powder and promoting it nationally.

In a famous utterance about how Hulman felt the Indianapolis 500 was integral to the Hoosier state, he said, "The Speedway has always been a part of Indiana, as the Derby is part of Kentucky. The five hundred mile race should be continued. I'd just like to be sure of sufficient income so we could make a few improvements each year and make the track something everybody can be proud of."

In November of 1945, a year after Shaw intervened, Rickenbacker closed a deal with Hulman, selling the Indianapolis Motor Speedway to a new owner for $750,000.

Once Hulman took control he put Shaw in charge as the new president of the Speedway. It was just six months until the next Memorial Day, but Hulman and Shaw pledged to have the track ready for roaring engines for a 1946 race.

The song was written by Ballard MacDonald and James F. Hanley and was published in 1917. Despite being recorded by a jazz band, it was described as a Tin Pan Alley pop song and included reference to the already-famous song "On The Banks Of The Wabash, Far Away," which was written in the 19th century.

On the track the winner was George Robson. Robson was English-born, had moved to Canada, and immigrated to the United States in 1924. He twice raced in the Indy 500 before World War II and gained his greatest renown by capturing this return to racing at the Speedway.

Although Robson demonstrated dominance, leading for 138 laps, Ralph Hepburn led forty-four laps and Mauri Rose led eight laps early before being eliminated in a crash.

Roughly thirteen weeks after his great triumph Robson was killed at age thirty-seven in a race in Atlanta.

1947

Mauri Rose's turn came in 1947. He had been lurking in the pack for years, shared co-ownership of a title, but finally won a championship outright. However, there were surprising developments near the end of the race that gave Rose the crown.

Owner Lou Moore entered more than one car. Rookie Bill Holland had qualified eighth, but was running in front after leading 143 laps. There were less than eight laps remaining in the race when teammate Rose pulled up to him. The pits flashed messages to the drivers, but they were not clearly understood.

Rose was making a play for the lead, but the inexperienced Holland thought he was a lap ahead of Rose. So when the veteran pulled even with him on the track he actually waved. Rose zoomed past and Holland realized his mistake too late and could not rebound. Holland was quite angry after the race since he had just given away the Indianapolis 500 title without a fight.

Once again there was the death of a driver during the race. Shorty Cantlon crashed and died on the 41st lap. This was Cantlon's eleventh Indy 500 and the accident that cost him his life revolved around swerving his car to avoid hitting Holland, whose car was spinning. Holland corrected his car, but Cantlon could not and died at forty-three. As a grim reminder of the crash, Cantlon's car was left in place leaning against a wall for the rest of the race, something which would never be condoned today.

Just thirty cars went to the starting line even after officials re-opened qualifying for an extra day in hopes of getting the field up to thirty-three.

1948

Compared to the early days of Indianapolis 500 racing, the cars were sleeker. The Marmon Wasp was boxy. When Mauri Rose won the race for the second year in a row (and third time overall including his shared victory) and Bill Holland took second again, he was driving a vehicle that was lower to the ground and more aerodynamic. In a way it was shaped like a slightly pudgy hot dog.

Rose joined Wilbur Shaw as only the second driver to capture the *500* twice in a row. This year he led eighty-one laps and Holland did not lead a single one, even if he duplicated his finish.

Mauri Rose featured next to the Borg-Warner Trophy after his 1948 victory.

The fourth place finisher was Ted Horn, who led seventy-four laps, and was in the last year of his nine year stretch that came in one lap shy of perfect attendance. During those nine years (after a no-finish and a sixteenth), Horn finished second, third, or fourth every single time, an unprecedented record of success.

Rose, who was born in Columbus, Ohio in 1906, was in his forties and nearing the end of his Indy career.

1949

Lou Moore's cars were the fastest ones around during this era and Mauri Rose and Bill Holland showed the world that each May. There was a twist to this race, though, that included disintegration of the partnership when it ended.

This time Holland obtained his long-sought goal and won the *500* after leading 146 of the two hundred laps. He clearly was the dominant driver that year, easing his frustration after two close calls.

As the race wound down and Holland had the victory in hand, a message was flashed from the pits to both he and Rose. The instructions were to drive carefully and cruise in. However, Rose chose to ignore it. He wanted one more win for himself. So he took a run at Holland, seeking to pass him and consign him to second place once again.

On lap 192, with Rose coming hard, his car suffered mechanical failure, throwing him out of the race. Instead of the team finishing 1-2, the Holland-Rose combination finished 1-13. An infuriated Moore fired Rose from the team immediately after the race for ignoring the game plan.

In a milestone breakthrough, the *500* was telecast from the Speedway for the first time. Some form of radio reports had been filed on the race as early as 1922, but Channel 6, WFBM-TV in Indianapolis broadcast live. The station itself was brand new. Appropriately enough, its first programming aired that day and it was a documentary about the race called "The Crucible Of Speed."

Illustrating the limited reach of television during that time period, it was estimated that viewership was about three thousand.

This new venture actually marked the birth of commercial television in Indianapolis and the station remains on the air, although its call letters changed to WRTV in 1972 after changes in ownership.

Tom Carnegie

The famous, deep-voiced Tom Carnegie was actually not named Tom Carnegie at all. He was born Carl Lee Kenegay. Kenegay grew up in Norwalk, Connecticut, but when he went into radio broadcasting his boss at the Fort Wayne, Indiana station told him the name Tom Carnegie sounded better on the air, so he adopted it.

Carnegie also adopted the Indianapolis 500 in 1946, and it could be said that the Indy 500 also adopted him. Although Carnegie was the voice of Indiana high school basketball, almost a public trust in the hoops-mad state, and had a decades-long career as a radio and television personality, he was perhaps the most known for his duties as public address announcer at the Indianapolis Motor Speedway for an astonishing sixty years.

The announcer's trademark delivery was to extend key words in his pronouncements, exaggerating selected letters. "It's a neeeeeeeww track record," Carnegie said, his emphasis giving import to the wording.

Distinctive in tone, informative in message, Carnegie had a special rapport with drivers and fans.

"He's got one of those voices that send chills down your spine," said racer Tony Stewart, an Indiana native who made his mark more in stock-car racing, but previously was an Indy 500 racer.

While some believed Carnegie came into being along with the track and had been its deliverer of news at high volume since the doors opened in 1909 that was not quite an accurate perception. Carnegie was born in 1919. He did stay around long enough that his nickname became "Voice of the Speedway."

Carnegie was a rookie announcer in 1946 and while he did possess one of those signature radio tones, a baritone of sorts, not even he could compete with the roar of the engines. The cars were powerful enough to drown him out if he chose the wrong moment to speak.

Wilbur Shaw, in his new role as an executive at the track, discovered Carnegie and sold the idea of hiring him to track owner Tony Hulman.

Carnegie was an insecure announcer for a time. The track was so enormous that he could not see all of it from the pagoda, so sometimes he hoped the words he uttered were correct. One of Carnegie's least favorite tasks, though he felt a sense of obligation, was speaking at the funerals of Indy 500 drivers, crew members or workers. He did so twenty-seven times.

His philosophy was a simple one.

"I play to the audience," he said.

In all, during his tenure, Carnegie was the PA system caller of sixty-one races. Carnegie retired in 2006 and died in 2011 at age ninety-one.

Prosperity, but Carnage

1950-1959

The nation was at peace and more than ever Americans took to the roads driving their new family automobiles in their free time.

Beginning with this decade, the legendary starting call of "Gentlemen, start your engines" was introduced to the lexicon of the *500*.

Once again the Indianapolis 500 gripped its Memorial Day slot on the sports calendar and a new generation of drivers became public figures. Tragically, several of them perished on the track in high-speed crashes that left fans depressed and dismayed even as they cheered new champions.

Bill Vukovich was the new hotshot on the track, winning the race in 1953 and 1954. However, he died in a fiery accident during the 1955 race.

In 1958, Pat O'Connor, who was from an Indianapolis suburb and was becoming a popular driver, was killed from a head injury in a fifteen car accident.

1950

Johnnie Parsons outran the other thirty-two cars and the rain to capture the 1950 Indy 500 title. The five hundred mile, two hundred lap race ended after 345 miles and 138 laps. Parsons was the only driver on the 138th lap when the race was flagged to a premature end.

In an unusual development, the Indianapolis 500 was tied to the AAA National Championship Trail race series and the first World Drivers Championship points event. This meant points scored at the Indianapolis Motor Speedway would help a driver on those two circuits.

As a sideshow, actors Clark Gable and Barbara Stanwyck, who were filming the movie "To Please A Lady," were around the Speedway during the month of May and rode parade-like in the pace car. Also, Stanwyck was in victory lane when the winner received his congratulatory kiss. Both posed for pictures with the Borg-Warner Trophy.

Gentlemen, Start Your Engines

The most famous phrase in automobile racing, "Gentleman, start your engines," has spilled over into the public lexicon.

Ironically, no one truly knows who said it first, or during the ceremonies before which Indianapolis 500. There have been suggestions that race starter Seth Kline first used the similar phrase, "Gentlemen, start your motors" in the 1920s.

Kline was first starter for the 1925 and 1926 races and returned to the job in 1934. He maintained that role through 1953.

John Francis "Irish" Horan was on the microphone as a public address announcer in 1950 when "Gentlemen, start your motors" was employed and noted. Kline did the honors in 1951. One of those two gentlemen said it again, but by 1953 the phrase had been permanently altered to "Gentlemen, start your engines." Motors were no more.

In 1953 and 1954, Wilbur Shaw announced, "Gentlemen, start your engines." Soon after, it became unthinkable to start the *500* without employing that command. Shaw died in 1954 at age fifty-one.

Track owner Tony Hulman tended to be more reclusive than predecessor Eddie Rickenbacker, but Hulman stepped into the role of reciting the command that took hold in American race fans' minds and he stuck with it through his death in 1977. His wife, Mary F. Hullman, took over, followed by daughter Mari Hulman George.

Precedent was set in 1977 when Janet Guthrie became the first woman to qualify to race the Indianapolis 500. Initially, it was stated that the track would not change the wording of the command. But suspense grew as the moment for actually starting those engines approached.

Tony Hulman said, "In company with the first lady ever to qualify at Indianapolis, gentlemen, start your engines."

Guthrie qualified again in 1978 and 1979 and Mary F. Hulman said, "Lady and gentlemen start your engines." Mary Hulman only issued the command through 1980. Mari Hulman George took over in 1981.

In 1992, Lynn St. James became the second woman to qualify for the *500* and she asked for the command to be changed to "Drivers, start your engines." The alteration was not approved and it remained "Lady and gentlemen start your engines." In the years since, when a woman has qualified to drive in the race that has pretty much remained the starting phrase.

In 2014, when long-time "Back Home Again in Indiana" singer Jim Nabors was on hand for his farewell performance, Mari Hulman George invited him to give the command with her. That was the first time since 1954 when Shaw delivered it that anyone outside of the Hulman family had officially voiced, "Gentlemen, start your engines."

Some Indianapolis figures showed up in the background of the film, including past winner Mauri Rose, who was third. Fifth place finisher, Joie Chitwood had a credited role.

Parsons had finished second in 1949. He raced the Indy 500 through 1958, but his next-best finish was fourth in 1956.

Parsons' son, Johnny, tried to enter the race twenty-four times, but only succeeded in qualifying twelve times. He finished as high as fifth twice.

1951

Lee Wallard was forty when he won the 1951 Indy 500 on his fourth attempt. He led 159 laps in a race where all but six cars fell short of two hundred laps and only eight were still running at the end.

Noting that other drivers had suffered serious burns in accidents, Wallard created his own fire-retardant uniform by soaking it in borax crystals and water. But the top portion of his outfit caused him to incur such bad chafing that he had to seek medical attention at the Speedway. The outfit must have been exceptionally hot, as well, since Wallard lost fifteen pounds during the race.

Merely a week after the Indy 500 while racing in Reading, Pennsylvania, Willard's fear came true. His car burst into flames after a crash and he suffered such severe burns that he needed twenty-seven skin grafts.

One of the drivers who did not finish that year's Indianapolis 500 was Mauri Rose. He crashed on the 126th lap. That was Rose's final auto race. He retired after the accident.

1952

Troy Ruttman won the 1952 competition when he was less than three months past his twenty-second birthday, a youth record. He averaged 128.922 mph to best runner-up Jim Rathmann.

However, the real challenger was Bill Vukovich, who led for 150 laps before his steering broke on the 197th lap.

Ruttman competed in twelve Indianapolis 500 races, but was also a renowned racer on other circuits. He was a dirt track racer before becoming an open-wheel man at Indy, entered U.S. Auto Club events, and even tried out the NASCAR stock cars periodically in the 1950s. Ruttman's younger brother Joe was a NASCAR driver.

Rathmann, whose given first name was Royal Richard, was a fixture at the Speedway for fourteen years and produced several top finishes. The most unusual thing about Rathmann's background was how he and his brother traded first names when they were teenagers. Dick became Jim and Jim became Dick.

This Rathmann wanted to race, but was too young, so he borrowed his older brother's identification and talked his way onto tracks. They kept the swapped names throughout their racing careers.

Art Cross, who was born in Jersey City, New Jersey, finished fifth this year. One way that was commemorated was with the first official Indianapolis 500 rookie-of-the-year award, a tradition that has continued ever since.

Cross, who competed in four *500*s, came to open-wheel racing through midget cars. He won a Purple Heart during the fighting at the Battle of the Bulge during World War II, and after retiring from racing ran a family farm in LaPorte, Indiana.

1953

For some reason Bill Vukovich acquired the nickname "The Mad Russian," even though he was not Russian and the main reason he got mad was because somebody called him that. Vukovich was of Yugoslavian descent and had been born in Fresno, California. He liked his other nickname, "The Fresno Flash" much better.

While he was regarded as a superb racer by his contemporaries, Vukovich failed to qualify when he showed up in Indianapolis for his first *500* in 1950. His second run was the go-for-broke ride when he led 150 laps in 1952.

This time he was ready for anything, including an official temperature in the high nineties and a track temperature claimed to be 130 degrees. That was a higher number than the 128.740 mph average speed. Vukovich was in command almost all day, leading 195 laps.

Conditions were so oppressive that several racers used relief drivers. Carl Scarborough not only had a relief driver in Bob Scott, he took himself to the Speedway medical area. Scarborough died in the infield hospital from heat prostration.

Bill Vukovich in his car with an Offenhauser engine before winning the 1953 race.

1954

Bill Vukovich became the rare driver to win Indianapolis two years in a row. This was a more competitive race. Although Vukovich led for ninety laps, his top foes also spent a portion of the day racing at the front.

Vukovich may have been the defending champion, but he almost did not qualify for a next chance. Vukovich did not qualify for the race start until the third day of qualifying and his time only placed him nineteenth. Whatever was bugging his car pre-race apparently vanished during it.

Second placer, Jimmy Bryan led for forty-six laps. Third placer, Jack McGrath, who was the pole sitter after setting a new mark at 141.033 mph, led for forty-seven laps. On the hot day McGrath was actually going too fast and had to pit for new tires because his original ones were wearing out too fast.

The first eleven cars made it through the two hundred laps, but that eleventh place finisher was a car started by the same Art Cross who won honors the year before. The car out-lasted its driver.

Cross started the race thirteenth on the starting grid after putting up a qualifying time of 138.670 mph. Cross took the lead briefly, but was feeling woozy and asked for a relief driver. In stepped past winner Johnnie Parsons. Then Parsons yielded to a third driver, Sam Hanks, who in turn was subbed for by Jimmy Davies. All of that trading off was due to the extremely hot and humid weather conditions, so severe that it sent many drivers to the sidelines to recover.

Less than six months after the race Wilbur Shaw was lost to the Speedway. He died after suffering injuries in a plane crash. No one else was tabbed to be president and general manager. From then on Tony Hulman ran the show himself.

1955

In this haunted year for racing, there had also been some strange doings during Indy qualifying, though not nearly as tragic.

It was windy and rainy on pole day and many drivers watching the conditions in Gasoline Alley decided to sit out qualifying. There was no formal meeting, however, and not all drivers learned of the unofficial agreement. Jerry Hoyt rolled his car into position for qualifying, took off and recorded a time of 140.045 mph. Seeing what was happening, one other driver was able to rush to the line in time to complete qualifying.

Drivers were angry at Hoyt because they felt the agreement was breached, but he was completely unaware of what was going on. So Hoyt got the pole and Tony Bettenhausen was second on the starting grid. When qualifying resumed the next day, Jack McGrath was faster than Hoyt at 142.58 mph, but that only got him the third starting spot. Hoyt was out of the race by lap forty and McGrath was gone by lap fifty-four.

Gone, too, for good, was Vukovich, prematurely in the grave at thirty-four. Before the race he had even mused at what he felt might be his final Indy 500 before possibly retiring.

"Maybe I'll retire soon, at that," he said. "If I won once more at Indianapolis you can bet that's the end for Vukie. I'm thirty-four now, not too far to go."

Only sadly he did not go out on his own terms.

Bill Vukovich was the two-time defending Indianapolis 500 champion when the 1955 race began. He started the race, leading fifty of the first fifty-six laps, and it seemed likely that he would become the first driver to win three straight events.

Instead, May 30 turned into a day of horror at the Indianapolis Motor Speedway. Rather than become a triple champion, Vukovich died of a fractured skull that day, due to his speeding automobile plowing into three cars involved in a previous crash.

On lap fifty-four, cars driven by Al Keller, Rodger Ward and Johnny Boyd, were littering the track as Vukovich sped forward and drove right into the mess and his car shot into the air, cleared the wall along the back straightaway and hit the ground upside down, causing a fire.

Vukovich hit Ward's car, which was stuck in place in front of him.

"I don't know that I could really explain to you how badly I felt," Ward said. "To me, it was an absolute disaster."

Given the large periods of time running in front, coupled with his two victories, Vukovich had been the *500*'s dominant driver for four straight years. His death was a devastating blow to racing.

After the accidents, Bob Sweikert took control of the race, leading eighty-six laps and besting runner-up Tony Bettenhausen by nearly three minutes.

Sweikert was from Los Angeles, but began street racing after his family moved to the San Francisco area when he was a teenager. He made his living as an auto mechanic, but began racing in 1947. He was in the Indy field for the fourth time. Giving him hope for success at the Speedway was victory in the Hoosier Hundred at the Indiana State Fairgrounds in 1953.

In 1956, a year after his Indy triumph, Sweikert finished sixth in the *500*. But only a few weeks later he was killed in a crash at Indiana's Salem Speedway. He was only thirty.

By 1955, the Automobile Association of America had been sanctioning auto racing for more than a half century. The death of Vukovich, following in the pattern of so many racers being killed in their cars, soured the attitude of the AAA. Even worse, a racing holocaust of sorts occurred at the 24 Hours of LeMans, which began on June 11, less than two weeks after Indianapolis.

In a tragedy of unimaginable scope, a car slowed heading into the pits and then swerved in front of driver Pierre Levagh. Levagh was traveling at about 150 mph when his car struck the other. Not only was Levagh killed, but his car disintegrated with large chunks soaring into the stands. Some eighty-three fans were killed, some decapitated by slices of the car, and another 120 were injured.

After that horrific incident, the AAA organization withdrew its involvement from racing altogether and focused on passenger travel.

That year the United States Automobile Club was formed by Speedway owner Tony Hulman Jr. and beginning in 1956 it became the supervising agency of American automobile racing. Its reach included sanctioning of the Indy 500 from 1956 through 1979.

Even now, forty years after its founding, the USAC still sanctions many races in the U.S., including the Silver Crown Series, the National Sprint Series, National Midget Series, HPD Midget Series, and Traxxass TORC Series.

The USAC recognizes national champions in events and the Silver Crown, Sprint Car and Midget Car are considered a triple crown of American racing. Only two drivers have ever won this trio of titles in the same year, Tony Stewart of Columbus, Indiana in 1975, and J.J. Yeley of Phoenix in 2003. Both are still active stock-car racers in NASCAR.

Stewart is considered the most versatile driver of the modern era, with three NASCAR season championships to his credit and victories in the IndyCar series, as well.

In 1955, the race went on after Vukovich perished and Sweikert fended off challengers whose cars gave out, and led from lap 160 on, winning the race.

1956

Between the end of the 1955 race and the start of the 1956 race, the Indianapolis Motor Speedway was paved with asphalt. Just six hundred yards of the 2.5 mile surface still had brick showing.

The United States Automobile Club was overseeing its first Indianapolis 500 and wanted to have a good show. The biggest impediment to that, however, was heavy rain that poured down drenching the track, leaving so much standing water that the event could have been converted into a sailboat race.

Infield dirt had been churned into mud and resembled quicksand. The pedestrian tunnels entering the track were flooded. Anyone hoping to reach the track on foot would be required to swim. There seemed no way possible that the Memorial Day race could go off on time.

Groundskeepers and maintenance workers are generally underrated throughout their careers, but this was one time that applause from thousands greeted their work. Speedway superintendent Clarence Cagle rounded up every worker available, put them to work around the clock and in the last forty-eight hours to race time, cleared hundreds of thousands of gallons of water and made the premises and the track useable. They did the impossible.

Although some qualifying was rained out and sometimes scheduling runs depended on the raindrops, a previously expected new track record on the new surface was achieved. Pat Flaherty claimed the pole with a run of 145.596 mph. Limited qualifying kept out some likely members of the field.

Flaherty also claimed the race title. In his fifth *500*, the California-born racer took the crown by leading for 127 laps. Sam Hanks was twenty seconds behind. The high group of finishers included former champs Johnnie Parsons (fourth) and Bob Sweikert (sixth).

The superb clean-up operation came to be known as "Cagle's Miracle."

While the rain could have spoiled everyone's parade, the grand opening of the new Hall of Fame Museum on Speedway grounds was a logical place to take a break from the weather. When the museum opened it had six cars on display. In 2015, approximately seventy-five vehicles were displayed at the same time.

1957

Sam Hanks raced his first Indianapolis 500 in 1940 and competed thirteen times. His early starts were not especially encouraging. In his first seven Speedway races he finished between twelfth and 33rd and never led a lap.

Since he was born in 1914, Hanks wondered if he would ever make an Indy breakthrough before he got too old. Then, starting in 1952, he began contending. He put up two third place finishes before slumping again for two years.

In 1957, Hanks was going on forty-three and with part of qualifying rained out he did not make himself a favorite, he placed sixth and his speed was 142.81 mph. In his entire *500* career up to that point Hanks had led four laps total.

But May 30 was Hanks' long-awaited day. He fended off all comers, led for 136 laps and fulfilled his dream of winning the Indianapolis 500. Hanks chose a good year to win since the winner's purse was a record $103,844 out of a total payout of more than $300,000, also a record.

Hanks knew he had a good car going into the race. Owner George Salih told him he was building a new car.

"The car was a real gem," Hanks said. "It was not only lower and lighter, but it allowed me to see better."

In a dramatic finish to his career, Hanks announced his retirement from racing while in the winner's circle. The only other racer who had ever done this was the first victor, Ray Harroun, in 1911. But Harroun had come out of retirement for the inaugural *500*.

Hanks did finish out the racing season at other events, but the next time he came to Indianapolis it was as the pace car driver. He returned as defending champ for the task in 1958 and kept up this other kind of driving at the Speedway through 1963.

"I had almost retired the year before when I finished second," Hanks said years later. "I decided it was time to hang up my goggles for keeps."

Unlike so many of his fellow drivers from the same era, Hanks avoided fatal injury in an automobile race and lived to be seventy-nine.

1958

Sam Hanks stuck to his pledge to stay retired, resisting the entreaties of his car owner. Instead, the car came into the hands of Jimmy Bryan, who led 139 of the two hundred laps.

Although much younger than Hanks, Bryan had paid his dues, seven times running the *500* before capturing it.

The biggest problem Bryan – and everyone else – had however, was getting beyond the first lap. Almost as soon as the race started there was a huge fatal crash. Seven drivers did not complete the opening lap of the race at the 42nd annual event.

Qualifying was tight through May, but Dick Rathmann, Jim's brother, emerged with the pole position after recording a speed of 145.974 mph. For all of the energy and effort expended, he might as well have stayed home on May 30. At the least it would have been safer.

Calamity began when Ed Elisian from Oakland, who had been involved in the accident that killed former Indy champ Bob Sweikert in 1956 at Salem Raceway (though he was not blamed), sought to get the jump on Rathmann at turn three. It was a bold stroke with disastrous results.

Elisian lost control of his car and numerous vehicles pinballed all over the track, ricocheting off each other and the wall. Fifteen cars were caught up in one of the largest accidents in Speedway history. Seven were credited with zero laps completed and one with a single lap completed. The other eight cars resumed racing.

Drivers who could not brake quickly enough literally ran over the tops of other cars that had slowed and in some cases were launched into the air like Evel Knievel trick drivers, although hardly by choice. Rathmann was finished on the first lap.

"Cars everywhere," said fourteenth place finisher Bob Christie.

Elisian's car was knocked out and due to another crash eighteen months later in Milwaukee, he was dead in less than a year-and- half. He died at age thirty-two.

Jerry Unser Jr., brother of Al and Bobby, both future Indy champions, shot over the wall in his car, but almost miraculously walked away with a simple dislocated shoulder.

Not so fortunate was Pat O'Connor. O'Connor was a very popular area driver, from tiny North Vernon south of Indianapolis. Just twenty-nine years old, O'Connor was viewed as an up-and-coming star and was actually on the cover of Sports Illustrated in the week leading up to the race, as part of the Sports Illustrated race preview. The article inside was not about O'Connor, but did include a minimalist phrase referring to him as "the lad who smiles from this week's cover."

His career and life were aborted in this massive crash. O'Connor's ran over the car belonging to Jimmy Reece, soared fifty feet in the air, landed on the roof and rolled over. The car the caught fire, burning O'Connor's body, but medical examiners said he was probably already dead from a head injury. The news of O'Connor perishing was made public before the end of the race and many spectators were visibly affected, walking out even as the race roared on.

Well aware of what took place, winner Bryan said, "It was a nightmare. I lived with it for two hundred laps."

He did not live very long, though. In 1960, Bryan perished in a crash in Pennsylvania at age thirty-four.

Fifty years after O'Connor's death, his son Jeff and his widow, then-named Ann Stiening, were present for the race to honor the driver's memory.

1959

Not so lucky this time, Jerry Unser Jr. who had escaped serious harm at Indianapolis in 1958, suffered fatal burns during a practice run on May 2, 1959. He lost control of his car heading into turn four. The car spun out, bounced down the track and burst into flames.

At first the burns Unser received did not seem quite so threatening since they were concentrated on his arms. But complications set in. Unser stayed alive in a hospital for fifteen days.

Two days after Unser died a rookie named Bob Cortner, from California, was the victim of high winds as he entered turn three. The car crashed, his head violently bounced off the steering wheel and he was taken to a hospital with "massive head injuries." He bled extensively and those reports reached other drivers, who were preparing to donate blood when word was received that Cortner had passed away and was only twenty-two.

It seemed the entire decade of the 1950s was a bloody one at the Indianapolis Motor Speedway.

Rodger Ward prevailed in the race itself. Although Ward was born in Kansas, his family moved to California before he was ten years old. Ward began auto racing after World War II service in the Army. He began slowly in midget racing, gradually improved, and won a 1951 national AAA driving championship.

That year also marked Ward's Speedway debut. He raced in the Indy 500 for eight years with just one top ten finish before his 1959 breakthrough. He never led a single lap until then, but led 130 of them in his victory. For the next six years in a row Ward never finished below fourth.

It had been a steep learning curve for Ward, who was thirty-eight when he captured the '59 race. Although he had paid his dues during the 1950s, a time of much gloom and sadness around the track due to the deaths of so many drivers, Ward was actually a herald of the future. He peaked in time for the golden era of the 1960s.

A Decade of Greatness

1960-69

Many of the greatest drivers in the history of the sport and the history of the Indianapolis 500 introduced themselves to the fans in the 1960s. They kicked off a golden era at the Speedway that rolled over into the 1970s.

Among the big-name winners of the Greatest Spectacle in Racing during the 1960s were A.J. Foyt (three times), Parnelli Jones, the first man to break the 150 mph barrier, Jimmy Clark, Bobby Unser and Mario Andretti.

The 1964 race was remembered for several important reasons, some of them terrible. While Foyt won and the race marked the end of the front-engine racing car, a horrible accident that took the lives of drivers Eddie Sachs and Dave MacDonald, marred the day.

1960

Nobody died on the track, the first time in a long time. That was the good news. However, the bad news was that a heavily weighed down scaffold collapsed with spectators on it during the parade lap and resulted in the death of two fans.

Once the Indianapolis 500 began, it was all racing on the track, one of the finest competitions in Speedway history, with twenty-nine lead changes between five drivers and a last hundred mile pursuit that demonstrated how automobile racing at its best could be such a thrilling sport.

There was no dust on an asphalt track, but when things settled, Jim Rathmann was the new Indy 500 champ, finishing about twelve seconds ahead of 1959 champ Rodger Ward. And that was only after they disposed of early challenger Johnny Thomson and put some distance between them and Paul Goldsmith and Don Branson. Neither of the duo actually led at first. But Eddie Sachs, who captured the pole with a mark of 146.59 mph, led twenty-one laps before his car broke down on lap 132. Tony Ruttman, another exiled from the race because of a broken axle, led eleven laps.

The 1-2-3 finishers, Thomson, Sachs, and Ruttman exchanged the lead during the first half of the race, but later the suspense was between Rathmann and Ward. This was the moment Rathmann had been waiting for in his eleventh Indy 500.

One by one the other cars dropped off and it was Rathmann and Ward head-to-head. They drove fiercely, Ward leading fifty-eight laps and Rathmann leading for one hundred. Ward's aggressiveness caused his tires to wear down and when he had to pit to make a change Rathmann seized the lead for the last time, lap 197 on. Ward could not make up the lost time.

As the new decade began Rathmann was completing the five hundred miles in just over 3.5 hours. In the first race, it took Ray Harroun nearly seven hours to finish the course.

Unlike several drivers who were prodigies, jumping into race cars as youths, Sachs, who was from Allentown, Pennsylvania, was a late bloomer. It took him a long time to gain success as he worked his way through the ranks. That was also true at Indy.

Sachs flunked his rookie driver's test twice before qualifying for his first Indy 500 in 1957. He was always a threat to swipe the pole, but once the race began, except for some stretches, he was basically a non-factor, finishing no higher than seventeenth in his first four races, including 1960.

Off the race course Sachs could be goofy, which endeared him to fans, and out-spoken, which alienated him from other drivers. In both cases his blabbermouth ways shaped his image. Eventually, he was named "The Clown Prince of Racing."

Sachs may not have been naturally talented, but he was driven, metaphorically, possessed of a great desire to learn and a determined work ethic. These traits were all on display in-between his jokes.

Early in his racing career Sachs witnessed two deaths at a track and was amazed by the other drivers' reaction.

"They seemed sad, but more determined than ever," he said. "Hell, they drove harder. It was remarkable."

Sachs had a strong sense of self-preservation. His number one goal in life was to win the Indianapolis 500, but he was married, saw how many drivers were getting killed in racing accidents and made a plan. He would win the race once and then get out of racing.

After winning the pole in 1960, Sachs believed the race belonged to him. Wrong.

1961

For the second year in a row, this time for the fiftieth anniversary of the first Indianapolis 500 race, Eddie Sachs earned the pole position. He averaged 147.481 mph. Once again Sachs felt great optimism when the gentlemen started their engines. This time, for sure.

Someone else felt differently about the likely outcome. A.J. Foyt of Houston, Texas, whom many believe is the greatest auto racer of all time, first appeared at the Indianapolis 500 in 1958. He finished sixteenth that year, tenth in 1959, and twenty-fifth in 1960.

For the moment, Foyt seemed like just another guy at Indy. That was despite a racing pedigree of great success as he experimented and learned how to handle a fast car in other disciplines. Foyt dropped out of high school to become a mechanic, but he began racing at eighteen.

This was the race where Foyt truly arrived on the Indy scene. Jim Hurtubise led for thirty-five laps. Parnelli Jones led for twenty-seven. Rodger Ward fought hard to stay in contention, leading seven laps before he finished third.

But as the end drew near it was a two-car race, Sachs versus Foyt. The experienced driver versus the youngster wanting to make his mark.

Other things were going on at the Speedway that year. The worst moment occurred in practice. Top competitor Tony Bettenhausen, was killed testing a car the day before the pole position was set. Bettenhausen, from the suburbs of Chicago, was nicknamed the "Tinley Park Express." He had been racing in the *500* since 1946 and had three finishes in the top four. Bettenhausen was forty-four when he died.

Also, a track worker named John Masiru, who was actually a junior high school principal in Danville, Indiana and was helping out as a safety worker, had his own safety compromised on the 127th lap. Masiru was riding on the back of a fire truck that headed to turn four to put out a small fire in driver Eddie Johnson's car. It was not clear if Masiru jumped off the fire engine in preparation for fighting the fire, or if he fell, but the truck backed over him causing his death.

Even in the early years of the *500*, racers from overseas were regulars. That pilgrimage was interrupted by World War I. The track reverted to form over the years, but World War II shut the operation down and Europeans were slow to return.

In 1961, Jack Brabham, an Australian two-time Formula 1 champion, who developed his own race team and was later knighted by the British crown, showed up in Indianapolis. He had become friendly with Rodger Ward and when Brabham heard about the type of cars in use he came to see for himself and perhaps show the Americans a few things.

Brabham brought an English-built car that was not only structured lower to the ground and bore a closer physical appearance to cars of the future than to boxier cars of the past, it startled competitors for two reasons. One reason was that the engine was in the rear. The placement of racing engines in the back of the car had been common in the 1930s and 1940s, but fell out of fashion. The last time even one Indy car raced with a back-of-the-machine engine was 1951.

After Brabham's re-introduction of the rear engine, that became the new rage, altering car manufacturers' approach all over again.

The second reason other drivers were put off was the color of the car. It was green and that was a forbidden color, by superstition considered bad luck since 1920 when Gaston Chevrolet died in a green car.

"There was a bright green car there," said a horrified Foyt of 1961. "I wouldn't even get close to it. I'm not a real superstitious person, but I have always believed – just like a whole lot of people – that green is a very unlucky color. You don't even wear green socks around the race track. Or drive a green passenger car."

Suffice it to say that Foyt was not driving a green car when he and Sachs dueled for the title.

There was also a five car accident on lap forty-nine, before the lead was whittled down to Foyt and Sachs, mano-a-mano.

Foyt seemed to be in control on lap 160 when he pitted to take on fuel. It was supposed to be enough fuel for him to go the distance. Only a mechanical problem developed and when he drove back onto the track unbeknownst to Foyt he did not have a full tank. The pit crew was aware, though. Sachs had also fueled up and the drivers believed they were done with pauses and one would have to outmaneuver the other.

Foyt began pulling away from Sachs because his car was lighter, carrying less fuel. However, on lap 184, the Foyt pit crew, knowing their driver could not make it all of the way on the gas he had, waved him into the pits. The stop was only to add gas, but Sachs kept zooming around the track and built a solid lead.

Charging back, Foyt seemed doomed. However, on lap 197, Sachs realized that one of his tires was failing and could cause him to crash and lose his hard-won position, he chose to pit and replace it. Foyt seized the lead and won by just over eight seconds over Sachs.

"At lap 194 or 195, I noticed that the right rear tire was wearing thin," Sachs said. "I admit I could have slowed down and might have made it with my twenty-three second lead, but I thought it would be better to win second place than be dead. I decided to take no chances and try to make first place next year."

For a driver who had told sportswriters that his No. 1 reason to live was to win the Indianapolis 500, it was a somewhat surprising choice. This was an era of macho driving where the men behind the wheel routinely took major risks. But Sachs had been around the Speedway long enough to see many men carried dead from their cars, so his comment was hardly hyperbole. If the tire gave out he could easily have crashed and lost his life.

Later, Foyt said he realized his fuel level was falling quicker than it should have been after the earlier pit stop. He hated the idea of coming in, but understood something must have gone wrong. His pit crew held up a sign reading, "Pit, A.J. 1." That meant he should go in on the next lap.

Foyt said there were tears in his eyes because he was certain the race had been lost. This time the pit crew did not fill the tank all of the way on purpose. Traveling light was about the only way he thought he could catch Sachs.

A.J. recognized something had happened to Sachs' lead when the crowd of about 300,000 let out such a mighty roar he was sure it vibrated his car. Although no one asked him that day, Foyt later said that despite the risk, the chance of winning the Indy 500 was too important to pass up.

"I would have stayed out there," he said of being in Sachs' shoes facing the same tire situation.

The legend of A.J. Foyt at Indianapolis had begun.

1962

As an indicator of how difficult it is to maintain a front-running position in the Indy 500 year after year, A.J. Foyt finished twenty-third in 1962 after his car lost a wheel on lap sixty-nine.

Parnelli Jones, a rookie in 1961 who placed twelfth became a sensation in 1962 when he broke the 150 mph barrier at the Speedway on May 12, with a record one-lap clocking of 150.729 mph. He turned four straight laps faster than 150 and captured the pole position with a speed average of 150.370 mph.

Leading up to qualifying, Jones did not believe he had the engine power to break 150 mph. The weather was also uncomfortable. On the thermometer it was around ninety degrees, but on the track it was 139 degrees.

When he coasted to a stop, fans screaming and officials in a tizzy, two members of his team rushed up to Jones and kissed him.

"To do something no one else has done is a helluva thrill," Jones said.

Jones was born in Texarkana, Arkansas, but grew up in California and that's where he got his racing start. By the time May 30 rolled around, Jones was the race favorite. He was at least the flavor of the month. But as has been shown many times, what happens in qualifying doesn't necessarily have anything to do with what happens during the race.

Parnelli got his moment of glory, but after leading 120 laps and averaging more than 150 mph with clearly the fastest car, the bugaboo of mechanical failure affected him. In a rather extraordinary bit of driving, Jones managed to coax his car to the finish line in seventh place – without the use of brakes. The exhaust pipe had burned a hole in the brake lining.

So Jones swerved in and out of traffic with his steering and his wits, slowing down when he needed to, but risking a crash at all times. Jones first realized he was driving with no brakes on lap seventy and held the lead as late as lap 125. Finishing at all, driving as hard as he did, was a monumental achievement, even if officials would have yanked him off the course if they had known.

"I'd be screaming into a corner and I'd be telling myself, 'You can do it,'" Jones recounted of how he reminded himself not to brake in the turns. "'You can get around without that brake. You got more guts than anyone. You don't have to hit that brake.'"

Jones admitted later that sometimes brakes are needed at Indy, and his foot involuntarily followed his training and tapped the brakes even when he knew it would do him no good.

"If an accident happens right in front of you, you might not be able to miss it without brakes," Jones said. "It was scary as hell."

Jones said he decided to keep going after the brake failure until he had to pit. But when he somehow coasted to a stop in front of his crew, it leapt into action, changed tires, filled the tank and pushed him out before he could even explain. He was frustrated because his car was handling so easily at 150 mph, but said "I really felt sick" when he had to slow and others passed him. On his next pit stop Jones halted by bumping into some tires and touching the wall. By then he was angry and kept on going.

It was crazy stuff, but the capricious track did not devour him and Jones reached the end.

By then others had taken over the front. While much drama surrounded Jones, most of it unknown to his competitors until after the race, this was one of Rodger Ward's finest hours.

Ward led sixty-six laps, including the last thirty-one, and bested his teammate Len Sutton, in second, who led nine laps. Eddie Sachs finished third the year after his late-race loss to Foyt, but this time did not lead one lap.

This marked Ward's second triumph, adding another championship to his 1959 race. But he had been a high-level consistent player in the previous several *500s*. The second win followed finishes of second in

1960 and third in 1961. He was also forty-one in 1962, making him a graybeard by the standards of the times and also Old Man River in a sport where so many drivers younger than that had met death on the race track.

"Indy makes the race driver," Ward said. "You become famous when you come. I don't care where else you race in the world. I was pretty famous in my own territory, but when I came to Indianapolis, and the first time I ran here, I wasn't known as a driver from California. I was an Indy driver."

Racing in the Indianapolis 500 entered Ward into an exclusive club of drivers.

"Winning that race was the greatest thing that happened to me in my life," he concluded.

1963

Parnelli Jones had so much fun winning the pole in 1962 that he decided to do it again, clocking 151.153 mph in qualifying.

Once again driving the best car Jones nearly did not finish this time either, and how he did so is one of the most controversial non-calls by officials in Indianapolis 500 history. Jones won his only *500* in the 47th running.

What a cast he beat. There were fourteen cars still running that completed the two hundred laps. Speedway newcomer Jimmy Clark from Scotland who won two Formula 1 world championships, finished second as an Indianapolis rookie. A.J. Foyt took third and Rodger Ward fourth. Eddie Sachs had been near the front, but crashed on lap 181.

In the late going, Jones, in his superior car, began leaking oil from a crack in his oil tank at the back of the car. While trailing drivers said oil splashed on them, sometimes making it difficult to see and Sachs felt his crash was precipitated by skidding on an oil slick caused by Jones' car, officials did not black flag Jones ordering him off the track. There were protests at the time and many felt he should have been sidelined.

The scuttlebutt was that officials did not want a non-American to win the race and with Clark sitting in second a disqualification of Jones would have created that very scenario.

Jones was also enormously popular and was at the forefront of a new generation of top American drivers.

Clark and Dan Gurney were also driving new-fangled Lotus cars with rear engines that were seemingly more aerodynamic than the boxy, front engine cars that most of the field was using. Lotus crew members actually hoped their drivers could complete the entire five hundred miles without a tire change.

There was only one scheduled pit stop for Clark, on lap ninety-five, because the Lotus cars were expected to only need fuel once. Clark did change three tires. Gurney did have a worn-out tire.

Although some say the first signs of oil smoke coming from Jones' engine appeared as early as lap eighty, it was not yet believed to be a big deal. With fifty laps to go Jones led Clark by forty-three seconds. However, after that Clark began clipping seconds off the lead and he pulled within five seconds with twenty-five laps remaining.

Sachs was in the mix, but spun out on lap 179. He continued racing and spun out a second time on lap 189 and lost a wheel, knocking him out of the race. This was the moment when Sachs felt his loss of control was due to an oil slick. Jones' car was clearly leaking oil and smoke came from his car. Chief steward Harlan Fengler gave serious thought to waving the black flag.

Representatives of Jones' team and Clark's became embroiled in an argument while attempting to sway Fengler. J.C. Agajanian, owner of Jones' car, advanced the point that the leak had stopped once the oil level dropped below the crack and said oil on the track came from other cars, as well. Fengler went for the no-longer-leaking argument and said he did not want to take the win away from a driver "on a snap judgment."

Years later, Agajanian said his forceful talk with the steward was pivotal.

"I know I saved us by arguing with Fengler," he said. "I know if I hadn't run up to him and argued with him they'd have thrown the black flag and we'd have lost. I think I won the argument because I was right."

Sachs, who was always forthright in critiquing other drivers and situations, did not let up and a day after the race he and Jones had a fist-fight. Jones threw the first punch after Sachs yapped at him.

"He riled me up and I punched him and I'm not sorry," Jones said, "but I know he wasn't being vicious or anything like that. He was just the kind of guy who pops off."

Clark's team was gracious, saying Jones had the best car, and did not file a protest.

While it appeared Jones had the makings of a long-term repeat champion, it turned out that this was his only Indianapolis 500 victory.

"It's not really forgotten and I don't guess it ever will be, but it is in the books and that is what counts," Jones said. "The fuss died down and I was still the winner. We got the money and the trophies and the pictures. They tried to spoil it for me and they couldn't."

Jones did not try to pretend he wasn't leaking oil. That was obvious.

"Sure I dropped oil, but so did a lot of other guys," he said. "I started with six gallons and I finished with two. There were cars that finished with less than that. But how much is too much. Where do you draw the line?"

Parnelli Jones took the checkered flag instead of the black flag and that race victory is one reason he was one of the most popular of American racers.

1964

Things were getting faster. Rodger Ward set a one-lap record of 157.563 mph. Things were sizzling. That mark did not even stand up to win the pole. Jimmy Clark was back and the world champion showed what he could do at Indianapolis, zipping his qualifying time in 158.828 mph.

But what took center stage was one of the worst crashes in Indianapolis 500 history. The horror of the day focused around "Clown Prince" Eddie Sachs and rookie Dave MacDonald from California. MacDonald was young, but viewed as a natural behind the wheel with a bright future. Many felt the twenty-seven year old was going to be auto racing's next superstar.

MacDonald was level-headed, but determined, a hard driver, but prudent. He excelled at every type of racing and posted sixty-nine wins in 115 events across the board. Some were concerned that he was not yet ready for Indianapolis's challenges, but he cleared rookie test hurdles easily and qualified well.

Far from being the showboat kind who might revel in the spotlight, MacDonald was more shy and unassuming. But he had a gift for bringing his cars to the front of the pack and keeping them there.

While everyone in the sport agreed that MacDonald was likely to become an Indy champion, some felt he needed more open-wheel racing experience before going all in at the Speedway. Others believed the car offered to him had suspicious handling. MacDonald did not issue any overconfident quotes. Instead, he talked like a beginner hungry to learn, saying, "Well, I'll drive it this year and maybe it will lead to a better car next year."

Meanwhile, Sachs, who it might be said was temperamentally the opposite of MacDonald, had invested years in getting to the front at Indianapolis – and staying there. He had come close to realizing his dream of capturing the Indy 500 in prior races with top finishes, but he wanted to read that No. 1 next to his name.

The fun-loving Sachs was as serious as any other driver on the track, but his penchant for light-hearted utterances of it may have produced a false image. Sachs' motto was, "If you can't win, be spectacular." To him that also meant having fun and avoiding too much detail that didn't involve holding the steering wheel and putting his foot down on the pedal.

Leading up to this race Sachs was late to the mandatory drivers meeting, the last to arrive and everyone knew it, too, because officials basically sent out a search party for him.

"I haven't been on time for one of those in eight years," Sachs said. "I wait until they page me. Those other guys have to sit through all that stuff and I walk in when they get down to business."

This was the beginning of a period of change at Indianapolis. The owners, manufacturers and drivers were going back to cars with engines in the rear. This field was somewhat of a hybrid. A lot goes into an Indy car, from big money to uncountable hours of mechanical work, testing, and driver prep. In many ways the cars are equal, but fine-tuning can make the difference in saving time on each lap. Just tenths-of-seconds saved can make the difference in the outcome of the race.

Lest it be forgotten that the entire existence of the Indianapolis Motor Speedway stemmed from wanting to provide a place for manufacturers to test new products, experimentation was in the DNA of the track. This happened to be a time in the evolution of the automobile when car makers were intensely focused on building better and faster cars and appealing to new audiences to buy them.

When the AAA pulled out of racing after the 1955 race and the Le Mans tragedy, so did many manufacturers of passenger cars. The AAA put heat on them to stay away from Indianapolis. Gradually, the car makers returned and in 1964 atmosphere changed. It seemed as if everyone wanted back in.

Ford introduced the Mustang that year and it was seeking any kind of publicity to help sell the new model, so it sponsored the pace car. Pontiacs were stealing thunder in NASCAR races. Overseas, the Lotus engine manufacturers were making noise. Independent car makers, notably Mickey Thompson in California, wanted places on the starting line at Indianapolis, too.

Thompson was a creative thinker and passionate about making cars that would go faster. Above all, he seemed enamored by the land-speed record-breakers – he was one himself – but wanted to outsmart the big-boy car manufacturers. Rookie MacDonald was in a Thompson car. Some veterans watching its performance in practice and qualifying weren't so sure the car was race-ready.

Two-time champion Rodger Ward was a skeptic and offered gentle advice to MacDonald. Ward said, "Look, Dave, you're a young hot dog. Conceivably you could become a really great race driver because you have got everything it takes except maturity. But in the race car you are driving, you don't have a prayer to win the race. So, play it cool. Take your time and learn. Use this place as a learning experience."

Sachs had a mishap in qualifying, hitting the wall after he tried to squeeze too much speed out of his car.

"I had been running about 154 mph and decided to try for 158 mph," Sachs said. "I was trying to get the extra four mph all in one turn."

This was a star-studded field, including Ward, A.J. Foyt, Dick Rathmann, Parnelli Jones, Jimmy Clark, Dan Gurney, Jack Brabham, Bobby

Unser, Johnny Rutherford, Lloyd Ruby and Troy Ruttman. There were past champions, racers nearing the tail-end of their Indy 500 careers, and racers just beginning to make names for themselves. Given the typical rate of mechanical failure, many of the best did not come close to finishing the race.

Vic Damone sang "Back Home Again in Indiana," the pageantry of patriotism that always accompanied Memorial Day was the usual dominant theme, and the rear-engine cars showed their stuff (and took over the race from then on).

Plus, there was an accident so terrible, the entire race was black-flagged, halted in mid-lap shortly after the start, for the first time in history.

MacDonald, the man of the future, started fourteenth. Sachs, going for the gusto, certain he could at last win the Indianapolis 500, started seventeenth. Before the day was over, they both would be dead.

When the race began, MacDonald did not play it cautiously. Excited to be in the big race, which he told many people, he worked to start chasing down other drivers immediately. That meant he was swerving in and out of traffic as he quickly passed five drivers.

The start can be the riskiest time in the Indy 500 because so many cars are closely bunched and the drivers are keyed up, just getting into race mode. After one lap Clark was leading, but behind him, nearing completion of lap one, MacDonald lost control of his car and hit the wall in turn four.

Chaos ensued. MacDonald's car (called "radically designed" in one post-race commentary) slid backwards into traffic and Sachs' car violently struck it. The impact was so severe and the cars swerved so wildly that Sachs was killed on the spot, five other cars were swept up in the carnage, and MacDonald, although rushed to a hospital, died shortly after his lungs were burned. Fire and smoke billowed above the now-hushed Speedway as more than 250,000 fans sat appalled by the scene.

Sachs' death was announced over the loudspeaker at the track. On the syndicated radio broadcast, typically heard over about 450 stations nationwide, veteran broadcaster Sid Collins launched into a complimentary eulogy for Sachs.

"Race drivers are courageous men who try to conquer life and death and calculate the risks," Collins. "Eddie Sachs exits this earth in a race car."

The catastrophe caused officials to stop the race for the first time. It was delayed for two hours while the track was cleared before resuming. Despite the pall hanging over the track, it was almost as if a second, new, race was underway.

Rookie Bobby Marshman, who had excelled in qualifying, took the lead and was cruising along comfortably when he moved to pass another car and spun off the track, ripping out oil and water lines. That was after thirty-nine laps. Bizarrely, it was said that Marshman did not return to the pits for an hour, mingling in the grandstand while trying to stay incognito. He turned up carrying a race program and said he hoped to avoid being asked questions about what happened on the track. It sounded as if he may have been afflicted with a concussion.

Marshman was pinpointed as someone likely to become an Indy winner. Yet six months later he crashed while testing a vehicle in Phoenix and died. Sometimes it seemed as if there were more automobile drivers in heaven than in Indianapolis. Foyt, who had been good friends with Pat O'Connor, said upon that Indy death he would never again become close to other drivers because it hurt so much to lose friends. He was true to his word, always operating in his own orbit for the rest of his lengthy career.

Weary of the ranks of drivers being depleted in spectacular accidents that harmed the image of the race, as well as dramatically reducing the lifespan of competitors, Speedway officials desperately sought safety remedies. One adopted quickly, in time for the 1965 race, swapped out gasoline for methanol, although much more protection was needed.

Still, in 1966, Jim Murray, a Pulitzer-Prize-winning sports columnist for the Los Angeles Times, penned these words about the Indy 500: "Gentlemen, start your coffins." Murray's piece was not only sarcastic, but in places downright vicious.

"Ladies and gentlemen, welcome to the 50th annual Memorial Day Safety Contest, the world's fastest traffic jam," he wrote. "This year, in order to more nearly approximate road conditions on our nation's highways and test performance under authentic hazards, we have brought about several changes in the field:

> *"The driver in Car No. 4 -- the Schenley Special -- will be drunk. The driver in Car. No. 5 will just have had a fight with his wife. The driver in Car No. 7 will be color blind, the driver in Car No. 11 will have an IQ of 12 or exactly 490 points below his horsepower. The driver in Car No. Zero will have his arm around a girl and 19 traffic citations for reckless driving. He will be called upon to light her cigarette at 195-miles-per-hour."*

There was more, but that was enough.

Jimmy Clark's suspension went out on lap forty-seven. Jones was the casualty of a pit fire on lap fifty-five. Only five cars completed the 200 laps, with Foyt leading 146 laps and earning his second Indianapolis 500 title. Ward was runner-up and Ruby took third.

Jones was hospitalized with burns on his left arm and his legs.

"But it wasn't so bad," he said. "I mean, after what happened to Sachs and MacDonald, how could I feel it was bad?"

The biggest challenge to Foyt came from Ward, who actually averaged two mph faster around the oval than the winner, but who made five pit stops to Foyt's two.

"Victory lane is always a big celebration," Foyt said after his second win. "But this time it was quiet."

Driver Bobby Johns crashed during qualifying in the crash-filled 1964 Indianapolis 500.

At the time the *Indianapolis News*, (then one of three daily papers in Indianapolis) made a tradition of swiftly delivering a newspaper to the winner's circle with the new champion's name in big, bold letters. The paper was flown from the plant to the track via helicopter. The winner always posed for photographers holding it up. The paper set several contenders' name in type, and then went with the real winner in a fast print job, long before the Internet or other digital products superseded the luster of such a quick transformation.

That year the newspaper came, as usual, but when Foyt saw it before he held it up he was sad to see these words: "Foyt Winner in *500*; Sachs, MacDonald Die."

"It took a lot away from my second victory," Foyt said.

Foyt had had the opportunity to run a rear-engine car, but chose to stick with his old roadster with a front-end engine. He may have said at the finish that there was life left in the "old dinosaurs," but he knew change had come.

No front-end engine car has won the Indianapolis 500 since 1964.

1965

It took a few years after the arrival of the rear-engine cars for the revolution to be completed, but even though the foreign influence was being felt, the road to the finish line still ran through A.J. Foyt and some other top drivers.

In his few years at Indianapolis, interrupting his Formula 1 career to compete in the *500*, Jimmy Clark had gained respect and made friends in Indiana. In 1965, he made history. Nearly fifty years (since 1916) after the last non-American driver captured the crown in the Greatest Spectacle in Racing, Clark won the day on May 31.

As Clark was winning two world championships in the 1960s, twenty-five Grand Prix races, and thirty-three pole positions, he added his name to the roster of Indy champions by averaging 150.686 mph. He led a stunning 190 laps and was introduced to American sports fans by ABC's Wide World of Sports, showing the race for the first of many times.

Clark came from a farming background and began auto racing against the will of his family. Before he was done he was famous throughout

Great Britain, Europe and anywhere there was interest in cars going fast, which certainly included Indianapolis.

Foyt, who was in his racing prime, captured the pole at the Speedway in 1965 with a clocking of 161.233 mph. That was after his Lotus-Ford crashed in practice earlier in the month when a part called a magnesium hub carrier broke. The surprise made some question the reliability of the cars and the United States Automobile Club benched all of those models for examination and to improve the parts.

Clark broke the 160 mph barrier and set one-lap marks on successive laps, but Foyt edged him for the pole and set a new record. Rodger Ward, nearing the end of his career, had a terrible stretch trying to qualify, surviving a crash and three blown engines. That year he ended up as part of the Wide World of Sports coverage team instead of on the track.

For some time it seemed possible that Clark might lead wire-to-wire. He went to the front immediately and only fell behind on laps 66-74 when he pitted and Foyt kept going. However, Foyt had to drop out after 115 laps with a broken gearbox.

"I made the switch to a rear-engine car," Foyt said. "As much as I would have loved to have upheld the tradition of Indianapolis and kept driving Offy roadsters forever, it became apparent that they weren't competitive anymore."

Clark triumphed over a field of unbelievable depth, one that included the top racers of the time and was introducing the next generation of Indy stars at the same time.

Mario Andretti was a twenty-five year old rookie. On pole day he went out before Clark and Foyt and briefly set a new one-lap record of 159.406 mph. Not bad for a newcomer. Andretti became one of the greatest auto racing drivers of all. He finished third in his Indy debut. Although Andretti said only that his goal was to finish in his first *500*, he learned quickly he was better than that. He was in the hunt for the championship as much as anyone else.

"What killed me in the race," he said, "was the car got looser and looser (handling) because it was burning all the fuel from the left-side tank first, then the right-side tank. So when I was midway through the fuel load the car was bicycling because I had all the weight on the outside."

Since the car was fighting him all the way Andretti was tightly gripping the steering wheel as if it was a barbell he was trying to lift. His hands took the brunt of the punishment, becoming seriously blistered. Yet the result was very encouraging.

"It's too bad we didn't know the beast any better for the first race, but we still finished third," Andretti said. "It was a miracle that the thing ran all day with no experience at all."

Sandwiched between Clark and Andretti was Parnelli Jones, who finished second, but never led a lap. Rookie Gordon Johncock, another future star, raced in his first *500*. So did Al Unser. Brother Bobby was in the field, too. Farther back was Dan Gurney and Johnny Rutherford. It was quite the cast.

About five weeks after the *500*, Clark appeared on the cover of *Time* magazine in an artwork portrait with the teaser headline, "The Quickest Man On Wheels." Many people thought so. Clark was given the Order of the British Empire. Clark was so good in Grand Prix racing in 1963 that he led 71.47 percent of all laps he contested.

Demonstrating the hunger he had built up to win Indianapolis, Clark had to sacrifice competing in the Monaco Grand Prix that year to enter. The victory made it worthwhile and Clark still won the world championship. A half century later Clark remains the only driver to capture the Indianapolis 500 and the Formula 1 crown in the same year. A handful of other drivers, including Andretti, have won both prestigious titles, but not in the same year.

Clark was dashing - with dark brown hair, gracious in personality, and talented on a track. Even Foyt, who wondered what all these foreigners were doing showing up in American races, admired Clark's skill. Competitive and proud, though not completely comfortable with gregarious Americans who thought they knew him, Clark was in Indianapolis to win and profit. "Every lap I was in the lead I could see dollar signs in front of my eyes," he said.

In the end, a fast car killed Clark the way similar poignant deaths dotted the landscape of auto racing of the period. Clark, then thirty-two, died at a track in West Germany on April 7, 1968, the victim of his car's broken suspension.

A racing world that seemingly lost its capacity for shock was truly stunned.

"God, he was a great race-car driver," said Parnelli Jones.

1966

Mario Andretti learned fast. The native of Italy won the pole at 165.899 mph in 1966, but the miracles didn't last. Andretti was KO'd from the race on lap sixteen when a valve broke.

This was not a pretty Indianapolis 500. The first lap was a disaster with eleven cars involved in a pile-up. A.J. Foyt was injured and pulled out and others whose race ended almost immediately included Dan Gurney and NASCAR star Cale Yarborough. Only four drivers completed two hundred laps.

Graham Hill, from London, out-lasted the remainder of the field, led just ten laps, but won the race in his rookie year. Hill was no novice, however. A two-time Formula 1 world champion, during his career Hill won Indy, the 24 Hours of LeMans, and the Monaco Grand Prix.

Defending champion Clark finished second and led 66 laps, but twice during the race his car spun out. He was fortunate to recover and finish so well. Third went to Jim McElreath, but fourth went to a rising Gordon Johncock.

Tucked away in sixth was the legendary Jackie Stewart, at the time a rookie from Scotland, but in the big picture a three-time Formula 1 world champ and a two-time points runner-up. Stewart became better known in the United States for his television work, much of it on the Indy 500 for Wide World of Sports in the early 1980s, but also for the Daytona 500 stock-car race.

Actually, Clark, Hill, and Stewart were so revered across the sea that all three were awarded the Order of the British Empire.

In a famous comment made at the U.S. Grand Prix in Watkins Glen, New York in 1969, Hill, who suffered two broken legs in a crash, was asked if he wanted to tell his wife anything and said, "Just tell her I won't be dancing for two weeks."

Hill survived that crash and the hazards of his profession, only to die in a plane crash on his way home from a race in France in 1975, when he was forty-six.

After the 1966 race ended, Rodger Ward, who placed fifteenth, announced his retirement at the race banquet.

"I felt like it was time," said Ward, who was forty-five. "Some drivers go past their time."

A.J. Foyt's third Indianapolis 500 victory in 1967. A.J. would later become the first driver to win the *500* four times.

1967

It took two days to complete the 1967 Indianapolis 500.

It began on May 30, with Mario Andretti on the pole after recording a speed of 168.982 mph. He set new one-lap and four-lap records and claimed the pole for the second straight year. As always the race started with considerable fanfare and optimism, but this time it was halted because of rain after eighteen laps. The delay went on and on and officials threw up their hands. This could have been a blessing for Andretti, who was sitting in the pits with a mechanical problem.

The drivers picked up where they left off on May 31. By that time it was sunny out. Andretti was back in business, but his car still flared out with a lost wheel after fifty-eight laps.

There were some other unusual doings because of the race interruption. Lloyd Ruby had withdrawn before the eighteenth lap and so he was out of the race. However, driver George Snider got sick overnight and Ruby rejoined the race in Snider's car as a relief driver when it resumed.

Hill never came close to defending his title, out of the race on lap twenty-three because of a blown piston.

"I supposed we used up all our luck last year," Hill said.

Parnelli Jones got off to a quick start and led early. He faltered late and finished sixth. On lap 196 a bearing gave out and he did not make it to the end.

Lee Roy Yarborough, another NASCAR star giving it a go at Indy, had a spin-out on the first day. On the second day, as Jones was passing him on lap fifty-two, leading the race by twenty-five seconds, Yarborough spun out again and this time forced Jones into a spin.

"My car runs so quiet other drivers can't hear me coming," Jones said. "As I went to pass below Lee Roy, I'm sure he hadn't seen me because he started to drop down into the low groove. Our wheels touched and he began to spin and I spun with him. We spun so close I could have reached out with my hand to touch him, but our cars never touched again. I never in my life felt so in control of a spinning car as I did of this beautiful baby."

Jones lost momentum and A.J. Foyt passed him for the lead, but when Foyt entered the pits, Jones got back ahead and built a thirty second margin. Jones was confident of victory when abruptly his engine gave out. Instead of cruising to his second win he cruised into the pits in defeat as five drivers passed him.

"I just couldn't believe it," Jones said. "I was numbed by it."

For Foyt, it was a special vindication. After the 1966 race he was competing in a NASCAR race in Riverside, California when he was in a serious accident. He broke his back and other bones, including a fractured heel and he had a punctured lung. One doctor, who apparently had no knowledge of the resilience and will of race-car drivers, told Foyt he would never drive again. Of course Foyt came back too soon. A month later, after discarding a cane, but still in tremendous pain, he raced again.

Many were surprised to see him at the Atlanta track. Foyt said, "I'm a race driver, where else should I be?"

Less than a year after the terrible crash Foyt won his third Indianapolis 500, once again emerging as king of the Speedway and moving into elite company in race lore.

The tough Texan, who could be seen wearing a cowboy hat around the Speedway at times, had a reputation of being fearless, but he later admitted that was far from the truth.

"I get scared almost every time I get in a race car," Foyt said. "And if I'm not scaring myself, somebody else is doing it for me."

That was a very rational outlook given how frequently drivers minding their own business were collected in other drivers' crashes and had their race chances ended , health ruined, and sometimes were killed.

"But death is something every race driver has to face," Foyt said. "I tell myself it's not on my mind, but it really is."

In this Indianapolis 500, just pleased to be healthy enough to race again, Foyt believed the race was lost. Jones' car seemed too strong. He kept chasing Jones, but did not believe he could catch him.

"I followed Parnelli lap after lap," Foyt said, "driving harder than I'd ever driven. With four laps to go I felt it was all over, but I kept pushing Parnelli. I can't say that's the reason or not – the car may have broken anyway – but on the next lap Parnelli slowed down. By the time I went past him, he was coasting."

As one of the sideshows during practice and qualifying there were intense debates about the best tires to use on the track that year. Firestone had long been king. Goodyear was trying to elbow its way back into the picture. Foyt ended up running on Goodyear tires and that marked the first time since 1919 that the company had outfitted the winning car.

Three-time Indy 500 champ. The words sounded good to Foyt.

1968

When Bobby Unser won the 1968 Indianapolis 500, he was carrying on the Speedway legacy of his brother Jerry who had died there. But he was also kick-starting a family tradition in the world's most prestigious automobile race.

Bobby, his brother Al, and his nephew Al Jr. became the first family of the *500*.

Although Bobby was born in Colorado Springs, Colorado, the Unsers moved to Albuquerque a year later and that is the home they have been identified with ever since. Like others in his clan, Bobby was fascinated at a young age by racing, but he was not particularly attracted to Indy cars and open-wheel racing. He liked the local scene and he especially was fond of the annual Pike's Peak International Hill Climb race.

The 14,410 foot mountain in Colorado has a road to the top that is more than twelve miles long and includes 156 turns. The Unsers long dominated the event, winning year after year. In the end, Bobby surpassed all his relatives, winning the race 13 times. Unlike track races, this event requires driving straight up. A driver could actually get altitude sickness from a swift ascent. The Pike's Peak race is the second oldest race in the United States to the Indianapolis 500 and was celebrating its 100th anniversary in 2016.

Unser made his Indianapolis debut in 1963, but for his first few starts all he showed was promise, not results. In 1966 and 1967 Unser finished eighth and ninth, hinting at a possible breakthrough.

Things were in flux at Indianapolis, as they had been for a few years. By 1968, rear engines predominated. All but one car, belonging to Jim Hurtubise, was a rear-engine vehicle. Ever since, all entries have been front-engine cars. It was a new day. Engines themselves were changing, too. They had become turbocharged, meaning a turbine piece was installed in the engine, which produced more efficiency.

Each year in May, the action is heavy at the Speedway, team after team trying to coax every last mph of speed out of its car. Experimentation is constant, adjustments are steady, and by the time pole day arrives everyone hopes their car is set up just right for their driver.

Joe Leonard, whose nickname was "Pelican Joe," was a champion motorcycle driver before trying Indy cars. Racing for owner Andy Granatelli in 1968, Leonard captured the pole for the 52nd running of the Indy 500. He sped around the track at 171.559 mph, a new record. That gave Leonard confidence and when the green flag dropped he shot into the lead.

Bobby Unser hung with Leonard, though, and by the eighth lap he had gone to the front. Unser led through lap fifty-six when Lloyd Ruby came into the picture. Ruby, from Wichita Falls, Texas, was a legitimate threat. In 1966 he led the race for sixty-eight laps and he competed in the *500* from 1960 to 1977. Ruby was a top U.S. Automobile Club competitor who earned eighty-eight top ten finishes and seven wins.

Ruby was quite comfortable leading from lap fifty-seven through lap eighty-nine when Unser wrested the lead back and held it through lap 112. Then Leonard surged, leading from lap 113 through 119 until Unser could steal the lead back and hold it through lap 165. Back and forth the front-runners raced with Ruby holding down the front of the pack from 166 through 174. Engine problems slowed Ruby then and he gave up the lead.

At that point it looked as if it might be Leonard's race. He took over on lap 175 and was still in command through lap 191. And just like that, suddenly, on a re-start after a yellow caution flag, Leonard's engine wouldn't go. He stopped dead in place. The cause was a broken fuel pump drive shaft.

The last of the front-runners was Unser. His machine was still humming and he led the final nine laps to win the Indianapolis 500. Dan Gurney took over second and Ruby got going in top form again too late. Leonard fell to twelfth place.

One rookie in the field was Gary Bettenhausen, whose dad Tony had been killed at the track in 1961. Between 1968 and 1994 Gary was an annual presence at the Speedway. Although he was always there trying, he failed to qualify five times over those years, but competed twenty-one times. Bettenhausen was a versatile driver who won races in several different types of cars. His highest Indy finish was third. Plus he recorded two fifths.

In what may have been his best achievement considering the times, the younger Bettenhausen did not die in a race car, but lived to be seventy-two.

"He was a great ambassador of the sport," said Mario Andretti. "He was a total racer and I respected that."

Another new racer with a haunting name showed up in 1968. Bill Vukovich II completed 198 laps and finished seventh. The younger Vukovich was rookie of the year. Vuke II competed in sixteen Indianapolis 500 races. His highest finish was third. While Vukovich scored twenty-three midget car victories he won only once in Indy cars, though he recorded top tens.

Tragically, his son, Bill III, met the same fate as his grandfather, being killed in a race. Bill III was the 1988 Indy rookie of the year, but died in a sprint race in 1990. Bill III made the Vukovichs the first family to send three generations to the starting line in the Indianapolis Motor Speedway. He had never doubted that he wanted to race.

"I know I'm a lot luckier than most kids my age because I've never wondered or worried what I would do with my life," Bill III said.

The same could probably have been said for Unser, at least in a general way. He wanted to race from an early age, but he just didn't know his greatest fame would come at Indianapolis.

"Nothing could ever top a person's first win," Unser said of his triumph that day. "That was the day the Good Lord smiled on me. The Indianapolis Motor Speedway really made Bobby Unser. Without that nobody would know Bobby Unser."

For Unser, that huge win was really just a beginning. He had a lot of racing left in him and a lot of winning, too.

1969

This was the moment Mario Andretti dreamt about, one that obsessed him. As great as Andretti was as a driver, as versatile and accomplished, Indianapolis always meant the most to him. One of the greatest auto racers of all-time (named the driver of the 20th century by the Associated Press) Andretti's proudest moment at Indianapolis Motor Speedway came in 1969.

Born in Italy in 1940, Andretti's family immigrated to the United States in 1955. They were displaced by World War II and were almost broke when they settled in Nazareth, Pennsylvania.

Andretti has a twin brother, Aldo, and both boys were entranced by fast cars. Mario and Aldo had no money to spend, but somehow were able to build and race cars on dirt tracks while also keeping it a secret from their parents, who would have disapproved. They took turns racing the same revamped 1948 Hudson and each boy won two races.

It was not until Aldo was seriously injured in a race that mom and dad even discovered they were racing. Aldo was forced to retire, but Mario persevered, pledging to race for both of them. Mario was not yet a fluent English speaker, but he spoke a universal language behind the wheel of a car.

Andretti was slight of build and not very tall. Some car drivers didn't believe he would be able to handle the bigger, heavy cars of the day and wouldn't give him a chance.

"I can tell you there is not a hell of a lot I didn't experience in my days," Andretti said. "I've experienced rejection in the worst possible way and I experienced humiliation because the rejection came with incredible humiliation."

Andretti proved a lot of people wrong who didn't take him seriously as a driver.

"I never forgot it," he said, "and later, when I would see these people, I had no forgiveness for them. To this day I cannot forgive them because of what they said and how much they hurt me."

Once he was able to make a name for himself racing, Andretti scrapped and hustled and demonstrated his versatility. If a vehicle had four wheels, he could drive it fast. He kept winning at whatever kind of auto racing he tried, but his heart was set on succeeding in open-wheel racing.

Worried if he was ready for the extreme speeds of Indianapolis, Andretti got his first chance in 1965 and finished in third place. From that point on he was a fixture at Indy. While that splashy debut made his name known, Andretti had experienced three fairly frustrating years leading up to 1969, finishing no higher than eighteenth.

Dark-haired, friendly, and appealing with his accented English, the handsome young Andretti was a popular figure at the Indianapolis Motor Speedway. But inside he burned to win. He knew he had it in him to commandeer the five hundred mile race and be catapulted to the forefront of American drivers. By then, indeed, he was an American, becoming a citizen in 1964 after his wife Dee Ann, who met him at a dance in Nazareth, helped polish his English in the first part of the decade.

Andretti's family had farming in its background, but he eventually became the patriarch of a famous racing family in the U.S., carrying on and carrying out the boyhood aspirations he shared with Aldo.

After qualifying sessions A.J. Foyt emerged as the pole sitter by averaging 170.568 mph. By this time Foyt and Andretti were rivals. While some front-engine cars came to the Brickyard, none could qualify for the race. Andretti had an accident in practice that totaled his car, and suffered some minor burns, but nothing that slowed him down physically. Using another Andy Granatelli car, Andretti qualified in the front row. In a somewhat humorous maneuver, when the usual photograph of the front-row starters was snapped, it was identical twin Aldo standing in place, not Mario. It was all for one and one for all in the Andretti family.

Andretti had briefly been a car owner and driver because a death had caused upheaval in his team. It was not a role he wanted to play and he cut a deal with Granatelli to instead drive for him.

Normally, the thirty-three car lineup featured the cars that qualified on pole day up front, but there were always cars that qualified later that were faster. This year, for the first time ever, the cars started the race in the exact order that every single one of them recorded for speed. Things just broke that way.

By the time the field slid through the first turn Andretti was in the lead, just ahead of Foyt. Foyt passed him after five laps and held it through lap fifty-one. Wally Dallenbach took a turn and then Foyt roared back. Lloyd Ruby, hopeful of capturing his first Indy, led from seventy-nine through eighty-six.

Andretti, who was hovering, led laps eighty-seven through 102. Ruby slipped in to lead a few more, but Foyt's car had a broken manifold. When he went into the pits it was for a long stay. Although Foyt did run again he was too far back to make a charge to the lead. Foyt placed fifth. After Foyt was out of the way and Andretti had taken on fuel, he went to the front on lap 106 and stayed there, crossing the finish line ahead of runner-up Dan Gurney and third-place, Bobby Unser. Ruby went out with a fuel tank problem after 105 laps.

Mark Donahue was rookie of the year. This was more notable retroactively than people thought at the time because this was the first year in the *500* for car owner Roger Penske. Penske, who had been an accomplished racer, was launching a legendary career as a team owner with Donahue's ride.

What a sweet moment it was for Andretti in the winner's circle, even if Granatelli gave him a kiss out of joy.

"Winning that race was the ultimate feeling of relief," Andretti said. "I finished third in my first race at Indy in 1965 and I figured, 'God willing, I'm going to win a dozen of these races.'"

Andretti did not count on the gods of racing frowning at him so often.

While Indianapolis was always special for Andretti, he became a globe-trotting success in other big races and year-after-year grew his reputation by accomplishing things few other drivers in history were able to do. Andretti was hardly identified with stock-car racing, but he had won the Daytona 500 two years before winning Indy.

He also won a Formula 1 championship in 1978 and won a CART, open-wheel racing championship in 1984 and three IndyCar championships under the auspices of the U.S. Automobile Club. Andretti seemed never to tire. Altogether Andretti won 109 major races and was chosen the American driver of the year in three different decades, the 1960s, 1970s and 1980s.

Clearly influenced by Mario, sons Michael and Jeff raced cars, as did his nephew John, and Mario's grandson Marco is a current Indianapolis 500 threat.

Despite personally knowing many drivers who did not survive the racetrack wars, Andretti's overriding philosophy was, "If everything seems under control, you're just not going fast enough. You're safer in the race car than you are in cars going to and from the track."

ATTENDANCE AT THE INDIANAPOLIS MOTOR SPEEDWAY

From the beginning, the Indianapolis 500 was the most-attended sporting event in the United States.

When it drew 80,000 people no other sport had stadiums large enough to reach that figure. Over time the number of people who came to the Indianapolis Motor Speedway increased to fill all 257,000 seats. And then it grew some more. The infield, otherwise known as The Snake Pit, attracted the seat spillover. Ultimately, even though officials declined to give out attendance figures, it became accepted that the Indianapolis 500 attracted about 400,000 to each race.

There is no other sports stadium in the world that can accommodate so many spectators for a single event in racing or otherwise.

That was true by the 1960s as the post-World War II period brought new drivers to the course, many of them with big personalities and even larger credentials. For a time, the day in May designated for determining the pole position attracted 100,000 people. And that was not even a sporting event with a true winner and loser.

The Indy infield crowd has been characterized by drinking, singing, dancing, public and private parties general whooping it up, drinking, and more drinking.

Few other sporting events open the infield in their arenas to more casual spectators, though notably, Churchill Downs, which is the venue for the Kentucky Derby in Louisville, is one.

Most of the other biggest sporting arenas in the United States are now NASCAR stock-car racing locales.

For starters, the one stock-car race that stands out is the Brickyard 400 and it has the advantage of being staged at Speedway.

Other than the Brickyard, there are several very large NASCAR sites. Bristol Motor Speedway can hold 160,000 fans. The Daytona International Speedway capacity is 146,000. Las Vegas Motor Speedway can accommodate 142,000 fans. Charlotte Motor Speedway can handle 140,000 fans. Texas Motor Speedway comes in at 122,000. Talladega in Alabama has a capacity of 108,000. Kentucky Speedway holds 107,000

A bunch of college football stadiums are within a few thousand seats of one another in capacity, with Michigan Stadium in Ann Arbor, on top at 107,601. The Big House is ahead of the home fields of Penn State, Ohio State, Texas A&M, University of Tennessee, Louisiana State, University of Alabama and University of Texas, all of them at 100,000 or more.

When AT&T Stadium, home of the Dallas Cowboys, hosted the Super Bowl a few years ago, seating was crammed into every available space to get the crowd total up to and over 100,000. But the standard number for a Cowboys' regular season game is 80,000.

There are large stadiums in other parts of the world, but none of them match in size the Indianapolis Motor Speedway and that's even without factoring in possible infield demand. There is a 200,000-seat venue in China for auto racing. There is a 200,000-seat soccer stadium in Brazil. But if the Indianapolis 500 has a full house, or an overflow attendance, it is always going to host the largest crowd for any sporting event in the world.

More Greats Emerge

1970-79

In 1977, A.J. Foyt became the first driver in the history of the Indianapolis 500 to win the race four times. Although tied since, Foyt remains co-holder of that record.

That year Tom Sneva thrilled race fans by qualifying for the race at more than two hundred miles per hour. The barrier had fallen.

It was no easy trick to make it to the finish line first in the 1970s. Besides Foyt's milestone championship, Al Unser won three times and Johnny Rutherford won twice in the 1970s. Bobby Unser won again and Gordon Johncock won for a first time. So did Rick Mears, on his way to a record-equaling career.

Basically, to win at the Speedway during this decade a driver had to be a Hall of Famer.

1970

It was an Unser kind of year at Indianapolis in 1970, but this time it was not a race that belonged to Bobby. Instead, his five years younger brother Al, captured the title and showed the racing fraternity there was more than one Unser to worry about each May.

Al was not born until after the family moved to Albuquerque and he was just eighteen when he began racing cars. By the time he sat down in a Parnelli Jones car at the Indianapolis Motor Speedway, in the spring of 1970, he definitely knew what he was doing.

Perhaps Al Unser was destined to win the Indy 500 because his birthday was May 29. He got to celebrate his 31st birthday one day and his first Indianapolis 500 triumph the next day. He not only beat his brother to do so (Bobby was eleventh that year), but an intriguing field that included folks like NASCAR stars LeeRoy Yarbrough and Donnie Allison (fourth), but overseas stars Dan Gurney and Jack Brabham and Indy luminaries A.J. Foyt, Mario Andretti, Johnny Rutherford, Lloyd Ruby and Gordon Johncock. Allison was rookie of the year.

Others who made the trip were Gary Bettenhausen, Joe Leonard, Bill Vukovich III and the always-dangerous Roger McCluskey and runner-up Mark Donahue, improving on his rookie race.

Yet the way the month went all of them might as well have stayed parked in the garage on Gasoline Alley.

For starters, Al Unser captured the pole with a clocking of 170.221 mph. He was first on the starting grid and he was almost never out of first on the track. Unser led the daily speed charts for all five days, driving the only car faster than the 170 mph barrier. Andretti crashed during practice and that did his car no good at all.

On pole day, however, Unser was challenged. Rutherford made a superb run and was timed at 0.01 second slower. Foyt, too, made a game run for the pole, averaging more than 170 mph, but was third.

It had been a humid month and rain interrupted pole day qualifying. The rain affected the race start, too. The gentlemen did not start their engines on time, but were delayed twenty-five minutes. Once again the nightmare of a first-lap crash loomed. Just before the race was about to be flagged green the suspension on Jim Malloy's car broke. The cart swerved to the wall and crashed into, but barely missed hitting other cars. Finally, after track cleanup, the race began.

Rutherford, no doubt emboldened by his strong pole run, snapped up the lead into the first turn. But Unser, drafting behind, showed he was not intimidated and he took the lead before the end of the first lap.

Irritated by how rain cost him his qualifying run despite being in line waiting his turn on pole day, Lloyd Ruby showed he had something to prove. Stuck in the twenty-fifth starting position he decided to make up the deficit almost all at once. He passed ten cars on the first lap and moved into the top ten by the third lap. Ruby kept on coming and by lap twenty-right he was in fifth place.

Really, though, no one could compete with Unser. He led the first forty-eight laps, took a pit stop and gradually worked his way back to the front after Ruby. Moving all of the way to the front, Donahue, and Brabham took turns in the lead. Unser was back in charge between laps fifty-four and one hundred. Foyt and Donahue led the next five laps, but when Unser was loaded with fuel he took the lead again for lap 106.

This time he kept it all the way around for the rest of the day. Al Unser won the title with ease. He led 190 laps and averaged 155.749 mph. Al's win made the Unsers the first brother tandem to claim Indy 500 titles.

Al Unser was right where he wanted to be and right where he had always planned to be – in Victory Lane at the Indianapolis Motor Speedway.

"My Lord, when I went to school I told my teachers you can't teach me what I want to do in life," he said. "They asked me what I wanted to do and I said I wanted to be a race driver."

It was a natural enough ambition since his father, uncles and brothers all raced cars. Al also wanted to beat his older brother. That was part of his motivation.

"I wanted to outrun Bobby," Al said. "Bobby always was the oldest and he set the pace and I wanted to outrun him."

1971

With a Parnelli Jones race car at his disposal and his dominating performance of the preceding season fresh in mind, no one could have questioned Al Unser for thinking "Why not?" about sweeping the race for a second straight year.

Things did not go quite as swimmingly in the chase for the pole. Peter Revson won that with a speed of 178.696 mph.

Revson had an unusual background for an Indy car driver. He was born in New York City and he was Jewish, a member of a family that emigrated from Russia. And yes, Revson was an heir one generation removed from the Revlon cosmetics owners. His father was said to be worth more than one billion dollars. Revson could certainly get funding to race, but he could have chosen a different type of existence.

Known as a hot-shot playboy, Revson dated prominent beauties, including a Miss World. He was on his way to his greatest Indy performance in 1971, first taking the pole and then taking a solid run at the championship.

This particular year the *500* was run on May 29, which meant that Al Unser was racing on his birthday with little time to blow out candles on a cake, at least until late in the day.

Also, the federal government changed the observance date of Memorial Day from being locked in on May 30 to the closest Monday. That led to a race schedule change. Subsequently, the race was always scheduled for the closest Sunday to the holiday with the actual holiday becoming a rain date.

The only other driver even close to Revson trying for the pole was Mark Donahue, one mile per hour slower.

On race day there was tragedy on the track even before the first lap began. The driver of the pace car, Eldon Palmer, who was an Indianapolis car dealer, crashed into a photographers' stand. It tumbled down, throwing a few dozen people to the ground and causing twenty-nine injuries.

The car was a Dodge Challenger and Palmer had supplied the track with the pace cars. The car was also severely damaged and instead of being given to the winner as had become the norm, a substitute was provided.

Donahue led at the beginning of the race and for fifty laps, but he was grounded after sixty-six laps because of a broken gear. Joe Leonard, Bobby Unser, and Lloyd Ruby all got some up-front time, but as their cars slowed or suffered breakdowns, Al Unser pulled away. He took the lead for the fifth time on lap 118 and stayed right there until completion of two hundred laps.

Unser became a two-time champion and the rare racer to win the Indianapolis 500 twice in a row.

With family wins in 1968, 1970, and 1971, the Unser brothers were the hottest racers at the Indianapolis Motor Speedway.

Al Unser once famously said, "Dad taught me everything I know, unfortunately he didn't teach me everything he knows."

It was obvious, however, that he had taught Al quite enough.

1972

There was a lot of adventure in the 1972 race. Al Unser was vying to become the first driver to win the Indianapolis 500 three straight years. Gary Bettenhausen was seeking to accomplish something his father couldn't. And Mark Donahue, who had burst on the scene two years earlier as the top rookie, then come back with a second-place finish, hoped to replace the number two with the number one.

Also, a tradition began that no one realized would be a tradition. Jim Nabors sang "Back Home Again in Indiana" before the race for the first time.

Almost by magic there was also a quantum leap in speed recorded in the chase for the pole. In 1971, Peter Revson won the pole with a speed of 178.696 mph. In 1972, Bobby Unser won the pole at 195.940 mph. That was fast enough to part your hair.

Each year the United States Automobile Club set the rules for the structure of the cars. The big difference for 1972 revolved around what were described as bolt-on wings. That changed the downforce character of the cars, resulting in faster times. Additional downforce can help cars take the corners at a higher rate of speed. Drivers do not have to brake as much and they can maintain their speed without losing momentum. There was a hint of pole qualifying to come in March when Bobby Unser clocked a lap at the Speedway caught in 190.8 mph. That was a barrier-breaking time.

Before practice and qualifying in 1972 no driver had ever topped the 180 mph mark at the Indianapolis Motor Speedway. During the first week of practice that occurred routinely and several cars topped 190 mph.

It was perhaps no surprise that higher speeds could also result in dangerous conditions. Jim Malloy crashed into the wall, broke bones in his arms and legs and was taken to the hospital in critical condition from burns. Malloy was a Colorado racer who had played football and baseball as a younger man. He was trying to compete in his sixth *500*. After several years of non-descript finishes he recorded a breakthrough in fourth place in 1971. He came to the track this May thinking he could contend for the title.

Instead, Malloy was hospitalized and died four days later at thirty-nine.

Several cars were blistering the track with runs faster than 190 mph, but as always there was drama to see who made the cut for the thirty-three car field. Gordon Johncock somehow blew out five engines during practice and qualifying, but still made the field on Bump Day, squeezing past a previously qualified car.

Veteran Jim Hurtubise garnered some attention because nobody really understood what he was doing. Hurtubise had already qualified a car, but got in line for qualifying as if to do it all over again. When asked, Hurtubise said he might trot out another driver to drive it. Qualifying shut down at 6 p.m. and Hurtubise was far enough back in the pack that his car wasn't close to getting a turn.

After the end of qualifying, Hurtubise flipped off the engine cover of this car. There was no engine under the hood. Instead, Hurtubise, who was sponsored by Miller High Life beer, showed off an inner compartment filled with ice and cases of the beer. He gave out beers to pit crews and race officials on the scene. Some sober officials did not laugh as loudly. But the Beer Engine lived on in Indy lore.

One change from the 1971 race was the placement of an experienced Indy 500 driver in the pace car in place of the automobile dealer who wrecked the photographer's stand. Jim Rathmann was talented enough to keep the pace car going in a straight line.

Just before the race went green there was a problem, A.J. Foyt's car stalled out and didn't get off the starting line as the other cars began rolling to get up to full speed. Foyt's pit crew frantically worked on the car and it got started just in time to go.

No doubt feeling very good about his chances after his record run for the pole, Bobby Unser went to the front and led for the first thirty laps. His dream ended there with a mechanical failure. Also running up front were Gary Bettenhausen, Jerry Grant and Mark Donahue.

After Bobby Unser was out, Bettenhausen led laps thirty-one to fifty-three. Briefly, Mike Mosley took the lead between fifty-four and fifty-six, but then he wrecked. Leaping out of his car that burst into flames, Mosley suffered minor burns, but escaped a worse fate.

Bettenhausen re-took the lead, setting the pace from lap 57-161. Grant led 162 through 165 and Bettenhausen came back to lead from 166 to 175. It appeared Bettenhausen had the best car. He did not. After leading for 138 laps Bettenhausen was finished because of ignition problems.

When Bettenhausen's car failed Grant took over and led laps 176 to 187. He appeared poised to seize the greatest moment of his racing life. On lap 188 Grant had a tire blow out. His big lead evaporated and Donahue took over as Grant's pit stop became the focus of scrutiny.

Cruising into the pits, Grant overshot his assigned pit stop and did not come to a halt until he reached teammate Bobby Unser's pit slot next door. Grant's crew ran over and fixed up his car, and since they were members of the same team they used Bobby Unser's fuel. It was too late to catch Donahue, but Grant finished second.

However, Al Unser, who never led during the race, but steadily gained ground, filed a protest saying that Grant broke the rules by using another driver's fuel. The protest was upheld and Grant's standing was changed. Officials removed the credit of the last twelve laps following the pit stop and ruled that Grant's race had ended there after 188 laps. That dropped him to twelfth place. Al Unser moved into second with Joe Leonard third. Several other top racers flamed out with mechanical issues. Mario Andretti was eighth, Bettenhausen fourteenth, Johncock twentieth, Foyt twenty-fifth, and Bobby Unser 30th.

Mike Hiss, originally from California, was the rookie-of-the-year in seventh place. It was the first of his four competitions at Indy and easily his top result. The six months beginning with Hiss' best Indy finish jump-started his fifteen minutes of fame in life. He turned forty-one about a month later and he turned into a sex symbol the following January of 2013 when he posed as the first nude centerfield for Playgirl magazine.

The main photo of Hiss in the magazine was of him sitting halfway up on a couch balancing on his right arm – with his race helmet strategically placed on a table blocking his privates. Hiss wore only his broad smile.

The more modest Donahue was the victor. Donahue was from New Jersey and attended Ivy League Brown University in Rhode Island. As a senior he began racing Corvettes and became an expert mechanic working on his own cars. In fact he earned a degree in mechanical engineering.

His first reputation was earned as an engineer who was considered a genius at tinkering with the machinery to make it go faster and a perfectionist to make sure that it did. That expertise initially left some believing he was a better engineer than driver, though that perception changed gradually. It turned out he was good at both.

Patrick Bedard, the driver and racing writer, watched Donahue work over what seemed to be a slow Ferrari and coax extra miles per hour out of it.

"He gained 11.5 seconds, the quickest Ferrari in the field, and fourth overall," Bedard said. "He did it through sheer force of will. Mark told me, 'Sometimes you've just got to get it done.'"

Donahue moved into racing, got noticed at the 24 Hours of Le Mans and did well in the 24 Hours of Daytona and the 12 Hours of Sebring.

Roger Penske was a good driver who never ran the Indy 500, but would become one of the legends of the race as a car owner. In 1965, he moved in that direction and targeted young Donahue because of his talent. By 1966 they were racing partners and Donahue dominated the USAC road racing championships with wins in six of the seven races he started. In 1969, they tackled Indy together. In 1971, the Penske-Donahue team produced a rookie of the year award and a second place finish. In 1972, Donahue delivered Penske's first Indianapolis 500 title and during the triumph he averaged a record 162 mph.

Donahue had the makings of becoming a great at Indy. He was well-liked at the time, too, acquiring the nickname "Captain Nice." But the continuous parade of driver deaths in the sport altered Donahue's outlook and in 1973 he retired. Penske was able to lure Donahue back with the promise of a full-time Formula 1 ride.

That was the driver's undoing. Donahue had difficulties with the new car and during practice at a track in Austria, he lost control and the car crashed. A track worker was killed by a piece from the car, but Donahue walked away with a headache. Later, however, Donahue felt ill – he had suffered a concussion. At a hospital Donahue was diagnosed with a cerebral hemorrhage, fell into a coma and died at age thirty-eight.

The Penske racing headquarters in North Carolina is decorated with murals of Donahue and his cars.

JIM NABORS

For the uninitiated Jim Nabors seemed the perfect fit to play the loveable TV character Gomer Pyle and a misfit to sing a serious song.

But Nabors was multi-talented. He grew up in Alabama and had the syrupy accent to prove it. A graduate of the University of Alabama, Nabors, who was born in 1930, moved to Southern California because he hoped it would help his asthma condition.

Living near ground zero of the acting profession Nabors was actually working in a theatrical technical job as a film cutter while moonlighting at a cabaret theatre. It wasn't Schwab's Drugstore and it wasn't because of his legginess, or chest size, but Nabors was discovered there by Andy Griffith.

Nabors was already fine-tuning his Gomer Pyle character and Griffith hired him to play Pyle on the air. Later, Nabors got his own show featuring the character's name. In 1972, Nabors was attending the Indianapolis 500 as a guest when he was introduced to track owner Tony Hulman.

Over the years many different singers performed "Back Home Again In Indiana" during the event's pre-race ceremonies. Many of those singers were just passing through and have been forgotten by time. Given the way one succeeded the other and then disappeared, it was obvious that Hulman did not give much thought to the selection of the singer.

As it so happened, Hulman met Nabors on the morning of the race, was told he was a singer, and asked him to perform. The Purdue University band – also an institution – was playing the National Anthem and Nabors thought he was being asked to sing "The Star Spangled Banner" as the band played.

Once the misunderstanding was cleared up Nabors had to scramble because he did not even know the words to the song "Back Home Again in Indiana". He obtained the lyrics, wrote them on a piece of paper and without any rehearsal sang the popular tune. Those fans who only knew Nabors from his goofy, thick accent portrayal of Gomer Pyle never suspected he had the same type of golden pipes of an Andy Williams. He was transformed from one Jim Nabors to the other and transfixed all of those listening.

Nabors was such a hit that he was asked back. And asked back again and again. Between 1972 and 2014, even as he moved into his eighties, Nabors always tried to make room on his calendar for late May in Indianapolis. Nabors truly was back home again in Indiana each year even if he had never lived there. He became a beloved figure at the Indianapolis Motor Speedway, and only missed performing a few times over the years, sometimes for health reasons.

When Nabors appeared in 2014, it was his pre-announced swan song, a last go-around at the Speedway on a day thick with nostalgia. He was introduced to the throng as a "cherished icon" for race day, singing for the 36th and last and scheduled time. As Nabors waved to the crowd, a simultaneous goodbye and thanks, a message was spelled out in a portion of the seats by cards reading, "Thank you Jim."

Once again Nabors hit all of the right notes in a song that he had become closely identified with. Fans provided a roaring ovation as an era came to an end.

For a long time it was as if the Indianapolis 500 could not begin without Jim Nabors, but now it had to learn how to live without him.

1973

Sometimes the Indianapolis 500 is over within a few hours. The 1973 race took three days to complete and it didn't cover the full miles either.

The scene was a mess, rain pouring down intermittently all month and at inopportune times. Coming off a year when the drivers had been very fast, there was no reason to believe that speeds would not increase again. That meant that the two hundred mph mark was within reach.

Huge crowds, as usual, descended on the Indianapolis Motor Speedway, totaling somewhere between 300,000 and 400,000 people. That meant that there were a lot of soggy and disappointed people the way matters turned out.

The race for the pole was compelling as speeds inched up and drivers did their best between raindrops. Yet disaster after disaster befell the race that year.

Those new rules from the year before which increased downforce and made the cars faster were still in effect. During practice Gordon Johncock nearly eclipsed two hundred mph, hitting 199.4 mph. Unofficially, that was the fastest lap ever turned at the Speedway.

While the drivers felt liberated by the speeds they also took on a kind of wariness.

"Because of the downforce or pressure on the back of the car the rear wheels were achieving better traction than the front wheels, which caused the car to push," said up-and-coming racer Johnny Rutherford.

That pushing shoved the car towards the outside of turns, meaning drivers had to be vigilant.

Pole day brought out 250,000 fans, a larger-than-usual crowd for the occasion because it was believed the two hundred mph barrier was going to be broken that day and those attendees wished to witness history. Alas, before qualifying even began they witnessed a horrible accident.

Practicing for his sixth Indianapolis 500, Art Pollard crashed into the wall coming out of turn one, spun halfway around, slid onto the infield grass, turned upside-down and slid back onto the pavement, traveling about 1,450 feet.

Wheels broke off the car, the chassis was smashed and the car caught fire, burning Pollard on his hands, face and neck. He likely suffered burning in his lungs, as well. Although rushed to the hospital, Pollard died at age forty-six.

The drivers followed that tragedy with the fastest Speedway laps of all time. Swede Savage set a one-lap record of 197.152 mph and a qualifying time of 196.582 mph. Rutherford, though, was faster, setting a new one-lap mark at 199.071 mph and a four-lap mark of 198.413 mph to take the pole.

Rutherford, who hailed from Texas and sported the nickname "Lone Star JR," had been a regular in the *500* since 1963, gradually working his way into contention. He was looking very good at the end of qualifying.

"We lined up for qualifying and I was raring to go," Rutherford said. "On several occasions during the past month of practicing I had unofficially reached speeds of up to 200 mph and had even run two or three 200 mph laps in a row. I drove flat-footed around the track and people in the stands went crazy. I had fun, too."

Rutherford was close, but did not top two hundred mph for the record book.

Plagued by rain off and on all month, race day was no different. It rained in the morning and delayed the start to mid-afternoon. When the race finally began things immediately went afoul. Problems began with Salt Walther, who had qualified seventeenth.

Walther's real name was David, but everyone called him Salt. The nickname stemmed from his days racing hydroplanes. On the first lap Walther's car swerved to the right, caught the wheels of another driver, and then climbed the wall into the fencing above. The vehicle spewed burning fuel, which showered on spectators, injuring thirteen of them.

The car broke apart, the front end coming off completely so that fans could actually see Walther's lower body in the vehicle. After hitting the fence the car ricocheted back onto the track, landing upside-down, but still spinning. Two more cars hit Walther's vehicle and then other cars trying to slam on their brakes bounced off one another.

Pieces of metal, some of it burning, and hot fuel and oil all littered the track in what appeared to be a battlefield scene. Altogether eleven cars were involved in the accident and to complicate matters, it began to rain again. The race was halted and Walther was rushed to a hospital. In such circumstances race fans had become used to (and some said inured) to hearing that drivers died from their injuries within an hour or two, often while the race was still going on. Walther, whose hands were severely burned, was the only driver seriously injured, being burned over forty percent of his body. However, he was aided by the fact much of the fuel spilled out of his car.

With rain drenching the Speedway, the Indianapolis 500 was shuttered, postponed to a fresh start the next morning at 9 a.m., a Tuesday.

Meanwhile, doctors feverishly worked on Walther. For once, no announcement was made telling the world about another *500* driver who died. In one of his greatest accomplishments, Walther, then twenty-five, survived. He spent more than two months in hospitals, lost some fingers on his left hand and was forced to cope with a damaged right hand.

Remarkably, Walther returned to auto racing and successfully qualified for the Indy 500 the next year and for several years thereafter, although his final results were never outstanding.

It was raining again that Tuesday morning, pushing the start to 10:15 a.m. Officials wiped out the start from Monday to begin again from the starting grid. After the cars took the track and were completing their warm-up laps headed into the green flag, it started raining again. Speedway officials waited until 2 p.m. and again postponed the start of the 57th Indy 500.

That pushed the race over to Wednesday morning. Memorial Day was very much in the rearview mirror. This was unprecedented. It would have been instructive to know the attendance, but since the Speedway never announced it when it was packed, it was definitely not going to announce it when the stands were comparatively empty. It wasn't even clear if the drivers wanted to race again. Sportswriters penned the sarcastic comment, comparing the *500* to Le Mans with the phrase, "The 72 hours of Indianapolis."

The weather was neither sunny nor cooperative Wednesday morning either. Officials anxiously watched the sky and at last at 2:10 p.m. the Indianapolis 500 began a few days late.

Indianapolis 500 cars are extremely sensitive and to run at top speeds and hold together they must be very carefully set up. Whether the delays or the weather affected mechanics, or the cars just got tired, they began malfunctioning at a high rate.

Bobby Allison, the great stock-car driver, was credited with one lap. Peter Revson made it through three and then crashed. Mario Andretti went out with a bad piston after four laps. Lloyd Ruby lasted twenty-one laps. A.J. Foyt ran for thirty-seven laps. Al Unser dropped out after seventy-five laps. Mark Donahue completed ninety-two laps. Bobby Unser made it halfway.

Bobby Unser led the early portion of the race from laps 1-39 before Gordon Johncock edged ahead for a few laps. Swede Savage took over for laps 43-54 before Al Unser led laps 55-72. He relinquished the lead to Johncock.

Savage was twenty-six years old and had been in racing almost his entire life. That included Soap Box Derby competition at age five. He had already competed in the Daytona 500 and tried as many types of auto racing that he was able to fit into his schedule.

Savage was on turn four, heading from the 59th lap to the 60th when he crashed at Indy. He had just completed a pit stop a couple of laps earlier with a new load of fuel and one new right tire, but lost control. He hit the wall almost head on and with seventy gallons of fuel in the tank, it erupted into flames. The car exploded, but the force expelled Savage out of the car and onto the track where he lay in a puddle of fuel.

All driving ceased and emergency vehicles and personnel, plus concerned pit crew members rushed to the scene to aid Savage. One of those men, Armando Teran, was part of the same team as Savage, though working with driver Graham McRae. He was on foot headed to the crash site when a fire engine roaring towards the flames compounded the tragedy by smashing into Teran, hurling his body fifty feet. Teran was killed.

Savage was evacuated to the hospital, the prognosis apparently bleak. However, he was conscious and actually joked with medical personnel as he was transported. Seasoned driver Dan Gurney was one of several people who termed this *500* "jinxed."

After a delay of more than an hour the race continued. Car after car went back to the garage with mechanical issues. Once the race passed the halfway mark with 101 completed laps the race was official. There were only eleven cars of the original thirty-three still running.

Johncock grabbed the lead after Al Unser's engine blew and built a large lead. On lap 129 it began to rain still again with just ten cars rolling. The yellow caution flag came out and cars slowed. The rain did not. Johncock won the race with just 133 laps in the books, completing a shortened, demoralizing, Indianapolis 500.

The scene was so discouraging that the traditional victory banquet was cancelled. It was later reported that Johncock ate a hamburger at a fast food restaurant for dinner that night.

At the hospitals doctors stabilized Savage. Days passed, then weeks, and his health seemed to improve, but on July 2, he died from the injuries incurred during the race. There was disagreement over the cause of death between doctors and family, with reasons mentioned including lung damage from the burns, infection and in some quarters the belief that he developed hepatitis from a blood transfusion.

"That whole series of events was a terrible tragedy," said Rutherford, who lasted in the race through 124 laps.

1974

A.J. Foyt went into the 1974 race thinking he had a better chance to win than he had in a few years. Nothing that happened during qualifying should have altered his thinking. Foyt won the pole with a speed of 191.632 mph. In fact, his car was the first one out and that mark stood up all day.

Also, when the green flag dropped and Foyt rolled off the starting line he set a record with his seventeenth Indianapolis 500 start. In his case they were also all consecutive. That may have been a new record, but Foyt was just warming up. He continued with his regular annual visits until he started thirty-five straight Indianapolis 500 races.

Despite the fanfare over Foyt in his seventeenth straight race some luster was lost because the car did not make it to the end. Foyt was sidelined after 142 laps with a mechanical problem and finished fifteenth. So Foyt was the man of the hour in May, right up until then.

Often, the Indianapolis Motor Speedway seems to be in its own world with a large number of people invited to visit during May. This year, though, there were things going on in the outside world that could have seriously affected the race.

The United States faced a gasoline crisis. The country had long gotten used to cheap and abundant gasoline for the drivers who loved to fill it up and cruise around the neighborhood or who preferred driving a thousand miles to visit grandma. Unified Arab countries of the Middle East declared an oil embargo in the fall of 1973.

They were angry the United States supported Israel in the Yom Kippur War. As a result, the price of a barrel of oil went up four hundred percent and supplies became scarce. President Richard Nixon and federal employees put a lid on unlimited driving and buying and Americans were faced with the prospect of only being able to purchase gasoline at selected times.

An off-shoot of the situation led to the creation of a national fifty-five mph speed limit and a new stated policy of conservation so there would be less reliance on the Middle Eastern countries for U.S. oil in the future.

This all produced a ripple effect in the auto racing world. For the 1974 season, NASCAR cut back on the distances of stock-car races by ten percent and limited practice time. Indy 500 officials did not want to trim the length of the race, but made other voluntary changes with practice schedules to save fuel. A week of practice was eliminated and time trials were cut in half. Individual days of practice were also shortened.

If the drivers felt shortchanged, they had to live with it in the context of the problems of the country. However, fans would not really notice much of a difference. Pole day was still popular. Race day was even more popular. As they had year after year when rules or plans changed, fans adjusted. They were even willing to come on Sunday, the new permanent day of the week for the *500* starting in 1974.

Rules changes, date changes, day changes, the Indy 500 management could cope with all of that. The one thing officials did not want to see was a replay of the horrors of 1973 when two drivers and one pit crew member were killed at the Speedway. They were fortunate in 1974 that nothing of the kind occurred. Death took a vacation at the track and all were relieved. The race was supposed to be safer and it was.

Wally Dallenbach started second and he made his intentions clear. He shot to the front ahead of pole winner Foyt and led the first two laps. Dallenbach set a race record with his opening lap clocking of 191.408, but his car had no interest in the pace. A piston broke and Dallenbach was gone by lap three.

Once that was settled, the lead was exchanged for the next 198 laps by three drivers. Foyt (five times taking a turn), Bobby Unser (twice) and Johnny Rutherford (four times), alternated at the front of the pack while cars belonging to other competitors suffered problems that KO'd drivers.

There were no major accidents, but Jerry Karl hit the wall after lap 115 in turn three. He only eliminated himself. Karl competed in seven Indy 500s and was at the Speedway for years, failed to qualify for others. His best finish was thirteenth in 1975.

Stunningly, Salt Walther, who cheated death in the 1973 race, returned to Indianapolis, qualified fourteenth and finished seventeenth. It was a gutsy showing for someone who had been so seriously injured and incurred permanent damage to his body only a year before.

"A.J. and I dueled throughout the middle stages of the race," Rutherford said. "His car, with its four-cam V-8 engine, was a little stronger down the straightaways than my car was. He made it very difficult for me to get by him. However, I was all over him in the turns because my car handled so much better than his."

Once Foyt dropped out of the race, Rutherford took command, leading laps 141 to 175. Unser led one more lap during a Rutherford pit stop, but the lead reverted to the Texan on lap 177 and Rutherford took over again, leading from lap 177 to the finish. Only Rutherford and Unser completed the 200 laps. Bill Vukovich II finished third and was the only other driver to finish 199 laps. Gordon Johncock was fourth.

It was a special day for Rutherford. He had been racing the *500* since 1963 and this was his eleventh start. The year before his ninth place finish was his best to date. Rutherford was thirty-six, but seemed to be just entering racing prime.

"We had a great deal of confidence coming into the race," Rutherford said. "It seemed everything had started to come into focus, and the entire team, myself included, felt an eagerness that was hard to hide."

Rutherford had won the pole, been timed in over 199 mph, and had good cars before. He had even driven through fire because of others' accidents. So he was definitely not taking anything for granted until he actually piloted the car across the finish line. Winning wasn't real until it was real.

Despite that early optimism Rutherford did have to overcome a blown engine in practice. That put plenty of pressure on the McLaren team to have his car set up just right for qualifying. The pole winner from the year before, Rutherford, only qualified twenty-fifth this year. That was a comparative downer for a guy with such high hopes. But once the race began and Rutherford drove in competition everything fell into place. He avoided the bad luck that afflicted so many other cars.

"Soon I had just fifteen laps to go," Rutherford said. "Then ten. Then five. Those last five laps were like hours to me. I had witnessed plenty of drivers run out of fuel on the last lap, or have their engines go."

Rutherford worried all of the way until he saw the flagman leaning over the side of the wall and waving the checkered flag.

"That was the prettiest sight in the world," Rutherford said.

1975

Up until this point in his Indianapolis 500 racing career, Bobby Unser was a regular who had distinguished himself with one win. It is a dream come true for any driver to capture an Indy 500 title even once, to be the star at the Speedway on one Memorial Day.

But anyone who wins the Indianapolis 500 more than once begins to move into the realm of open-wheel racing royalty. Unser took that step in 1975 by capturing his second win at the Brickyard.

Appropriately, on the morning of the holiday, the Indianapolis Motor Speedway received an honor of its own. The 1909 structure was placed on the National Register of Historic Places. It accompanied the 30th anniversary of Tony Hulman's ownership of the track and owed considerably to his efforts to restore the track to its former glory after World War II.

Although the race was not televised live, but on a delayed basis, ABC certainly had the "A" team in the broadcast booth with Chris Schenkel, Keith Jackson and color man Jackie Stewart sharing duties and helped from the track by Chris Economaki and Sam Posey.

At the end of the 1974 Indy Car season Firestone tires, which had been a staple of the race for decades, pulled out of sponsoring the series, leaving the circuit to Goodyear. For two decades starting in 1975, Goodyear was the only tire supplier for *500* race cars.

Pole day was packed with excitement. One driver after another took off and superseded the clocking of the previous drivers. At one point Mike Mosley had the inside track. Then Tom Sneva took over. Bobby Unser drove faster. But Gordon Johncock went faster still.

A.J. Foyt put an end to all discussion by taking the pole with a speed of 195.313 mph.

Johncock took the early lead, laps one through eight. Foyt took over for a little while and Johnny Rutherford and Donnie Allison led briefly. Foyt regained the lead for laps 25-58, but Wally Dallenbach, hungry to push himself into the top echelon of Indy drivers, led laps 56-69.

Dallenbach, who was from New Jersey, ran thirteen Indy 500s in his career. Mostly, his cars were not good enough to best the very top drivers' cars, but 1975 shaped up as his best chance to capture a title. While other cars went back to the garage Dallenbach kept fighting back to the lead.

Between lap twenty-five and 161, with the exception of lap 124, nobody besides Dallenbach or Foyt led the race. However, on lap 162 Dallenbach's car blew a piston. He drove off into the sunset frustrated over the setback and having led ninety-six laps that day with nothing to show for it.

In the middle of all that there were two crashes.

Sneva, who had been a math teacher in Spokane, Washington, was in his second Indy 500, though he went on to have a long career at the track. However, he was fortunate to survive the 1975 race. After completing 125 laps Sneva was attempting to pass a lapped car driven by Eldon Rasmussen, but they touched wheels. Sneva's machine went haywire, flipping over, and going over Rasmussen's car before taking off into the air, coming down on the wheels and then smashing a wall and fencing rear-end first. Large chunks of the car, including the engine, were ripped from the guts of the car and it caught fire. Sneva was still in the driver's seat as it kept skidding along the track, doing somersaults twice. The seating area traveled still longer before stopping next to the track.

Remarkably, Sneva was able to loosen his seat belt, but not knowing the rear of the car was on fire he lifted his helmet visor and burned his face. Unsteady, he then put his fingers into a puddle of methanol, incurring more burns. Although he attempted to lift himself out of the remains of the car, he could not do so without help because his legs were pinned.

Sneva actually walked on his own to the ambulance waiting for him. The frightening scene wreaked havoc on Sneva's car, but after all of that bouncing around his most serious injuries were the burns on his face and fingers acquired after it was all over.

The second crash occurred later on lap 170, another event that could have ended in much worse fashion than it did. The hub on Gary Bettenhausen's right rear wheel exploded, but somehow he kept control of the car, running it to a stop, on just three wheels.

Rutherford took over the lead from lap 162 through 164 and as the race denouement loomed the showdown shaped up as being between Unser, Rutherford and Foyt. All were on lap 174 with engines still running and spaced out under a yellow caution flag.

Abruptly, it began to rain and rain hard. Some areas of the track flooded and cars began skidding. The sky was so dark visibility became an issue. Starter Pat Vidan surveyed the conditions above and in front of him on the track and halted the race. The trio of racers going one, two and three, Unser, Foyt, Rutherford, completed 435 miles.

"I wish that race had gone the full two hundred hundred laps," Rutherford said. "We were right there. We had a chance to win, but coming in second at Indy after winning the race the year before showed that our win wasn't a fluke."

1976

Johnny Rutherford moved into elite company with his second victory in 1976. He owned the month, taking the pole with a speed of 188.957 mph and then capturing the race by outrunning A.J. Foyt, who took second, and Gordon Johncock in third.

However, it was the shortest race in Indianapolis 500 history, ending after 255 miles and 102 laps because of rain. It was barely official, with not much more than fifty percent of the scheduled distance completed.

In a milestone development, Janet Guthrie became the first woman to enter the Indy 500. However, with minimal funding to back her car when it ran into trouble she could not make the field of thirty-three in qualifying.

She had a newsworthy attempt, but not everyone at the track was warm to Guthrie. The Indianapolis 500 had always been a man's bastion and drivers were not all accommodating to the arrival of a woman on the track. Some fans were also insulting. Sexism was still very prevalent in American society.

Born in 1938 in Iowa City, Iowa, Guthrie graduated from the University of Michigan and worked as an aerospace engineer before she broke into auto racing. At the time she was easily the most qualified female driver and people who believed it was time for racing to become integrated turned to her. Guthrie simultaneously broke into both Indy Car racing and NASCAR.

Although she knew theoretically that some opposed her, Guthrie was surprised when she ran across vocal taunts at the Indianapolis Motor Speedway and elsewhere.

"I was very surprised," she said. "It just wasn't an issue to me. I was astounded. Sometimes I got mad. Mostly, I laughed it off."

Practice and qualifying strain the stamina, concentration and focus of all drivers in May, and that can be multiplied by a large factor if the driver is not part of one of the richer teams with seemingly unlimited resources. And all of that can be compounded if the driver is a rookie. Guthrie was in a much brighter spotlight than the average rookie because of her gender .

Guthrie did experience engine trouble and mechanical breakdowns that hindered her practice sessions. But she passed her rookie test, driving as fast as 171.429 mph, although speed alone was not what her performance was judged upon.

Janet Guthrie was the first female driver to race in the Indianapolis 500 in1977.
Photo Courtesy of Janet Guthrie.

When Guthrie passed the rookie exam and it was announced, she was swarmed by reporters, but was also greeted by Tony Hulman who shook her hand in public.

"I admit I never thought I'd see a woman driving at Indy," the track owner said. "But it's OK. If she's able to drive out there, she should."

For a time Guthrie was rescued from her car problems by A.J. Foyt allowing her to run his second car in practice. But he did not agree to let her race the second car, saying his pit crew did not want to take care of a second vehicle and his partner did not want to let her either. The second car was supposed to be for Foyt's use at Pocono and the others all wanted him to focus on winning a record-breaking fourth Indy 500. However, Guthrie had run the other Foyt car at more than 180 mph.

So Guthrie was out of the game for 1976. Instead, she spent Memorial Day at Charlotte Motor Speedway competing in the NASCAR World 600. Guthrie finished fifteenth. The next February she ran the Daytona 500 and finished twelfth, winning rookie of the year honors. The 1976 Indy experience coupled with the good results in NASCAR set Guthrie up for another Speedway try in 1977.

Once Guthrie departed the premises and the pole was won, full attention turned to the 1976 race.

Rutherford led the first few laps and Foyt took over for about ten. Pancho Carter, the 1974 rookie of the year in seventh place, led a few laps. Wally Dallenbach jumped in for another few laps. Johncock took a turn in front for seventeen laps, Tom Sneva led one lap and then Rutherford flexed some muscle. He moved to the lead on lap thirty-nine and kept it through lap sixty. Foyt, the win in mind, led through lap seventy-nine. But the rest of the race, before the deluge of rain, belonged to Rutherford.

All of that was wrapped around a rain delay and then, finally, rain too strong to fight off, compromised the safety of the track.

Normally, the driver guides his car into Victory Lane, but Rutherford stopped and was surrounded by reporters. Instead of following the usual procedure the driver got out and walked into Victory Lane.

"It was a real frog-strangler," Rutherford said of the pelting rain. "We had run only 255 of the five hundred miles, but it counted."

Foyt and Johncock were determined about waiting out the rain. Even Rutherford wanted to keep going despite being the beneficiary of the early stoppage.

"With three fiercely competitive racers chomping at the bit to go wheel to wheel for 245 more miles the race was shaping up to be a real thriller," he said. "But sometimes being in the right place at the right time is the name of the game."

JANET GUTHRIE

American society has changed dramatically over the last forty years. The concept of a woman driver was just too much to grasp for many when Janet Guthrie first tried to qualify for the Indianapolis 500 in 1976 and did so in 1977.

In some quarters she was viewed more as an alien than simply just another driver, which is all she was interested in. Guthrie saw herself as just another driver, even if no one else did. But she became a symbol for women, in auto racing, in sport, and in daily life just because no other woman had even come close to starting the Indy 500 before.

From there, as others commented and encouraged her, Guthrie did come to look at herself as a barrier breaker who could help all women with her effort, performance, and demeanor.

While the Indianapolis 500 was the centerpiece of the racing world, wherever Guthrie showed up to race an IndyCar or a stock car, she was mobbed by reporters. There was no such thing as flying under radar or arriving at a track without fanfare.

Title IX, the federal legislation, which transformed the landscape for girls and women seeking opportunity in sports and tremendously boosted high school and college sports involvement nationwide, was only four years old in 1976. It was still a novelty for women to be competing in big-time sports and the Indianapolis 500 was as big as it got.

By the time Guthrie returned to Indiana for round two in 1977 she had greatly burnished her credentials in the minds of many. Being rookie of the year in the Daytona 500 was a major feat. Completing the World 600, which is a hundred miles longer than the Indianapolis 500, certainly indicated there was nothing wrong with her stamina.

Now all she had to do was go fast enough at the Indianapolis Motor Speedway to qualify. Newspaper attention at the time was phenomenal, creating an avalanche of words on the likelihood of success or failure of a woman making it into the field, if one should be allowed, and what it all meant. Initially, Guthrie was flabbergasted by the coverage she received, but by this second time around she was fairly used to it if not

still a bit peeved at some patronizing tones.

"My own position was that of course women could do these things and why in the world did anyone ever think otherwise?" she said. "But many people seemed to perceive it as a defining moment in the evolution of women's cultural role."

One of Guthrie's defenders was A.J. Foyt, who in 1977 established the record for winning the most Indianapolis 500 races with four, a mark yet to be surpassed. Foyt, who was hardly seen as a backer of women's rights, was forthright in saying Guthrie could drive and her biggest problem was the same problem faced by many male drivers – lack of funding for equipment.

Guthrie was neither a soloist as a female driver, nor did she unleash a tidal wave of female drivers flooding the course at Indy. As of 2015, women who competed in the Indy 500 included Guthrie, Lyn St. James, Sarah Fisher, Danica Patrick, Pippa Mann, Milka Duno, Ana Beatriz, and Simona de Silvestro.

Four of them have finished in the top ten, with Patrick's third place finish in 2009 as best in the group. James finished sixth and Guthrie and Fisher each finished ninth.

In retirement, Guthrie was chosen for the International Motorsports Hall of Fame and the International Women's Sports Hall of Fame.

Those elections, plus the fact that Guthrie's racing helmet and suit are in the possession of the Smithsonian Institution, testify to the significance of what role she played in advancing the cause of women. Those who said so in the beginning were right to take note in claiming that Janet Guthrie racing in the Indianapolis 500 was more than just a sports story.

1977

Longevity, perseverance and talent were some of the characteristics that combined to make A.J. Foyt the first driver to win the Indianapolis 500 four times.

It is a career achievement for a race car driver to win the Indy 500 once. Although Foyt's accomplishment has been matched a few times, nearly forty years after he set the mark no other driver has exceeded it.

The Texan was the first driver to win the Indy 500 on the Indianapolis Motor Speedway's newly paved asphalt surface. The track had experienced considerable wear and tear and in the interests of keeping things in tip-top shape and with safety in mind the improvements and maintenance were part of doing business intelligently.

Although the clocking was unofficial, Gordon Johncock hit 200.401 mph during a tire test in March, two months before qualifying began for the 1977 race. Indications were that the 200 mph barrier-breaker was coming soon on official timing devices.

During qualifying, Tom Sneva, who was previously fortunate to walk away from a devastating crash, set a new one-lap Speedway record for the 2.5 miles by clocking 200.401 mph. On his next lap Sneva topped it by recording 200.535 mph. He did slow over his next two laps, dropping his pole-position winning time to 198.884 mph, which was also a record.

To some the instant when a driver at Indy officially ran two hundred mph was a now-I-have-seen-everything moment. It was a magical number and although surely cars would run somewhat faster in the coming years it was the last true barrier anyone imagined would ever be eclipsed.

In other good news for the Sneva family, the 1977 race was when Tom's younger brother Jerry made his *500* debut and with a tenth place finish, he recorded his best work in five races. Jerry Sneva became rookie of the year.

Much attention before the race was focused on Janet Guthrie again. Guthrie had made an aborted effort at qualifying in 1976, but she was back and gunning for a spot in the thirty-three car field.

This time Guthrie made it, establishing a first in a race that was so steeped in tradition. The Purdue Band played the National Anthem, as usual. Jim Nabors sang "Back Home Again in Indiana," as usual. Tony Hulman was scheduled to say, "Gentlemen, start your engines," as usual. However, once Guthrie qualified there was widespread speculation on just what Hulman would say to account for a field that included thirty-two male drivers and one female driver.

What Hulman said was, "In company with the first lady ever to qualify at Indianapolis, gentlemen, start your engines."

That was good enough. If the situation came up again (which it did) it could always be modified. It was Hulman's last delivery of the start-up message, however, because he died a few months later from a heart attack at seventy-six.

Sid Collins, whose voice was the famous voice of the Indianapolis 500 on radio since 1951, was absent. Collins had been diagnosed with amyotrophic lateral sclerosis, which had come to be called Lou Gehrig's disease in public vernacular and just before the start of the 61st running of the *500*, Collins committed suicide.

To demonstrate how difficult it was to make it into the field, nineteen drivers who tried failed to pull it off. Included were future star Rick Mears, past rookie of the year Gordon McRae, Salt Walther, and Jim Hurtubise.

Tom Sneva had the pole, but Al Unser went to the front when the race went green. Sneva tucked in behind him and Bobby Unser was running third.

Johnny Rutherford, who had repeatedly done so well in recent years, was shut down early with gearbox problems. Rutherford finished 33rd, almost as if the standings had been turned upside down. He completed just twelve laps.

"Chicken one year, feathers the next," Rutherford said. "We had gone from first to worst at Indianapolis. I sat and watched the rest of the race from the pits and stewed in my own dejection."

Guthrie wasn't much cheerier. Engine problems knocked her out after twenty-seven laps and she placed 29th.

On lap forty-nine, Lloyd Ruby crashed, without significant injury, but that was his finale at Indy after a long and distinguished career at the Speedway.

Gordon Johncock took the lead, but the number of cars trailing kept dwindling. Although no major accidents contributed to the attrition, cars were coming up with creative ways to fail and drive pit crews insane. By the halfway mark of the race sixteen of them were sidelined.

To this point in Johncock's career the highlight was his 1973 victory, but in a rain-shortened race. Each year he was a threat to win and he sought the satisfaction of winning a full *500*. This appeared to be his time. Johncock grabbed the lead on lap ninety-seven and held it through lap 179. A.J. Foyt and Tom Sneva were in the hunt, also on the same lap as the leader, but as the cars pulled out of the pits with twenty laps to go, Johncock led by more than fifteen seconds. Johncock was suffering from dehydration, and knew something was wrong with his body. His crew even threw water on him on his last two pit stops.

Sneva, and especially Foyt, were charging. On lap 184, Johncock's car belched a huge plume of smoke from a broken crankshaft and he was done. Foyt rode a thirty second lead over Sneva to the title, jubilant over his fourth Indy 500 victory.

"I talked to the car," Foyt said. "I talked to the good Lord and everybody that would listen that I could win and nobody would get hurt today."

That last was important to Foyt since the day he won his first Indianapolis 500 his celebration was muted, as was everyone else's, because of the deaths of Eddie Sachs and Dave MacDonald in a fiery wreck. Foyt always remembered the Indianapolis newspaper headline about his victory also noting the driver deaths. What should have been a great day for Foyt was not a good day for many others.

Foyt was forty-two at the time and after the demise of Johncock's car he actually had time to think as he drove the final laps alone in front, un-pressured by any other driver. He later said he reflected on how far he had come from his poorer days in Texas, as an unknown at Indianapolis, and how winning the big race four times was more than anyone would have imagined. Maybe, he said, it was time to retire.

Foyt had come to Indianapolis in May many times believing he had a good shot to win and he had come out of qualifying with the same belief only to be disappointed because of one mechanical breakdown or the other. Not this time.

"It had been one of those races I felt I was going to win from the start," Foyt said. "I mean, really felt it. There are days like that. I felt it with my steak and eggs that morning and I felt it as my challengers fell off, one by one."

There had been rumors Foyt might retire if he won with the new record, but Foyt said that thought was merely a passing thought over the final laps. He knew even by the time he took the checkered flag it was not going to happen. He was enjoying himself doing what he loved too much to quit.

Foyt never won the Indy 500 again, but he was far from finished as a driver. He competed annually, without a miss, through the 1992 race, and often was a contender again. And then he stuck around as a car owner. In that sense Foyt never left Indianapolis even when he did step out of the car.

1978

Now they were over two hundred miles per hour. Tom Sneva broke the barrier the year before in qualifying, but still averaged less than that for the entire four laps. This year Sneva took the pole again, but averaged 202.156 mph, a new record.

By the time Sneva made his official runs Mario Andretti had clocked 201.838 mph in practice. Then along came Danny Ongais at 201.974. Ongais was in his second year at the track after an impressive debut in 1977. He finished twentieth after qualifying seventh that year. A native of Hawaii, Ongais was nicknamed, "The Flyin' Hawaiian." He came to open-wheel racing from a motorcycle background and after serving in the military. He became a Hot Rod champion and competed in Formula 1.

A new face was thrust into the mix when a rookie topped two hundred mph. That fellow was Rick Mears, poised to write his own Indianapolis 500 history. Andretti upped the ante once more at 203.482 mph, but again it was in practice. So were the other two hundred plus mph speeds of Sneva again, A.J. Foyt and Pancho Carter.

During this stretch, two of the best-known Indy 500 drivers showed their versatility. When they weren't in practice or qualifying, they were elsewhere. Andretti competed in the Grand Prix of Belgium and A.J. Foyt entered the Winston 500 stock-car race.

On pole day Sneva topped the field with all four of his laps going over two hundred mph. The second time around Janet Guthrie qualified at 190.325 mph.

By this time, car speed had increased sufficiently that Speedway officials required a minimum practice showing of 180 mph to even sanction an attempt. Qualifying ended with a bizarre dispute. Jim Hurtubise, who had been a fixture at Indy for years, but was also a thorn in officials' sides, had not proven his car could go that fast. Qualifying was coming to an end with one spot left in the thirty-three car field when Bob Harkey was readying to go out.

As time was running out, Hurtubise argued with officials and then startled everyone by climbing into Harkey's car yelling, "If I can't qualify, no one can!"

Eventually, Hurtubise got out of his fellow competitor's car, Harkey got in and started up. But Hurtubise jumped in front of the car to prevent Harkey from approaching the track. Members of the track safety patrol stepped in and Harkey got away. Everyone thought that was that, but Hurtubise wasn't finished.

As Harkey rolled the car onto the track, Hurtubise jumped over a restraining wall and ran out onto the Speedway. In a scene that resembled cops and robbers, law enforcement personnel ran after him. Hurtubise was tackled, led away, and banned from the Speedway for the rest of May.

That was the fourth straight year Hurtubise failed to qualify. He did not give up and his ban was lifted, though Hurtubise did not run fast enough to qualify for another three more years. His last try was in 1981.

Hurtubise died of a heart attack at fifty-six in 1989, but in his years he was no dilettante. He did win one NASCAR race and compile ten top tens. He finished as high at thirteenth one year. Hurtubise was inducted into the National Sprint Car Hall of Fame in 1993.

Still, that was as cuckoo as it ever got in qualifying at Indy.

Tony Hulman had passed away since the previous race and the starter role fell to his wife Mary T. Hullman. With Guthrie in the field the command called for something out of the ordinary and she proclaimed, "Lady and gentlemen, start your engines."

Car trouble and his travel responsibilities led to Andretti starting from the 33rd and last position. Starting fast, Andretti gained twenty places very quickly, but then a faulty spark plug sent him to the pits and he was never a front-of-the-pack factor again. Ongais took over the lead, but was pitting when a Spike Gelhausen crash on lap twenty-three shook things up.

Ongais came out of the pits at a fortuitous time, passed Sneva, and led for sixty-eight laps out of the first seventy-five. But his car had pretty much peaked and Al Unser zoomed ahead.

It was a scorching hot day and cars began overheating. By lap 120, thirteen of the thirty-three cars were sidelined. Unser was cruising. Ongais and Sneva were trying to catch up, but on lap 145 Ongais' engine blew. He left the track with billowing smoke trailing him. Unser and Sneva were alone on the lead lap. Other challengers were disposed of one by one. Those two hundred mph speeds from practice were distant memories for most cars.

Unser seemed a sure bet when he built his lead to thirty seconds over Sneva with nineteen laps to go. But as anyone who had ever watched an Indianapolis 500 knew, no race was over until it was over. It was even truer in the *500* than when Yogi Berra made the original comment about baseball. Unser may have appeared home free, but hit a spare tire on a pit stop. When he pulled onto the track he realized he had damaged a piece of his car's front end.

The effect of that seemingly minor incident threw his steering out of whack just enough to make it difficult for Unser to handle the car at the previous high speeds. Unser frantically tried to steer, keep his speed up sufficiently and coax the car to the finish line before Sneva could catch him.

Realizing something was off Sneva kept his foot on the gas and gradually began to reel in Unser. Gordon Johncock, who had been a lap behind, got on the same lap as the leaders. Unser was now a tortoise and not even a truly steady one.

Sneva made up twenty seconds. Going into the last lap, the final 2.5 miles, Unser led by ten seconds, but was still fading. Sneva was still coming. If Unser tried to go any faster there was a good chance he would wreck. Somehow, he made it to the checkered flag first. Sneva finished eight seconds arrears. Johncock took third. Steve Krisiloff, who led the only five laps in his long Indy career despite recording five top ten finishes between 1971 and 1983, placed fourth and Wally Dallenbach fifth.

Past winners Bobby Unser, A.J. Foyt, and Andretti finished sixth, seventh and twelfth, respectively. Guthrie finished ninth. That should have been enough to forestall snide comments for a lifetime. Johnny

Rutherford was thirteenth. Mears placed twenty-third.

While it probably didn't matter in the end because of his engine woes, Ongais lost his two-way radio in the first half of the race and communicated the old-fashioned way with his crew, reading sign boards.

Al Unser in victory circle, 1978. Al Unser was the second driver to win four Indianapolis 500s.

The triumph was Al Unser's third, though first since the second of his back-to-back victories in 1970 and 1971. He joined the small group of drivers with three or more Indianapolis 500 championships, ranking just one behind Foyt for the record.

One thing characterizing Unser's win was his engine choice. The British-made Cosworth DFX V8 engine was a first-time victor, but the beginning of ten straight years of supplying the engine to the championship driver .

Unser was on a spectacular run when he claimed that third title, one that transcended the Indianapolis Motor Speedway. He won the California 500 seven months earlier and later in 1978 he won the Pocono 500 before winning the California 500 again that fall. That was referred to as the "Triple Crown" of Indy car racing and no other driver has won all three in the same competitive year.

CREATION OF CART

During its earliest days the Indianapolis 500 was conducted under the auspices of the Automobile Association of America. AAA pulled its sanctioning after the disastrous 1955 race.

The United States Automobile Club was formed by Speedway boss Tony Hulman and it supervised the *500* beginning in 1956.

After the 1978 race, and after Hulman passed away, there was dissension in the ranks. Compounding the situation was the death of several key officials from the USAC in a plane crash.

Car owners grew dissatisfied with operations of the race and wanted bigger paydays.

Driver-turned-owner Dan Gurney authored a so-called "white paper" outlining what the owners felt should be done, patterning it after Formula 1. The proposal was sent to the USAC operators, but was rejected.

That action provoked a split and the owners formed the Championship Auto Racing Teams organization that was immediately shortened to CART in references. The change met with widespread, but not universal approval, from owners and drivers, A.J. Foyt being an exception.

However, when the 1979 season got underway thirteen of the twenty events were under CART supervision. Gradually and steadily CART grew in strength and influence. Although primarily a North American phenomenon over time again European racers began coming to the United States in growing numbers and entering CART events.

Acrimony still lingered, as well as disagreements between haves and have-nots. Open-wheel racing is incredibly expensive and some of the smaller operations started believing CART was really all about the big-time guys with rules changes and policies favoring the monied operations. These feelings simmered over years and sometimes came to the forefront in arguments at big races.

There was behind-the-scene resentment, jealousy, backbiting, all the usual elements of a good soap opera. But while feelings ran high there was a limited effect on the Indianapolis 500 experienced by spectators. The knowledgeable racing fan understood the attitudes of many of those involved, but as long as the Indy 500, the jewel of open-wheel racing, came off as planned each Memorial Day, they did not worry too much about the rest of the operation.

Indeed, to them, eventually adding such luminaries from other countries as Emerson Fittipaldi, Nigel Mansell and Alex Zanardi to the scene had some appeal. But that was later.

What the CART creators did was fill a vacuum in power and leadership by taking advantage of the death of Hulman and some of the USAC strong men. Under Hulman, who controlled the Indianapolis 500 and the Indianapolis Motor Speedway and more or less all open-wheel racing in the United States, there may have been restlessness, but there was no rebellion.

It is unclear what may have transpired if Hulman had not died, but once he did and the USAC that he had established had lost influence following the plane crash, certain elements of the racing community began agitating for change.

Although this appeared to be a quick-fix changeover, the implications were much broader longer term than anyone may have anticipated. It took years for the change in supervision to be truly felt and that eventually led to complete upheaval in the sport. But that was still to come.

1979

Rick Mears emerged as the new star of the Indianapolis 500 in 1979. He captured the pole with a speed of 193.736 mph and he won the race itself, outshining the off-track controversies that surrounded the *500*.

Mears was born in Wichita, Kansas, but grew up in Bakersfield, California. He first made his mark in off-road racing which could include dirt and desert or just about any surface that wouldn't rip up tires. Always on the lookout for the next big thing, Indianapolis owner Roger Penske liked Mears' potential and brought him into the team fold.

It took just two Indy 500 races for Mears to win one. It took just two Indy 500 races for Mears to capture a pole. Ultimately, both of those accomplishments became habits. During his career Mears won four Indianapolis 500 titles, tying for the most-ever.

While Mears was scorching the track with his wheels in 1979, others were busy arguing administrative and rules issues.

This was the first Indianapolis 500 since CART was created and sought to usurp the USAC. The long-time sanctioning body fought back and announced it was going to prohibit entry in the *500* by any of the CART racers. The battle grew nasty. CART officials submitted forty-four entries to the Indy 500. Included were six team owners involving nineteen cars and the USAC board rejected their participation on the basis of being "harmful to racing" and not in good standing with the governing body.

That group went to federal court seeking an injunction based on restraint of trade and antitrust laws. The court agreed and issued an injunction allowing them to enter the race.

CART drivers were permitted to race, but most of them who entered only competed in the Indianapolis 500 that season and spent the rest of the year competing in new CART races instead of USAC races.

The entry issue was resolved by May 5, weeks before the start of the race. The atmosphere remained testy and a fresh uproar began over rules regulating turbocharger wastegate inlets, which had to do with the size of exhaust pipes. Some drivers discovered what they thought was a way around the manner in which the rule was written governing the size. Some drivers accused the USAC of changing the rules in the middle of qualifying.

At last, attention turned to the action on the track. But the activity was hardly satisfactory. Rain basically washed out most of pole day. Danny Ongais would have been happier if it had been complete since he got his car out near the end of the day and promptly crashed in turn four. He could not be freed from his car for twenty minutes and was taken to a hospital with a concussion.

Due to Ongais' crash no car even made a qualifying attempt on pole day, so everything began anew the next day. The next day was much nicer, sunny and mild and forty-five cars made qualifying attempts. The best times were all in the high 180s and with only minutes to go to determine the result Mears became the last driver out. He blistered the track with his 193-plus mph to grab the pole. During his career Mears set a record by claiming the pole six times.

Ongais had needed some recuperation time and missed pole day. He came back later in May to compete for a spot in the field and initially was turned away by the track for not being sufficiently healed. He insisted he was OK and finally was allowed to drive. He made it.

Even after the field was set, peace did not reign. Eight teams complained the waste gate inlet rules were too vague and they had been treated unfairly because of them. A protest was made to the USAC and was turned down with one provision.

If all thirty-three qualified teams allowed another qualifying session those eight would be allowed to run again. One of the three other non-qualifiers went to county court saying if those teams were allowed another qualifying session, he should be permitted in, too. The suit was dropped.

Two of the thirty-three teams refused to sign the deal. Reviewing the situation USAC officials declared it would sanction one bonus day of qualifying for the eleven teams that were on the outside looking in. All previously, officially qualified thirty-three teams were in the field regardless. The field would be expanded if the other cars produced a swift enough time.

Cars belonging to Bill Vukovich II and George Snider did record times quick enough and that increased the field to thirty-five cars.

After this entire exhausting series of events, there was finally a race on May 27. However, for a little while it appeared there might not be. It rained overnight, but the storm halted in time to get the race going in sunshine.

There was a new car on the block driven by Al Unser, called a Chaparral 2K Chassis Cosworth. It was exceptionally sleek with a wide wing on the rear, built close to the ground (described as a ground effects car), the Jim Hall design had superb aerodynamics, and on the underside was shaped like the top surface of an airplane wing. To some extent the car looked exactly like what most casual fans think an Indy 500 car should have been shaped like.

The net result was a very fast car and Unser broke for the lead immediately when the green flag dropped and stayed there for the first twenty-four laps. While several drivers had to pull out early because of car failure, Unser did not shake many of the stars. He was trailed by Mears, his brother Bobby, and Johnny Rutherford.

What seemed too good to be true was. Al Unser was riding behind Bobby just after the halfway point when his transmission oil fitting blew out and finished his day. Bobby held his lead ahead of Mears as

A.J. Foyt moved into the picture in third. This other Unser looked to be in command, but a gearbox went out of synch and Mears took the lead with nineteen laps remaining.

Foyt was far behind, but clipped seconds off the lead, dropping it to thirty-eight seconds when Tom Sneva crashed. The yellow caution flag was displayed and stayed out until the last four laps. Foyt frantically tried to work his way through traffic to catch Sneva, but then his car failed and it was all he could do to coast across the finish line second ahead of Mike Mosley. Ongais overcame his tribulations of early May to place fourth.

Mears led just twenty-five laps while the Unser brothers combined led for 175 laps.

Jim McElreath finished 35th and last and Janet Guthrie was 34th. While George Snider made it into the field with that last-gasp qualification, he placed 33rd. However, Bill Vukovich II made up ground on most of the early qualifiers to finish eighth.

It was a messy year all around, but in the end kicked off Mears' spectacular career.

Old Winners Hang In and New Ones Grab Titles

1980-89

One of the most spectacular moments in Indianapolis 500 history occurred during the 1985 race when Danny Sullivan spun 360 degrees, but instead of crashing, as was likely, he straightened out his car and drove it to victory.

It took until 1987 for Al Unser to capture his fourth Indy 500 crown and tie A.J. Foyt for most victories. Unser was forty-seven at the time, the oldest winner ever.

Much like the 1970s, winners seemed to come from a small pool of repeat champs with stars such as Bobby Unser, Johnny Rutherford, Gordon Johncock and Rick Mears twice, joining Al Unser as familiar champs.

In the 1980s, disputes in the management of open-wheel racing operations led to a split in the sport, and began drastically impacting which drivers competed in the Indy 500.

1980

In a year when popular veteran Johnny Rutherford won the title after also winning the pole and Tom Sneva came close to winning the race after starting it last, there was peace off the track.

Compared to 1979, the scene at Indianapolis Motor Speedway was a lovefest between CART and the USAC. Their reconciliation, an agreement to merge schedules for racing, was welcome and a positive step in inter-organizational relations. It was in place for the Indy 500, but it didn't last. By July the groups were no longer following the same path.

After the 1979 Indianapolis 500, Al Unser split up with the Chaparral manufacturers. Rutherford got the second car in 1980 and it proved just as fast, but also more reliable than Unser's had, because it stayed together for the distance.

Naturally, supervisors of the race couldn't go a year without tinkering. Turbocharger boost levels were reduced, an action that did not meet with approval from all drivers, which was hard to achieve no matter what the issue. A.J. Foyt famously said because the change would slow speeds by about ten mph, it would result in "taxicab racing." Rutherford chimed in and said the rule would make it tougher for drivers to pass other cars.

Unhappy with the alteration of the rule or not, Rutherford was the best out there on pole day, qualifying at 192.256 mph. It was obvious Jim Hall's cars were doing something right. The car, which looked pretty much just like the yellow auto that Unser ran with the year before acquired the nickname "The Yellow Submarine," a takeoff on the Beatles' song and cartoon movie.

Sneva, who was doing everything but winning each May, from capturing the pole to breaking the 200 mph barrier, to finishing as the runner-up, made a different type of news this time. His qualifying time for the pole was fourteenth, a non-descript, middle-of-the-pack placing.

However, in the days after the pole was taken he crashed in practice, ruining the car he had used. Under the rules Sneva could still race, but if he utilized a second car it had to start in the rear. So his starting position was dropped to 33rd. It was not ideal for a driver with designs on first place.

Sneva came off as a down-to-earth guy with a good sense of humor. He said he was such a rank beginner when Roger Penske invited him to drive for his team that he had no idea what that meant.

The driver once told the story that Penske offered him $2,000 to sign and Sneva thought, "I don't have $2,000." Then he realized he would be the one actually getting paid.

The owner and the driver did discuss what Penske expected from him and Sneva told Penske what he needed to be a driver for the company. Sneva said later they compromised...doing it exactly Penske's way. It was a profitable pairing, however.

That 1980 race was an off year for Janet Guthrie, who did not qualify. That meant the starting command returned to the original, "Gentlemen, start your engines."

Ten different drivers led laps in the *500*, an unusually large amount by recent standards. Rookie Roger Rager could always tell his family he led the Indianapolis 500 for two laps. Which was one more than George Snider that year or rookie of the year Tim Richmond.

Pancho Carter led for five laps, Mario Andretti and Rick Mears each for ten, Gordon Johncock for eleven, remarkably, the last-place starter Sneva for sixteen, Bobby Unser for twenty-six, and winner Rutherford for 118 laps.

Andretti, who was beginning to curse his bad luck at the Speedway a decade after his victory, was hot at the start, but was KO'd by engine trouble after leading those ten laps.

Bobby Unser was the halfway leader, but his car failed him after 126 laps. In the latter going Sneva wisely used his pit stops and kept himself in contention. Mears tried for an extra quick pit stop taking on only fuel, but it didn't help him. Rutherford was stronger and over the last 20 laps he was merely maintaining his lead, accelerating to a faster speed only when necessary.

In taking his third Indianapolis 500 crown, Rutherford bested Sneva by just under 30 seconds. Sneva gained much admiration for his effort. No other driver had worked his way through the field from 33rd to finish second.

Richmond was on lap 197 when he ran out of gas. Rutherford was already on his victory lap and pulled up alongside Richmond. He offered a ride and Richmond jumped on for a lift to the finish line as the crowd cheered and applauded and he and Rutherford shook hands and waved.

Richmond was one of the most flamboyant race car drivers of his era. He started in open-wheel racing, but became much better known in stock-car racing. Richmond was showy, dressed flashy, cracked jokes and was viewed as a playboy, and he always seemed to find a way to irritate the old guard in NASCAR because of his nature and flair and so gained the nickname "Hollywood".

Humpy Wheeler, the prominent NASCAR racing promoter, once said that Richmond reminded him of the hip actor James Dean and he also thought he was good for stock-car racing. Wheeler ran the Charlotte Motor Speedway and was always interested in highlighting fresh faces who differed from the southern conservative, driver mold. Most of Richmond's success came in stock-car racing, but he proved early on in 1980 that he was skilled enough to do well at Indy style racing, too.

"Here comes a cat that looks like he's straight from 'East of Eden,' and New York City, Greenwich Village," Wheeler said. "I thought, 'This is perfect!'"

One reason for that Hollywood feeling was a small Richmond part in the movie "Stroker Ace." Later, the Tom Cruise character in "Days of Thunder" was supposedly partially modeled on Richmond. Anyone who hung out with Richmond had a fun time. Perhaps too much fun. Eventually, the driver who won thirteen NASCAR races was infected with the AIDs virus which caused his death in 1989 at age thirty-four. Richmond would never admit the reason he became ill, but it was commonly known amongst many close to him what was behind his demise.

Richmond once said, "I'm trying to prove that I was put on this earth to have fun. To succeed at the fun department."

Richmond was a tremendously talented driver and he fit into the category of the many drivers whose careers were cut short by death. The only difference is that Richmond did not die due to a race car accident.

1981

The best guys seemed to be taking turns winning the Indianapolis 500. There were no one-hit wonders, only drivers who kept winning championships, enshrining themselves prominently in the history of the Indianapolis Motor Speedway and in *500* lore.

A.J. Foyt was already up to a record four wins. Al Unser and his brother Bobby Unser were winning their share. So was Johnny Rutherford. Gordon Johncock was in the mix and Rick Mears was coming along. If you wanted to win the Indianapolis 500 it wasn't going to come cheaply. You were going to have to beat the best of the best, guys who were considered all-time greats.

It was like that in 1981, too. This year it was Bobby Unser's turn, but once again things going on off the track influenced things on the track. In fact, this result took on a surreal nature for that reason.

Things began with rain hovering over the race track off and on all May. The weather heavily interfered with pole qualifying spread over three different days. Ultimately, Bobby Unser won the pole by averaging 200.546 mph. The altered schedule, because of bad weather disrupted Mario Andretti's plans to quickly qualify on the first day and then fly to Belgium again to compete in that Grand Prix before race day.

However, the postponements and the constant rain did not allow for him to accomplish that. Andretti flew to Europe and because of all the interruptions ended up with a car qualifying 32nd.

Complicating the entire scenario was the record number of 105 drivers seeking to qualify for the thirty-three positions. The track was jammed with cars and hopefuls trying to dodge raindrops.

Unser flashed the most speed almost daily, proving his pole position was no fluke. Mike Mosley, hopeful of a race breakthrough, qualified second at 197.141 mph. But after only sixteen laps his radiator went bad and he finished last.

The race began the way qualifying went, with Bobby Unser rushing ahead. Johnny Rutherford tailed him after starting in the second row. Even more impressive was Tom Sneva who started in twentieth place, but was in third by lap twenty. Rutherford, given his track history, looked as if he was going to be around all day, but he suffered a breakdown after twenty-five laps and he finished second-to-last.

It drove Rutherford nuts. He had been driving the Chaparral, won a national championship in it, and was poised for success at Indy again.

"Things were looking pretty good after a couple of dozen laps," Rutherford said, "and then the car just quit on me. I coasted to a stop on the backstretch and the car was towed back to the pits where the crew discovered a $4.50 belt drive had busted."

Rick Mears was still running up front on lap fifty-eight when he made a pit stop that almost cost him his life. When the pit crew attempted to start fueling, the hose flew away from the tank and sprayed the car with methanol. Then the fuel ignited. But unlike gasoline, which burns with orange flames, methanol fires are invisible. Mears caught fire, but no one could see it. He frantically sought help, but neither pit workers nor safety workers on the other side of the wall immediately recognized his predicament. Spectators nearby ran, but Mears' father Bill picked up a discarded fire extinguisher to spray him down and saved him.

Mears and four mechanics needed hospital attention, but despite the danger he was in, Mears did not suffer as badly as he might have. He did require plastic surgery on some parts of his face, but recovered well to continue his racing career.

Gordon Smiley was in his second Indy 500 and briefly took the lead when Mears headed to the pits while the fire raged. The next year Smiley was killed in a crash at the Speedway during the race.

Only a handful of laps after the drama of Mears' pit stop a major accident occurred. Danny Ongais was in the lead after lap sixty-three and when he emerged from a pit stop he tried to pass a slower car at the end of the backstretch heading into turn three. Ongais was going too fast and the rear of the car began sliding. He tried to correct and the car moved sharply right and then collided with the wall.

The contact was vicious. The front end of the car was torn off and Ongais knocked unconscious. But the car did not stop, traveling around turn three in flames. Fans feared Ongais had been killed. Rescue workers needed to employ the Jaws of Life to lift him out of the car. Ongais suffered a concussion and broken legs and feet, but he returned to race another day at Indianapolis.

For a while the race was comparatively uneventful, but then a complex serious of events played out that affected the outcome of the race in an unexpected manner.

Tony Bettenhausen's failing tire caused him to lose control of steering and he clipped wheels with Smiley. That knocked Smiley into the wall and out of the race on lap 141. The yellow flag came out and leaders Bobby Unser and Mario Andretti ducked into the pit area.

Unser beat Andretti out of the pit. The pace car was circling the track with cars traveling in a line under the caution flag. Unser, who had been the leader, drove on the track apron below the white painted warning line and passed fourteen cars until he resumed his position as leader just in back of the pace car. Andretti apparently also passed a few cars before drifting into line.

Andretti said later he immediately radioed his pit crew that Unser passed cars under yellow. Officials either didn't notice any of these doings or did not react. Similarly, no comment was made on the national radio broadcast. However, ABC TV announcers Jim McKay, Jackie Stewart, and Don Diles did discuss the situation. They pointed out that Unser had incorrectly passed cars under the yellow flag. The race was not shown live, but on tape delay, so no TV viewers were watching at the time. There were no penalties assessed and the race continued.

In the late going Johncock made a move, but a blown engine finished him. Unser took the lead for the last time on lap 182. Andretti was running second and Austrian Vern Schuppan was challenging him. That's how it finished, Unser, Andretti, Van Schuppan, 1-2-3.

During the post-race interview in Victory Lane someone brought up the possibility of a penalty to Unser, but he didn't believe such a thing would happen.

"We didn't cheat," Unser said. "We were the best car all day. I beat Mario all day long. The good Lord meant for me to win today and we beat Mario fair and square."

The telecast was not viewed until hours after the finish and it was closing in on midnight when Andretti watched it and announced he was going to file a protest.

"Currently, there is a protest in process," Andretti said, "because we're talking about an unusual violation of the rules. The one particular rule spoken about during the public drivers meeting about not passing under yellow."

Race officials began studying the broadcast video overnight so they could make a determination of what happened before posting the official results (a normal procedure) at 8 a.m. the following morning.

One of the key players in this tense review was Tom Binford, who was the chief steward. Binford was a well-known, wealthy Indianapolis resident, who briefly ran the Indiana Pacers NBA team and was prominent for his philanthrophy. He became chief steward in 1974 – and held that post through 1995.

It was later learned that although the *500* was taped as it ran, the commentary was not added until later, after Unser had become the winner and after it seemed likely a protest was to be filed. It was later shown that Andretti also indeed had passed cars when rejoining the pack under yellow.

This was a controversy with legs, or wheels, as the case may be. It was not in-house haggling over equipment and mechanical changes. This was a direct challenge that would change the first-place result and possibly take away a title from an esteemed champion.

Yet nonetheless, in the morning, that is exactly what the United States Automobile Club did. A statement was issued declaring that Unser had illegally passed cars under yellow and his penalty was to be demoted one place. That was to second and the result of that was to elevate Andretti to first and give him his second Indianapolis 500 crown.

Perhaps in anticipation of more uproar to come, when Andretti was introduced at the Victory Banquet, his pay envelope was empty and when he was presented with the pace car he was not given the keys. Unser did not attend the dinner.

Ironically, Andretti had once had an Italian Grand Prix victory taken from him by an officials' decision based on him leaving the start too soon. At the banquet, Andretti said, "I am glad the officials did the right thing, but it is still sad."

Unser wasn't finished yet. Roger Penske, his team leader, filed a protest of the decision stripping his man of the *500* title. A couple days later officials denied the protest. Penske kept right on going, filing paperwork with the USAC Appeals Board.

Unser made it sound as if all of the doings were too much for him and that he no longer cared what happened, although that might be a bit strong.

"It's already been ruined for me," Unser said. "I'm very bitter."

A hearing began on June 12, about two weeks after the race ended, on Penske's appeal of the USAC decision. Testimony was taken for hours, but no resolution was reached and part two of the hearing was continued until July 29.

Unser's testimony provided revealing information about the race's rule about blending back into traffic under yellow while coming out of the pits. Unser said he understood that as long as the car stayed beneath the white line of the apron it was proper to regain position at the exit of turn two. Andretti testified that he believed the proper place to merge into traffic was at the south end of the pits.

Those who read the rules and understood them agreed that the guidelines were vague. There was also considerable discussion about the lack of a penalty being administered during the race when the alleged infraction took place rather than waiting until later.

No word came out of the USAC until October 9. On that day it was announced that officials erred in not assessing a penalty promptly if they were going to do so. The track officials had not noted a violation, they said. If there was going to be a one-lap penalty at all it should have been given when the cars were still racing.

In a twenty-three page opinion, the appeals board took the win away from Andretti and gave it back to Unser. However, it also fined Unser $40,000.

While not many people focused on other results from that day, Mexican Josele Garza won rookie of the year honors even though he finished twenty-third, behind several other rookies. Garza led the race for thirteen laps before going out in a crash. The big surprise with his situation came two years later when it was revealed he had lied about his age to gain entry. At the time the minimum age to race the Indianapolis 500 was twenty-one, and Garza had twenty-two on his racing license. It turned out he was nineteen in 1981. The rule was later changed, but only one younger driver has ever competed in the *500*, A.J. Foyt IV.

Three Europeans, Schuppan, Geoff Brabham, and Dennis Firestone, placed in the top ten.

By winning the Indianapolis 500 in 1968, 1975 and 1981, Bobby Unser completed a special triple, capturing the title in three decades.

However, he was soured by his experience with the protests and bad feelings emanating from the 1981 victory. That was his last Indianapolis 500 and he retired from racing at forty-seven.

1982

One reason the Indianapolis 500 is the most famous auto race in the world is its unpredictability.

Not all of the surprises are good ones. Many turn out to be tragic. But there is no doubt that any race fan considers the Indy 500 to be compelling theatre each year. Truly, it is impossible to predict what might happen once the cars gather at the Indianapolis Motor Speedway each May.

It took one day for Bobby Unser to win the *500* in 1981, but nearly five months for everyone to acknowledge it. In some ways the 1982 race was even closer, though happily for everyone it was decided on the track.

As a rookie in 1981 Kevin Cogan finished fourth. His fine performance was partially overlooked by all of the controversy. Cogan was also overlooked for rookie of the year, but he was just beginning an all-around racing career.

Cogan showed up at Indy in 1982 ready for more and on pole qualifying day he blasted out a record 204.638 mph one-lap time. He also set a four-lap record of 204.082 mph. However, the times did not stand up. Rick Mears bested him and took the pole at 207.004 mph.

Pole qualifying was marred by the death of Gordon Smiley, who rammed into the same wall in much the same way as Danny Ongais did in his own previous serious accident. Smiley hit the wall so hard it was believed he died instantly and observers of the scene likened it to an airplane crash. Smiley was so violently broken up that the announcement of his death was made to fans a little more than a half hour after the crash, one that did not include fire. It took more than two hours to clean up the track and fix it up sufficiently for more driving.

Smiley, thirty-six at the time of his death, was from Nebraska. His background mostly revolved around road races.

In an unusual qualifying development, three brothers, Don, Bill and Dale Whittingham, all made the thirty-three car field, an Indianapolis first.

When the race began on May 30, it took only a short while to be interrupted by a crash. The culprit was Cogan, who was in the middle of the front row between Mears and A.J. Foyt. The green flag had not waved to start the race when Cogan turned right, hitting Foyt's car during the warm-ups. Then the car slid in front of Mario Andretti and took him out. Tightly bunched cars began bouncing off each other.

The race was immediately flagged to a stop before it could even start and Cogan, Andretti, Dale Whittington and Roger Mears, Rick Mears' brother, all had their cars wiped out in the chain-reaction crash. Foyt's car was damaged, but his team was able to repair it and get him to the starting line for the re-start.

There was no apparent reason for Cogan's faux pas and when he tried to explain what did happen to Andretti, the veteran driver pushed him away. Foyt and Andretti were infuriated about the mishap and highly critical of Cogan. Andretti was promptly interviewed by the broadcast media and had not cooled one bit, saying, "This is what happens when you have children doing a man's job up front."

Cogan was twenty-six at the time. Andretti kept up a stream of criticism directed at Cogan after he returned to the garage area, exceedingly unhappy that his race ended with zero laps covered. Foyt was later interviewed, as well, and wasn't much friendlier, saying, "The guy pulled a stupid trick."

While there was also much discussion about how slowly the pace was being set before the green flag – the pace car brings the speed up to ninety to one hundred mph before swerving off – most of the blame seemed to fall on Cogan. Cogan said something in the rear of his car broke and radio broadcaster Rodger Ward, the former two-time champion, suggested there might have been brake failure. Foyt later suggested that Cogan may have been preparing to jump the start that he might well have been readying to take off just before the green flag, and the slower pre-race pace prevented it.

Cogan continued to race at Indianapolis through 1993, with best finishes of second in 1986 and fifth in 1983, in addition to that rookie-year fourth.

Perhaps because he was angry and perhaps because he just wanted to get away from traffic as soon as possible, Foyt went to the lead on the re-start, though his car was patched together. Foyt led for thirty-two laps, but his transmission went out after ninety-five laps, ending his race.

Although Rick Mears accumulated seventy-seven laps in the lead, most cars had a tough day with mechanical problems. Tom Sneva led for 31 laps and despite his engine blowing out after 197 laps he still finished fourth. Pancho Carter was in the hunt for a long time, but didn't get beyond 199 laps. The only two cars to complete the two hundred laps belonged to Gordon Johncock and Mears.

At that point in their careers, each driver owned one Indianapolis 500 title, with Johncock's coming in a rain-shortened race.

As the race passed the 180 lap point, it was obvious that the closing miles would be a showdown between Johncock and Mears unless their cars broke down and ended their dreams. They both needed one more pit stop before churning for the finish. Mears had a problem in the pits as he rolled up to his crew, hitting the rear of Herm Johnson's car. The mistake cost him several seconds.

Johncock was on the track leading when Mears rejoined the fray, but he knocked off his pit stop with sixteen laps remaining. Johncock's stop was faster and he had a lead of eleven seconds. Then his greatest fear seemed to be coming true. The sweet-driving car began giving him handling problems. Mears gained one second a lap.

With three laps left Mears was within three seconds. Then Mears caught up and the cars rode side-by-side as they took the white flag signaling one lap left. Mears took a run at passing Johncock, but the leader fought him off.

"I had him set up," Mears said. But not well enough to get by.

Commentator Jim McKay's voice conveyed the sense of excitement felt by the 400,000 fans.

"I've never seen anything like it," the sportscaster said.

On the final backstretch Mears made one more try for the lead, but again Johncock held him off. Johncock said if Mears had chosen another spot for the pass, when he dropped very low on the asphalt, "he would have had me."

Johncock won his second Indianapolis 500 crown by 0.16 second. Some sixty-six races into *500* history that was the closest finish yet.

"It was a race you're never going to forget," Johncock said. "It gives me goose bumps when (any time he watches it again)."

It's still close on those replays, but Johncock still wins every time. Experts consider the 1982 Indy 500 one of the greatest finishes of all because of the head-to-head racing by the two leaders and the narrow margin at the end.

1983

Tom Sneva, who had been posting super clockings for years and three times had finished second in the Indianapolis 500, finally got his name and face etched onto the Borg-Warner Trophy by capturing the 1983 title.

Italian Formula 1 star Teo Fabi crossed the ocean to give the *500* a try and won the pole at 207.395 mph. It was a good beginning for the newcomer and a satisfying race for the veteran Sneva who had come close so many times.

As they always seemed to be doing, Indy 500 officials tinkered with the rules that set parameters for cars. The rules governed aerodynamic systems and meant cars had to be built in a certain manner. Not all cars that showed up for practice met the new standards and were not approved in technical inspections. As the number of cars failing grew to fifteen, interaction between drivers and owners with officials grew testy.

The new March chassis appeared and the design superseded the Chaparrels. The old yellow cars were squarer and the March's were thinner and more needle-nosed. Sneva drove a March in 1983 and March cars won the Indianapolis 500 for five years in a row.

While Mike Mosley, Rick Mears and Sneva drove fast in pole qualifying, it was Fabi who gained the most attention. He was already a successful racer, but no one could predict how his success elsewhere would translate to the Indianapolis Motor Speedway. Quite well, as it turned out, based on his taking the pole and thrusting himself into the race picture as a rookie.

In a history-making occurrence under the modern qualifying system the entire field of thirty-three cars was filled in one day of timing.

Only Dennis Firestone of Great Britain was successful on bump day with a run of 190.888 allowing him to sneak into the field in 33rd place and John Mahler being bumped out.

Fabi was not shy about being in Indianapolis for the first time. When the green flag was dropped he raced straight to the front and led for the first twenty-three laps. He was moving impressively until a broken fuel gasket consigned him to 26th place after forty-seven laps. Although four rookies placed higher, some completing many more laps, Fabi was given the rookie of the year award. Most likely his pole position, fast speed in qualifying and early leading of the race tipped the vote his way.

Among those gone from contention before the first half of the race was completed were Mario Andretti and Johnnie Parsons, who crashed, A.J. Foyt, who suffered from mechanical issues, Firestone, former rookie of the year Josele Garza, and Steve Krisiloff.

As the race approached its final thirty laps, Sneva was in the lead, but Al Unser was hanging close and Kevin Cogan and Geoff Brabham seemed to be in the hunt. Sneva was headed to the pits on lap 172 for his final pit step, but just in front of him Mosley spun out and crashed. Sneva desperately sought to avoid the other car and did so. After the situation settled down Unser was in the lead.

This led to a curious and controversial situation. Al Unser Jr. was a rookie in the race and after a yellow caution flag was withdrawn he moved in front of the other cars although he had been lapped. Then Al Jr. let his dad pass him, but blocked Sneva. This went on for laps and it seemed obvious to many Al Jr. was trying to manipulate the situation to give his father the victory by preventing Sneva from catching up. Meanwhile, despite the clear track, Al Sr. could not pull away.

It was felt Al Jr. held back in front of Sneva to make him run through bad air and did not yield when he could have been passed. Eventually, when their vehicles caught up to other lapped cars Sneva was able to shed Al Jr. as he ran up behind Dick Simon's car. After disposing of the Al Jr. nuisance Sneva passed Al Sr. with ten laps remaining and pulled away from the threat, winning by more than eleven seconds.

After the race ended Al Jr. admitted he was trying to help his father, but did not confess to the rule violation of blocking. Al Jr. ran out of gas and finished tenth, the highest-finishing rookie that year. He took considerable criticism for his actions, but did not receive a penalty.

Sneva led for ninety-eight laps, Al Sr. led for sixty-one laps. Mears placed third, Brabham fourth, and Cogan fifth. Bobby Rahal, who led for fifteen laps early, went out of the race with a radiator problem after 110 laps.

ABC was still airing the race on delayed tape, later the same night after the race ended. One innovation was the first camera mounted on a car at the Indy 500.

Fabi made Indianapolis a habit after his first race, competing eight times over twelve years. His best finish was seventh in 1994.

"It looks so easy, but driving the ovals is not as easy as it appears," Fabi said. "You have to contend with traffic almost all of the time, the speeds are constantly high, and you must maintain your concentration for such a long time."

Al Jr. was just starting what would be an exceptional career. He was young, but matured into a top-flight racer and champion.

Someone once asked him if he had ever considered a Formula 1 path, but the son of Indy 500 champion Al Unser Sr. and the nephew of Indy 500 champion Bobby Unser, said it was logical to think of Indianapolis first.

"I dreamed of the Indy 500 when I was a kid," Al Jr. said. "I mean, look at my family – my dad and my uncle – that's where they were."

1984

No matter how talented and experienced a driver, there are infinite examples of how things can go wrong during the Indianapolis 500, from practice through qualifying and throughout the race.

But sometimes perseverance wins out and in 1984 Rick Mears, who hadn't won a title in five years despite coming close, earned his second Indy 500 championship.

During early practices, Mario Andretti, who could tell anyone a thing or two about Indianapolis 500 bad luck, zipped a lap over 212 mph. The talk was that Andretti would swipe the pole. Only on pole day, it was Tom Sneva sneaking in and recording the first official clocking over 210 mph. He grabbed the pole at 210.029 mph. This was the same driver who broke the 200 mph barrier in 1977.

While Mears leapt to the lead on the first lap he didn't shake any of the other contenders. Sneva, Al Unser Jr., Mario Andretti, and for the first time Michael Andretti, Mario's son, appeared in the field, and all were all mixing it up with Mears. The race was also crash free for the first 100 miles.

That changed on lap fifty-eight when Pat Bedard hit the wall, flipped and rolled, and broke in half. It was the type of crash that kills drivers, but Bedard, who was also a writer for Car and Driver, survived. Bedard, who wrote for the magazine for forty-one years, only competed at Indy one year.

Bedard said nothing can match the excitement of racing at the Speedway.

"I can't find anything that quite captivates me the way that did," he said. "You can't do it from writing. You can't do it from anything. When you're a race driver and you have speed at the Speedway, that's as good as life gets."

Halfway into the race Sneva was ahead with the group still the same, but the order shifting. Al Jr. was second, followed by Mears, Mario Andretti, and Michael. Between the Unsers, the Whittingtons, the Mears', the Snevas, and the Andrettis a broadcaster over the years had to learn to call drivers by their first names.

The attrition came late. Al Jr.'s car broke a water pump after 131 laps. Mario got cut off in pit lane on lap 153 by Josele Garza and the nose cone of his car was wrecked. Mears and Sneva put distance between themselves and others, but Sneva's car went out after 168 laps because of a broken joint.

Mears led 119 laps and was the only car to complete the two hundred laps. Rookie Roberto Guerrero took second. Al Unser Sr. finished third. Rookie Al Holbert was fourth and Michael Andretti placed fifth. Guerrero and Michael shared rookie of the year honors.

1985

Call it the Impossible Spin. If you are going to win the Indianapolis 500 once in your career you might as well do it in the most memorable fashion possible. That's what Danny Sullivan did in 1985.

Sullivan was born in Louisville, Kentucky in 1950, but it would be a stretch to say that the guy who won seventeen CART races, a season-long championship, and the Indy 500 was born to be a race car driver. In fact, Sullivan didn't really know what he wanted to do when he grew up and he did try out a few intriguing professions, including becoming a lumberjack and driving a taxi in New York.

Driving in Indianapolis, however, is what made the good-looking, swash-buckling Sullivan famous. Sullivan ran the Indy 500 twelve times between 1982 and 1995 and was a popular driver with the fans. His popularity peaked in 1985 when a legendary survival move prevented a crash and positioned him for victory. The maneuver was called "Spin and Win" and established Sullivan firmly in the history of the race.

The pole was captured by Pancho Carter with a clocking of 212.583 mph. That was after Mario Andretti at more than 214 mph and Bobby Rahal, nearly as fast, posted wicked practice times. When it came to actual qualifying Scott Brayton set the early pace. He set records for one lap (214.199 mph) and four laps (212.354), but they did not stand. Carter broke the four-lap record with his pole-grabbing run. Brayton clinched second on the starting grid.

Beginning in 1981, Brayton qualified for the Indy 500 sixteen times, though he started only fifteen of them. Brayton was born in Coldwater, Michigan and raced for Brayton Engineering, the company his father Lee ran, for the first five years of his career, driving Buicks. He later changed to two other teams.

The 1985 race figured to be a breakthrough for Brayton after his superb qualifying day. But after leading one lap, a cylinder wall in his engine broke and Brayton was out of the race after nineteen laps. He placed 30th.

Brayton recorded four top ten finishes and in 1995 and 1996 he captured the pole. However, after taking the pole in 1996, Brayton was on the track practicing with his team's other car. He was hurtling along the

Speedway track at about 230 mph when he crashed into the wall head-on. He was killed on impact at age thirty-seven.

Brayton was so popular that from 1997 through 2009, the Speedway named an award for him. The Scott Brayton Trophy was awarded to the driver who best exemplified the same spirit, attitude and competitive drive.

Janet Guthrie had already broken one barrier at Indy by becoming the first woman to race. Willy T. Ribbs nearly became the first African-American in the *500*. He participated in practice, as he had in 1984 briefly, but his speeds were not high enough to contend for the thirty-three car field. He withdrew with the promise that he would be back when he gained more experience. Probably several other drivers, some of whom were killed or injured in practice, might have wisely made the same call over the years.

Even though Carter and Brayton both excelled on pole day in 1985, some questioned the staying power of their engines. In both cases the doubters were correct. Carter exited the race on lap six, even before Brayton.

Mears, the defending champion, had been seriously injured later in the 1984 season and had competed only intermittently since. He did qualify in 1985, starting on the inside of the third row, but his car, too, gave out, after 122 laps.

It was sunny when the race began on May 26, and Bobby Rahal, on the outside of the first row, grabbed the early lead. After running strong, Rahal's car began troubling him. After attempts to fix it he dropped out after eighty-four laps.

About 250 miles into the *500*, Mario Andretti was in charge, with Sullivan running second. Emerson Fittipaldi, a Brazilian racing star who was just at the beginning of twelve years of competition at Indianapolis, had made a check-it-out foray to the Speedway in 1984 and placed 32nd. Running with the frontrunners in 1985, it was clear he was on hand trying to win.

Sullivan made his charge to pass Andretti on lap 120, believing that the race was closer to finishing than it was. Sullivan tried to pass Andretti on the inside, but Andretti fought back and gave him little room. Sullivan went by, but was very low on the track. What followed next was an incredible bit of car handling accompanied by heart-in-the-throat drama.

As Sullivan passed, the rear of his car began dragging, throwing the driver into a complete 360 degree spin. Sullivan made his high-speed circle right in front of Andretti, who somehow was able to steer by him by going low as Sullivan shot high. Sullivan did not hit another car and he missed the wall. The engine stalled out, but after the spin Sullivan was facing the right direction on the track.

Sullivan put his car in the proper gear and tried to start it. Indy engines are so fickle so often, but this time it started up. Sullivan picked up speed, once again trying to chase down Andretti. Neither the car, nor Sullivan was injured in any way, though an immediate caution flag sent him to the pits.

The astounding, quick series of events astonished the 400,000 fans and the nationwide TV and radio audiences.

Sullivan, who later called his race – and perhaps life-saving maneuver – fifty percent luck and fifty percent skill, said he was cursing himself for losing control. He was finally taking the lead from Andretti.

"I'm mad," Sullivan said, thinking to himself, "What a dumb mistake." He didn't have a whole lot of thinking time, however. He understood that the car was spinning.

"You could argue it wasn't much skill that got you spinning," Sullivan said twenty-five years after the race. "But when it first started to happen, I tried to correct it and I could feel I wasn't going to catch it. At that point you just jump on the brakes. It was just dumb luck that I looked and saw turn two suites and took my foot off the brake. I almost lost it on what gear to take because the engine was dead. Then the car jumped and I almost lost it again. Whether skill or dumb luck, it was 50-50. Maybe I give myself too much credit. What most racers know and people can't relate to is the whole thing took three seconds." He had made the comment about 50-50 luck and skill before, but he suggested that being able to react so quickly is part of a driver's skill.

Two red cars were side-by-side speeding along the track. As Sullivan spun, his tires threw out, billowing smoke.

"We looked like fighter planes in formation," Sullivan said.

Only for seconds. Andretti said he had to decide instantly what to do and plowing straight ahead proved the right choice.

"Danny spins and I see just a big cloud," Andretti said. "It was not skill that avoided that collision."

Sullivan thought he had just lost the race and he was greatly surprised when that tire smoke blew away and his car was in one piece and facing in the right direction. So he did what was natural. He put his foot on the pedal and brought the car back up to speed.

After the yellow was withdrawn and the green flag flew, Fittipaldi was in front. He would lead eleven laps, but he went out of the race due to low oil pressure after 188 laps.

Not long after the Sullivan spin – no one has ever seen anything quite like it before or since – another mishap occurred on the track. Rich Vogler hit the wall on lap 119 and was taken to a hospital. Tom Sneva could not escape the debris and went to the pits for good after 123 laps. There was a lot of action at the time. Mears exited because of mechanical damage after 122 laps and Chip Ganassi, who would gain much greater fame later as a team owner, suffered from a busted fuel line and went out after 121 laps.

There seemed to be as many drivers waving goodbye almost all at once as were vying for the lead.

It took until lap 140 for Sullivan to position himself for another pass of Andretti. This time his car ate Andretti up without any difficulty and as the last twenty-five percent of the race unfolded, it was Sullivan with the stronger car. Sullivan led sixty-seven laps and won it all, though Andretti held on for second while leading 107 laps. The only other driver completing the two hundred laps was Roberto Guerrero. Al Unser Sr. was fourth and finished 199 laps.

Arie Luyendyk made his presence known as rookie of the year, finishing seventh. Luyendyk, a native of the Netherlands who was dubbed "The Flying Dutchman," became a significant historical figure at the Speedway over the following years while competing in the *500* seventeen times.

Anyone who wins the Indianapolis 500 is regarded as an esteemed auto racing champion. For Sullivan, who was a new face in Victory Lane, the manner in which he won, by making what was presumed to be an unimaginable move, added to his luster. Sullivan became an overnight sensation.

Sullivan was even invited to act in a couple of television shows, one a soap opera and the second "Miami Vice." He also appeared in a western movie called "Outlaw Justice" with Willie Nelson and Kris Kristofferson.

Andretti, who burned to win a second Indianapolis 500, felt he had lost out on one of his best chances. He was so upset he did not talk to Sullivan for more than a year.

More than thirty years after the "Spin and Win" the startling stretch of driving is considered to be one of the most breath-taking moments in a century-old event.

1986

In an unusual twist rain called off the originally scheduled May 25 Indianapolis 500 and again on the rain date of May 26. The race was postponed an entire week and took place on May 31, pretty close to the original date it always happened on, before the federal holiday schedule was changed.

For the first time, long-time broadcast partner ABC televised the race live instead of on later-night tape delay. It was the 75th anniversary of the first Indy 500 of 1911 even though it was not the 75th race because of the World War I and World War II interruptions.

There was also a major change to the physical plant at the Speedway, which opened in 1909. Gasoline Alley garages were a distinctive green and white color and had been unchanged since the 1940s. The old ones were removed and new ones constructed. More space was provided and garage space itself was increased from eighty-eight to ninety-six cars.

The new garages were not the least bit fancy, however. The garages were pretty much concrete bunkers and they had modern but boring pull-down metal doors. To some extent they resembled storage units for the public. Still, during May the area was, as always, alive with the buzz of activity as cars were rolled in and out, repaired, fine-tuned, and readied for the big race.

This was also the 50th anniversary of the awarding of the Borg-Warner Trophy and it was spruced up and altered to be capable of having more faces and names engraved on it. There was now room for names of many future champions.

The first one that helped fill up space on the revamped trophy was Bobby Rahal.

After racing a limited schedule in 1985 because of the injuries he suffered in a later race, Rick Mears, the two-time champ, was back at full speed. Mears won the pole with a ride of 216.828 mph. He went even faster in pre-qualifying practice, hitting 217.548 mph. Others were flying too. Defending Danny Sullivan briefly set a Speedway track record at 215.382 mph, but he was eclipsed. Mears is the one who emerged from a fast day of qualifying with the new mark. Mears, Sullivan in the middle, and Michael Andretti, on the outside, filled out the first row. Rahal, Al Unser Sr. and Kevin Cogan made up the second row.

The worst part of preparation was the waiting that ensued when spring rain pounded the track and wiped out the original race date and the fill-in date. It wasn't as if the re-scheduled day forecast was encouraging. The National Weather Service predicted an eighty percent chance of rain and this time the agency was right.

It was a strange situation at the Speedway. The best drivers in the world were hanging around with the fastest cars available and almost no one did much high-speed running for a whole week.

While the weather was peachy May 31, in the eighties with sunshine, it took some effort to get underway after the normal command was issued by Mary Hulman. Tom Sneva crashed on the last pace lap bringing out a yellow flag before the green could be waved. When a re-start was configured a different person delivered the "Gentlemen, start your engines" order with the race starting thirty-five minutes late. It came from Tony George, grandson of Tony Hulman, and a man who in future years would play a tremendous role in the *500* and at the Speedway. In a few years George would be running the place, never mind making a one-sentence cameo over a microphone. In retrospect, this might have been considered a sneak preview introduction to him.

Michael Andretti went to the front and led for the first forty-two laps while his dad, Mario, who started from the 30th slot, seemed to be trying to make up for his way-back starting position all at once. It didn't work and the older Andretti flamed out after nineteen laps, becoming the second big name after Sneva, to have his car go off the board.

For 250 miles it was smoother sailing than usual, especially considering the problems that had beset the race a week earlier. The worst incident that occurred was a yellow waved because Michael Andretti lost a mirror from his car. Seventy-five years earlier Ray Harroun was the only driver in the field who even had a rearview mirror.

After Sneva and Mario Andretti's demise, no other driver dropped out until Phil Krueger and he had completed sixty-seven laps. At the halfway point twenty-eight cars were still running. Attrition began to mount after that, with mechanical flaws and spinouts removing such drivers as A.J. Foyt and Al Unser from contention. For the second year in a row Rich Vogler had a crash. Arie Luyendyk also departed due to a crash after 188 laps.

The top thirteen cars completed at least 192 laps, including rookie of the year Randy Lanier. Lanier sought to qualify the year before, but didn't make the cut. His tenth place finish in his debut in 1986 seemed to stamp him as a future star.

However, Lanier was indicted on drug trafficking charges in January, 1987, convicted, and sentenced to life in prison, although he was eventually released. Drivers Don and Bill Whittington, race team partners with Lanier, were also caught up in legal matters and were sent to prison, as well, Don for money laundering and Bill for income tax evasion and conspiracy to smuggle marijuana. Don Whittington's sixth at Indy in 1982 was the best family finish.

Four drivers were on the 200th lap together and only seconds separated them. Rahal won the championship and Cogan finished second, 1.441 seconds behind. Third was Mears, 1.881 seconds in back of Rahal and fourth was Roberto Guerrero, 10.558 seconds off the lead. Al Unser Jr. and Michael Andretti, sons of Speedway legends, were next, covering 199 laps, as did Emerson Fittipaldi.

Nearing the end it appeared Cogan had the race in his hands, but Rahal swooped past and took the white flag signaling one lap to go. This was the closest three-car finish in the three-quarters of a century of Indy racing.

It was such a clean race that Rahal's elapsed time of two hours, fifty-five minutes, forty-three seconds, was the first finish under three hours. The winning average speed, again due to a limited number of yellow flags, was a record at 170.722 mph.

At that age, Rahal resembled the later comic actor Sacha Baron Cohen, except for having large lens glasses that seemed almost as large as windows. It was the pinnacle of Rahal's Indy career, though he competed fourteen times and also posted two additional third-place finishes. He was a thoughtful and insightful man who was articulate in explaining his retirement from the car at age forty-two after twenty-four wins.

"I don't want people to remember me going through the motions," he said.

That was unlikely. Rahal didn't stray too far from the track, either. Later, he became an Indy team owner, and his son, Graham, has been a regular in the *500* since 2000.

"In racing I wanted to be a winner, and in racing you have to be willing to roll the dice," Rahal said.

1987

For those who believed that A.J. Foyt would hold the record of four Indianapolis 500 crowns in a career by himself forever, Al Unser Sr. proved them wrong. At a time when his son Al Jr. had already become a contender, the older Unser won his fourth title in 1987.

Although Unser had pretty much established himself as open-wheel racing royalty, it was believed he was past his prime and unlikely to contend again. Unser was forty-seven and his 48th birthday was only five days away from the May 24 start of the race.

It wasn't even a sure thing that Unser would race in 1987. He showed up at the Indianapolis Motor Speedway without a car or team and minus sponsorships. When practice began early in the month he was a spectator. He had retired from full-time racing, but was still interested in periodic rides, especially in the longest races.

Unser's fortunes changed when Danny Ongais' did, as well. A day after four crashes marred practice, though without serious injury, Ongais crashed. Ongais bashed into a wall and incurred a concussion. That knocked him out of the *500* and left the Roger Penske team one driver short in its three-person team. Unser got the ride.

For those who believe that showing up is half of life, Unser's experience was definitely testimony to that. He was right there when Roger Penske turned around. After Ongais' crash and before Penske filled the slot, several other drivers crashed. It was as if the Speedway was under a voodoo curse that May.

A week after the Ongais crash, Unser moved into the car. It wasn't as if Unser scorched the field in qualifying. He started twentieth. The pole was taken by Mario Andretti, still game to win his second Indy. He ran 215.390 mph to earn the right to start first on the inside of the front row. Andretti was impressive all month, burning up the track day after day in practice. It was obvious he had confidence in his car and he loomed as the favorite. Absolutely nobody was talking about the likelihood of Al Sr. winning his fourth Indianapolis 500.

George Snider's car caught fire on the pace lap. He didn't even get to start before being eliminated. To no one's surprise, Mario Andretti darted to the lead right away. Snider's was not the only early mishap. Josele Garza spun out and nearly hit Unser. Unser steered clear and Garza continued in the race.

Andretti was driving so fast and so well that he first began lapping racers after seven laps. Andretti's effort broke up the pack quickly, with only a half-dozen cars on the lead lap well before the halfway point. For mile after mile Andretti led. The only times he fell back was when he chose to pit for routine maintenance.

Compared to some cars Andretti was actually driving ten mph faster, a huge differential. Past 250 miles the only car on the same lap as Andretti belonged to Roberto Guerrero.

A tragedy interrupted the race on lap 130 when Tony Bettenhausen lost a wheel and it began its own journey along the track. Guerrero crashed into the fat tire head-first smashing in his nosecone, but worse sending the wheel soaring into the grandstand where it landed and hit a spectator in the head killing him. The accident happened during a TV commercial and the death was not announced on the air. Broadcaster Jim McKay appeared to have missed the accident.

Surprisingly, Guerrero was able to guide his car to his pit crew, which frantically made repairs and sent him back onto the track. He lost a lap while this was going on, but against the odds remained in the race. He also was able to make up ground and stay near the front, a remarkable achievement in itself.

Guerrero was back in second place with twenty-five laps to go, but he was now a full lap behind Andretti. Al Sr. had worked his way into third place. As more cars departed the track with ailments, there were just twelve still running.

Andretti led for 170 laps, raising the prospect of a wire-to-wire win. But suddenly, his speedy car slowed down. Aware that something was wrong, Andretti conserved speed, but stunningly, after 180 laps he was out of the race, a victim of a malfunctioning ignition system. It was another in a series of heartbreaks for Andretti, who often seemed to have the best car, only to see something thwart him.

Suddenly, the race was up for grabs. Guerrero, who had survived his own close call earlier, took the lead with twenty laps remaining. He was ahead of Al Sr. by a full lap, but he also needed to pit for fuel. What not everyone realized was that Guerrero's clutch was damaged when he hit the errant wheel many laps ago. Also, his third gear was broken. For a time, a frustrated Guerrero was stuck in the pits, his car refusing to go.

While the pit time ticked by, Unser moved ahead. The frantic efforts of Guerrero's pit crew revived the car, but Unser was a lap ahead by then. Guerrero was moving faster than Unser and with nine laps left he got back onto the lead lap. During this, Andretti's men were following the same procedure. They eventually got his car going again, but when Andretti sought to bring up the speed, it stalled. That brought out a yellow flag to the aid of Guerrero, who was able to tuck in behind the half-dozen cars ahead of him to make another run.

The last four laps were run under green. Guerrero swept past all of the cars between him and Unser, but ran out of ground before he could catch him. Al Sr.'s margin of victory was 4.496 seconds. He tied the record with four victories and became the oldest winner of the Indianapolis 500. If open-wheel racing was no country for old men, Unser defied the standard.

As an aside, almost as if proving the point, Al Jr. placed fourth in the same race his dad won. Little Al, as he came to be known, was twenty-five.

Andretti was disappointed once more when seemingly driving a guaranteed winning car.

"Al Unser Sr. was one of the smartest drivers I've ever raced against," Andretti said. "And I've often said 'I wish I could have had some of his patience.' I know it would have worked for me many times."

Al Jr. was about as savvy as anyone reading Al Sr.'s mood after the fourth victory .

"It means everything to dad," he said. "They called him retired and washed up and all that. I've got goose bumps. I'm ecstatic for dad."

That win gave Al Sr. new life at the track. He kept on returning and racing until 1994. When he was only a days away from turning fifty-five years old, Unser tried qualifying one last time, but retired before the race.

"I always said if the day came when I wasn't producing the right way, if I wasn't happy, I'd get out," Al Sr. said on that day in May. "I think the time has come."

1988

Rick Mears sped towards rarified territory, picking off his third Indianapolis 500 championship in 1988 and that was after claiming the pole with a speed of 219.198 mph.

At this point, as some of the older drivers began to retire and others seemed past their prime chances for winning, Mears' third triumph propelled him into consideration as the best of the best in the extremely chancy business of open-wheel racing.

Mears went plenty fast to claim the pole, before official qualifying started he posted a lap time in practice at 222.827 mph. That speed opened everyone's eyes. No one else could match it.

A.J. Foy, Rick Mears, Danny Sullivan, and Al Unser together in the 1988 race.

In official qualifying Danny Sullivan ran 217.749 mph, but Mears blew that away when it was his turn. Mears' opening qualifying lap was turned at 220.453 mph, a new track record. That made him the first driver to officially top 220 mph. It did not seem long ago that Tom Sneva had cracked the two hundred mph barrier.

There was a newcomer in qualifying with a familiar name. Bill Vukovich III, the first Bill's grandson, showed up. When Bill III made the cut the Vukovich family became the first three-generation group of drivers at the Speedway.

On race day, Sullivan was the first into the lead. However, right behind Sullivan and Mears, Scott Brayton spun, caught Roberto Guerrero and they both crashed as did Tony Bettenhausen. All three were wiped out of the race and posted zero laps covered.

Despite new faces and crashes, the first five were well-known to race fans. Sullivan led, but Mears, both Al Unsers, and Mario Andretti constituted the closest competition. Sullivan retained front-running status even as others faltered. For a time Mears was in trouble, fighting the poor handling of his car and dropping back. Mears was lapped. When Sullivan took a pit stop, Jim Crawford took the lead.

Crawford, from Scotland, had been coming to Indianapolis for four years without making a notable impact in the standings. In 1987 he was seriously injured, but returned for 1988 and was making a nice move. After one hundred laps Crawford was in the lead and kept it for eight laps. After getting his car fixed, Mears came all of the way back to the front of the back.

The fragility of these high-strung automobiles caught up to Sullivan, the 1985 winner, whose front wing adjusters broke on lap 102 after he led for ninety-one laps. Mears gained the lead on lap 113 after his earlier woes. As other cars encountered problems Mears got stronger.

In a confusing series of events, Emerson Fittipaldi was running in second place when officials slapped him with a penalty for passing cars under the yellow flag. They changed their mind and withdrew it. Then they changed their mind again and imposed it.

Mears pulled away to win. Al Unser Sr. took second and Michael Andretti third. Temporarily. Fittipaldi's team went to bat for him and said there never should have been a penalty. When the results were studied overnight and posted in the morning, there was Fittipaldi back in second place. It was a goofy sequence of events, but that became Fittipaldi's official placing .

Fittipaldi once enunciated his racing philosophy this way: "The racing driver's mind has to have the ability to have amazing anticipation, coordination, and reflex. Because of the speed the car goes."

He might have added patience to the list of components. Because of the slow speed the officials went.

Crawford's sixth-place finish in 1988 was his best in nine *500*s, though he missed qualifying three other times. After retiring as a driver, Crawford became a fishing boat captain in Florida. He died of liver failure in 2002 at age fifty-four.

1989

A year following his runner-up finish and the controversy surrounding it, Brazilian Emerson Fittipaldi conquered the Indianapolis Motor Speedway.

While Rick Mears was once again grabbing the pole position with a run of 223.885 mph, Fittipaldi outlasted him over five hundred miles.

Before Mears took the pole, Al Unser Sr. was the man to beat at 223.471 mph. At the end of qualifying there were three Andrettis in the thirty-three car field, Mario, his son Michael and nephew John.

Once again, between the 1988 and 1989 races, Speedway officials resurfaced the track with a fresh blend of asphalt setting up faster speeds.

Regardless of how fast the others were going for the longest time nobody could stick with Fittipaldi, the two-time world champion driver. For about four hundred miles it was all Fittipaldi. But another driver with patience kept nipping away at the lead and with ninety or so miles left, Michael Andretti took the lead. Andretti led for thirty-five laps, but it is possible all of that hard work to catch up stressed out his car because the engine gave out after 163 laps.

After that, the only other racer in hailing distance of Fittipaldi was Al Unser Jr. All other still-running competitors were a minimum of six laps behind. For any of them to win it would take a minor miracle or a major breakdown of the two leaders' cars.

That did not occur, but when Fittipaldi took his final planned pit stop, Al Jr.'s crew made a calculation and thought there was a chance he could finish without taking on more fuel. So Unser stayed on the track when Fittipaldi ducked into the pits and that gave him the lead. It was a bold attempt, but Fittipaldi muscled his car back into the lead.

Unser stayed in pursuit and had one more move in him. By lap 193, with seven to go, Unser was on Fittipaldi's tail and on lap 194 the drivers went back-and-forth trying to establish control. At one point Unser's car touched Fittipaldi's, but neither paid for it. Al Jr. passed Fittipaldi for the lead on lap 196.

The problem both men faced was that they did not have a clear track. With all of the other cars lapped, they were constantly approaching slower traffic and had to swerve through it. Again, this time with two laps remaining, the cars touched wheels. Unser spun around and Fittipaldi took over. Although he was not hurt, Unser crashed and was out of the race after 198 completed laps. Fittipaldi, who led for 158 laps, earned his title.

Three rookies finished in the top ten and two of them, Bernard Jourdain and Scott Pruett, shared rookie honors.

Unser did not blame Fittipaldi for the crash after their fierce battle for the lead. Fittipaldi summarized what most drivers are very aware of at more than two hundred mph.

"You are going in one second the length of a football field," he said. "That means your brain is receiving information from your body what the car is doing physically, bumping, balance, performance."

This was the first time in twenty-three years that the Indianapolis 500 had a foreign winner.

Foreign Star, Another 4-Time King, and More Troubles

1990-1999

Brazilian, Emerson Fittipaldi heralded a new influx of drivers from other countries when he won in 1989 and again in 1993. He was joined in Victory Lane by Arie Luyendyk and Jacques Villeneuve in 1995.

Rick Mears picked off his fourth crown in 1991. This equaled the record for driver wins held by A.J. Foyt and Al Unser. A quarter of a century later, the same trio holds the mark as others have tried to match them, but could not.

By the mid-1990s, the poisonous administrative split between CART and the Indy Racing League kept some top drivers out of the Indy 500, a circumstance variously described as a lockout or a boycott.

1990

The drought for foreign winners ended with Emerson Fittipaldi in 1989 and his successor in Victory Lane was another foreign competitor, Arie Luyendyk. Although if anyone was asked to choose an out-of-USA winner beforehand they probably would have sided with Fittipaldi as a repeat champ.

That was because the defending titlist was extraordinary in qualifying. The Brazilian whiz took the pole position with an effort clocked at 225.301 mph. Rain plagued the Speedway during practice in May, but although the start of pole qualifying was delayed because of poor weather, some drivers capitalized on the late afternoon start.

Fittipaldi was one of them. From the moment his car opened up his times were fast and consistent. Fittipaldi set four straight one-lap records, going slightly faster each time around the 2.5 mile oval. His marks were 225.006 mph, 225.259 mph, 225.366 mph, and 225.575 mph. Fans wondered if Fittipaldi kept going if he might not hit 250 mph. After his dash everyone else was competing for the second spot in the starting grid.

The sloppy weather interrupted things repeatedly and it took some days to fill out the field. Practice kept getting rained out. Rick Mears qualified second and Luyendyk third.

After the weeks of rainy weather, race day was actually sunny. Fittipaldi, using the same tactics he employed in 1989, went to the front immediately. Others fell back and Fittipaldi set a record by leading for the first ninety-two laps. When 250 miles had been logged and one hundred laps counted, Fittipaldi had led for ninety-eight of them, the only interruption coming when he took a pit stop.

The day became unseasonably warm, and unexpectedly after the chilly preceding weeks. Tires began having difficulty coping and on lap 136 Fittipaldi had to pit to replace a tire. His was no longer such a smooth rider and Bobby Rahal took the lead.

Fittipaldi was running third on the 153rd lap when a second tire blistered and sent him back to the pits. Rahal had his own difficulties and on lap 168 Luyendyk took the lead. This was Luyendyk's sixth Indy 500 and first time leading a single lap.

By 170 laps it was a two-car race between Rahal and Luyendyk. Neither side wanted to spend time in the pits refueling, but neither side could be sure his man could complete the five hundred miles without adding more fuel. It became a war of nerves as the laps sped by.

The weak tires had dropped Fittipaldi back to not only third place, but a lap behind the leaders. He went for broke trying to make up the distance, but could not. Luyendyk was able to pick up speed and outrun Rahal. Rahal placed second, 11.878 seconds behind. Fittipaldi got within 41.719 seconds of the lead.

Luyendyk's winning average speed set a new record of 185.981 mph.

"I can't believe this," Luyendyk said in his post-race interview, sounding almost dizzy about the pleasing result. "It feels like a dream."

It was more of a nightmare for Fittipaldi, who learned one of the hard lessons of the Indy 500. The man with the fastest car doesn't always win.

"It was a shame," he said. "Everything was under control. The car, she was flying."

If Fittipaldi hadn't changed those tires, however, the car might well have been flying dangerously.

Only those three racers finished the two hundred laps. They had a Hall-of-Fame cast of drivers finishing just behind them, though, with Al Unser Jr. in third, Rick Mears in fourth, and A.J. Foyt in fifth.

The rookie of the year in eighth was Eddie Cheever, giving the Speedway a try after first and foremost driving as a Formula 1 driver. He competed in more of that division's races than any other American. Growing up in Italy influenced Cheever's early racing focus and he ran his first Formula 1 event at twenty.

Later, Cheever would make even bigger news at Indy.

1991

Rick Mears pulled a double. After winning the pole at 224.113 mph, he won the race, too. This was Mears' fourth victory, tying him with A.J. Foyt and Al Unser Sr. for most Indianapolis 500 triumphs. This was also Mears' record sixth pole.

This may have been Mears' most difficult challenge, too, because of a practice crash early in May. A crash during practice knocked the car that he planned to run out of commission and he had to switch to a back-up.

That crash also injured Mears' right foot and the injury did not heal quickly. On race day he had to fight through pain to keep his foot on the accelerator and later admitted that at times it hurt too much to do so. To combat that circumstance Mears sometimes used his left foot on the gas.

Such a maneuver is not advisable in a street car, never mind traveling at more than two hundred mph. It is also a contortionist trick at that speed, but Mears pulled it off.

There were several other, notable developments at Indianapolis that year. Mario Andretti was still chasing his second *500* win – it was almost unbelievable that he had not captured a second victory. But the Andretti family was out in force. Not only did Mario again qualify for the race, as expected, but the starting grid was practically a family reunion. Son Michael and nephew John, who raced in 1990, were back. The new Andretti in the mix was Jeff, another Mario son.

Jeff finished fifteenth, dropping out due to a funky engine after 150 laps, but he was rookie of the year. However, he was only fourth best in the family that day. Michael finished second, John fifth, and Mario seventh.

A.J. Foyt came to Indianapolis for the 34th straight year and said it would be his final race. But when he could complete only twenty-five laps because of suspension failure he changed his mind about retiring.

Curiously, at the same time Hiro Matsushita became the first Japanese driver to qualify for the Indy 500, a hullabaloo broke out because the vehicle chosen as the pace car was a Dodge Stealth. The United Auto Workers and others complained because the Stealth was a Mitsubishi model made in Japan and the pace car had always been an American car. Officials backed off and a Dodge Viper became the pace car. Matsushita finished sixteenth, completing 149 laps.

As promised several years earlier, Willy T. Ribbs was back at Indianapolis seeking to become the first African-American to qualify for the field. He did so, posting a clocking of 217.358 mph. Ribbs' attempt was closely followed by sportswriters and fans cheered him. Ribbs qualified 29th, but finished 32nd. Ribbs' engine blew after just five laps.

Ribbs had competed in NASCAR, which was rooted in the South, and did not always feel he got the same welcome on that circuit.

When he returned to Indianapolis, Ribbs said he did not do so to become a pioneer, although he was. He wanted to run in the most prestigious race in the world because that's what it is.

"I want to go because I want to win," Ribbs said. "Indianapolis is the big apple. Any driver who is a pro wants to win the big apple."

Ribbs had difficulty finding sponsorship and at times he was abrasive, though not more so than other drivers who had conflicts around the track. It seemed clear to Ribbs that the color of his skin was holding back his opportunities.

"It's like having chains around your ankles," he said.

Ribbs qualified for just one more Indy 500 the next year, placing twenty-first.

The African-American driver remains extremely rare in almost all divisions of the sport, with the vivid exception of Lewis Hamilton, the three-time Formula 1 world champion from England. As of 2015, when he turned thirty, Hamilton had never tried to enter the Indianapolis 500.

It was a messy start to the 1991 Indy 500 in more ways than one. Rain delayed the start by about an hour and Buddy Lazier crashed after one lap after Gary Bettenhausen turned into his car. Danny Sullivan incurred fuel pump damage and after a quick fix he accelerated into the action, but was already three laps behind.

Kevin Cogan and Roberto Guerrero crashed in turn one of lap twenty-five and their cars sprayed parts all over the track. Foyt hit a piece and that's what broke his suspension. Cogan broke his leg. Foyt waved to the hundreds of thousands of Speedway fans as if it was a final goodbye, though it turned out not to be.

After all of that shuffling, it was Michael Andretti smoothly dictating the pace up front. In a reversal of recent years Emerson Fittipaldi was near the lead, but in second, trying to hunt down Andretti. His persistence paid off when the Brazilian champion surpassed Andretti on the 113th lap. Fittipaldi's car looked strong and he led for forty-six laps. But to his frustration, the gearbox on the car gave out on lap 182, ending his shot at a second title.

Michael was seeking a second crown for the Andretti family and the typical attrition kicked in the longer the race lasted. Seventy percent of the way into the race, only thirteen of the thirty-three cars were running. A little later only Andretti and Rick Mears were on the lead lap.

Sullivan, who had recovered his deficit to chase back into the fray, blew his engine out on lap 183, throwing up more smoke than he ever had in his "Spin and Win" victory six years before. With the yellow caution flag waving Andretti made a pit stop. Mears led with Andretti a close second.

Three laps later Andretti made what he hoped would be the decisive move of the race, pushing past Mears on the outside. Andretti's car seemed to have what it took, but Mears came right back and passed Andretti three turns later on the 186th lap. Then things got tricky. Now it was Mears who seemed to have the necessary horsepower to leave Andretti behind. But on lap 189, Mario Andretti's car stalled at the entrance to pit row, causing the yellow flag to be hauled out. Some complained the older Andretti stalled on purpose to help Michael because after the green came out the leaders would be bunched up.

It didn't matter. The green was waved with six laps remaining and Mears had the power he needed. Michael's car was not in top form anymore and Mears won. The time differential was 3.149 seconds.

The result made Mears a four-time Indianapolis 500 champion, but it also showed his staying power. By notching victories in 1979, 1984, 1988 and 1991, Mears won in three different decades.

After Mears captured his fourth Indy title, driver Arie Luyendyk teased him, saying, "OK, Rocket, you've won four. Retire." Mears responded, "No chance, Arie."

Wise in the world of auto racing and witnessing dozens upon dozens of crashes and breakdowns beyond the bad luck he himself experienced, Mears had a simple philosophy.

"To finish first," he said, "you must first finish."

Luyendyk may have been kidding, but a year later, in 1992, after crashing in the race, Mears did retire. Compared to many of the other top drivers he was young, just forty-one. Al Unser Sr. was six years older when he won his fourth *500.*

"You'll hear a lot of drivers say they'll quit when they're not enjoying it," said Mears, who had experienced some racing-related injuries not long before. "That's pretty much what happened to me. It was a combination of things, but mostly it was losing that enthusiasm I always felt before.

Nearly a quarter of a century after Mears' retirement he still is one of three four-time champions of the Indianapolis 500.

1992

When it came to flat-out racing, head-to-head, and hard driving with a tight finish, the 1992 Indianapolis 500 was hard to beat. That's because Al Unser Jr. became a third member of his family to win the *500* in the all-time closest finish.

Son of Al Sr. and nephew of Bobby, Al Unser Jr. got his own winner's trophy, in the end holding off second place finisher Scott Goodyear by 0.43 seconds in what for many was an ordeal of a race - because of crash after crash.

Little Al was the big man on campus for this one after Roberto Guerrero posted a stunning pole speed of 232.482 mph.

So often the drivers faced ninety degree temperatures and rain in May as they tried to qualify. This year Mother Nature threw high winds and cold temperatures at the Indianapolis Motor Speedway. Those oh-so-delicate fast cars did not all cope so well. The accidents and crashes began in practice, before qualifying even started.

The first crash of the month involved Fabrizio Barbazza, the Italian driver with the euphonious name who was rookie of the year in 1987 had an accident on the second day of practice, Guerrero turned the first 230 mph in track history, though it was unofficial.

Two days after Barbazza's wipeout, Scott Brayton, Buddy Lazier and Paul Tracy all had some kind of accident.

For the first time since Janet Guthrie appeared on the scene another woman sought to qualify at Indy. Rookie Lyn St. James, born in Ohio in 1947, did not look as if she had enough horsepower in her car in the early going at practice. By auto standards she was moving fast at 217 mph, way faster than the cars were going in Guthrie's time, but some other drivers were fifteen mph faster.

The bad luck at the track kept on coming. Four-time winner Rick Mears, also the defending champion, crashed and suffered a broken foot bone and a wrist injury. A day later, Nelson Piquet smashed his car into the wall, damaged both legs, and was knocked out of his race attempt.

In between debris being strewn all over the track and drivers doing their best to skirt injury, 230 mph laps became routine. This had the makings of the fastest pole confrontation ever and possibly the fastest race. One out of two of those events came true.

Guerrero, who had been fast all month, set track records for the 2.5 mile laps on his first three circuits and his pole time was a new record.

Qualifying time trials in the latter going produced some surprises. Pancho Carter crashed, broke an arm, and eliminated himself. Lynn St. James, whose car did not seem up to the task, broke through instead of breaking a body part. James qualified after hitting more than 220 mph and became the oldest Indianapolis rookie at forty-five.

Mike Groff qualified a Walker Racing team car, but when teammate Scott Goodyear was bumped, the bosses turned the car over to him. There had been some back and forth with the cars during runs, so while this may have sounded ugly to outsiders, it was pre-planned. This proved to be a significant change for other competitors. The swift qualifying produced a front row of Guerrero, Eddie Cheever and Mario Andretti.

After the hectic practice and qualifying, the series of accidents, and shuffling of lineups, when the cars lined up to start the 76th Indianapolis 500 on May 24, there were ten past champions in the field of thirty-three cars, a record. Four of those drivers, A.J. Foyt, Gordon Johncock, Tom Sneva, and Mears, were driving their last Indy 500.

Guerrero had been strutting his stuff all month, with a lickity-split car that seemed capable of producing speed on demand … until he needed it most. As the pace car was circling the track, leading the cars up to full speed, Guerrero crashed. He owned the fastest lap in Speedway history, but completed zero laps in the race. In fact, he did not even start the first lap.

As others had learned throughout May, finding a way simply to get to the starting line at the Indianapolis 500 was stressful enough to raise blood pressure.

Usually the racers are sweating in their cars because they are often baked. At the start of this Indy the temperature was forty-eight degrees and the winds were blowing at twenty-three mph. At about 230 mph that could be a handling challenge, especially if tires did not grip in the colder weather.

In his last Indy 500, Sneva was out after four laps because of a crash. His was hardly an isolated incident on this day. Crashes also claimed the cars of Philippe Gache, Stan Fox, Mears, Crawford, Emerson Fittipaldi, Mario Andretti, Jimmy Vasser, Brian Bonner, Jeff Andretti, Gary Bettenhausen, and Arie Luyendyk. There were four ex-champs in that group.

Some sixty laps into the race Mario Andretti had a thirty second lead. Was this the race he had long-awaited? Even Andretti knew not to get too optimistic because there was such a long way to go. Eventually, a yellow flag slowed him, then on lap eighty-four Andretti also crashed. He was fortunate that his main injury was broken toes.

On lap 115, Andretti's youngest son Jeff also needed medical attention. His problem was battering his legs after his car went head-on into the wall. Jeff Andretti was lucky because his car did not erupt into flames. It took track personnel eighteen minutes to get him out of the wreckage and upon arrival at the hospital he immediately went into surgery.

Although two Andrettis had departed within a limited period of time, a third, Michael, moved into the lead. By the time the race passed one hundred laps almost half the field was sidelined. There were just seventeen cars chasing the prize. After 150 laps there were only five cars on the same front lap. Al Unser Jr. was one of them and he had put some time in on the front end under the seemingly rarely seen green flag.

After 188 laps the remaining Andretti, Michael, led by twenty-eight seconds. It was shaping up as a Michael Andretti victory. Scott Goodyear, who started 33rd, was sitting second. However, Al Unser Jr. came on strong and passed Goodyear. Soon, Michael Andretti went by Unser, so Little Al was a full lap behind.

Andretti's car was a smooth-running machine. Until all of a sudden it was not. On lap 189 Andretti's fuel pump gave out and the car stopped running. His 2.5 mile lead evaporated in a matter of seconds and Unser was ahead. Andretti's car was sitting dead on the track and the yellow flag came out.

The race did not go green again until there were seven laps to go. Neither Unser nor Goodyear was going away and the race became a for-the-duration duel. Quite a duel it was with only hundreds of seconds separating the nose of the cars. Goodyear tried to slip ahead, but Unser kept fighting him off. In the end Unser prevailed by the slimmest margin of their needle-nosed cars.

Although all eyes were on first and second, Al Sr. came up and grabbed third.

Goodyear couldn't quite pull it off, but he did advance from the 33rd starting position to second place, he would have been the first last-to-first driver if only he had snagged the title.

"I just needed a little more time to get him," Goodyear said. He said when Andretti relinquished his gigantic lead he thought "This is a real possibility" to win the Indy 500.

Instead, the championship went to Al Jr. As Little Al said several times, he grew up in a family that revered the Indianapolis 500, so winning the biggest race of them all was a natural goal for him.

His first from-the-gut reaction when celebrating putting his own name alongside the names of his famous relatives as an Indy champ was, "Well, you just don't know what Indy means!"

At that moment, looking upon his smiling face, everyone probably did think they knew.

1993

The 1993 Indianapolis 500 had one of its most distinctive finishes in history with racers from other countries outside the United States going 1-2-3 in the standings. Emerson Fittipaldi of Brazil won his second *500*, followed by Arie Luyendyk, who had already won an Indy 500, and then Nigel Mansell, who at the time was the reigning Formula 1 champion entered as a rookie in Indianapolis.

As famous as he was and as accomplished a driver as Mansell was, he was no Indianapolis 500 regular. He was just trying out this new forum, this new kind of racing to him.

Much attention was lavished on Mansell when he showed up for qualifying. It was an intriguing question being able to predict how he would do. A lot was expected, but as any sage Indy 500 observer was aware, anything could happen. Mansell was not just crossing the ocean for one race, however. He was committed to the CART season. He really wanted to see how he could do by focusing on this racing style.

Mansell's racing career was initially self-financed and it took him time to improve up through the ranks. His own father disapproved of his efforts and Mansell worked as a constable to support himself for years while racing.

When he came to Indianapolis in the spring of 1993, Mansell was at the peak of his fame and acclaim. He was the Formula 1 world champion and had eclipsed Jackie Stewart's record of twenty-seven victories by a British driver. However, Mansell had a dispute with his team owner and that paved the way for him to move to the United States and compete in CART in '93. He began winning races immediately and by the end of the season he had five victories, the most points, and became CART champion before relinquishing his Formula 1 title. That made him the only driver to hold both crowns simultaneously.

So Mansell was no rookie slipping into the Speedway unnoticed. But he did have one disadvantage besides not having done a single race on an oval. He crashed in practice at a race in Phoenix and hurt his back. He underwent surgery a month before the Indy 500.

Mansell was a tabloid hero in England, so the London papers chronicled his every move in Indianapolis. He arrived at a time when Indy officials implemented equipment changes to slow speeds. There were so many crashes in 1992 that could have had worse consequences that the point was to drop the speeds below 230 again rather than have them rise. Mansell found a quality team to sign with when Michael Andretti made the reverse move, transferring to Formula 1 in Europe. Mansell became Mario Andretti's teammate.

Luyendyk took the pole with a clocking of 223.967 mph. Mansell qualified eighth at 220.255 mph.

A.J. Foyt had twice suggested he was retiring, but showed up at Indianapolis and took practice laps. He was now a team owner and Robby Gordon was racing for him. When Gordon crashed the main car, although unhurt, Foyt examined his dual role as owner and potential driver and decided he couldn't do justice to both roles. The car went to Gordon and Foyt went into retirement on the spot.

Foyt drove a valedictory lap waving to the cheering crowd and then was interviewed live by public address announcer Tom Carnegie. Foyt, the he-man of the racing fraternity, shed tears in public.

"It's a hard decision, but there comes a time," Foyt told the spectators. "The fans have brought me back as many years as I've been back, but I felt like if I'm gonna run a team, I can't be in a race car. So if I'm going to be a successful car owner, I've got to spend 110 percent of my time with the car and not think of A.J. When Robby hit the wall was when I made my decision."

Raul Boesel of Brazil had one of the fastest cars all month and when the green flag flew he and Luyendyk gunned it for the lead. He remained with the leaders, but when he dove into the pits things went awry.

Boesel's stop was complete, but as he exited his area he was briefly headed off by Scott Goodyear. That put Boesel even with Mario Andretti as they tried to regain the track. Boesel passed Andretti, but officials then dropped the black flag on him for a penalty. At first Boesel was accused of speeding in the pits, but then changed to passing under yellow. Boesel had to return to the pits and he lost a lap.

The normal attrition through mechanical failures thinned the field, but at one point Mansell was leading the race. Mansell had a bad pit stop, overshooting his crew and lost time with a longer stay than planned.

When Jeff Andretti and Roberto Guerrero crashed and were knocked out of the race, the track went to yellow. Mario Andretti wanted into the pits, but they had been closed. The black flag was waved for him and he was given a stop-and-go penalty. That meant Andretti had to shut down his engine and start it over again, costly in time.

About forty laps later on 169, Boesel was guilty of the same infraction, nailed with a stop-and-go penalty. The circumstances of other guys meant he did not lose as much time.

Mansell's inexperience in racing on ovals showed when he was the leader on a yellow flag going green on lap 184. He went too slowly and was promptly passed when the color of the flag changed. By lap 192 Fittipaldi was in command. Mansell came out of turn two too high and scraped along the wall. Although the yellow was waved, he was still in the race.

Fittipaldi won the race, 2.8 seconds ahead of Luyendyk. Mansell hung on for third and Boesel made up his deficit to take fourth. It had been twenty-three years since a rookie at Indy had completed the two hundred laps.

Although he had done so after his first victory, Fittipaldi committed the faux pas of refusing to drink from the bottle of milk, the longstanding Indianapolis 500 tradition. The milk bottle is almost immediately thrust into the hands of the winner, who takes a gulp and then does a television interview.

Three times the milk man tried to give Fittipaldi the bottle and he refused to take it. When the TV cameras and interviewer Jack Arute caught up to him the questions focused more on the ignored milk bottle than the race.

"No, I'm not going to have the milk," Fittipaldi told viewers.

"Now there's a first!" said Arute. "Emerson, you're not going to drink the milk?"

It was not an allergy or any such thing. Fittipaldi chose to drink orange juice to promote the Brazilian citrus industry.

"I'm going to drink the orange juice," Fittipaldi said. "That's my producer. I'm going to help this time orange juice. I produce orange juice."

So Fittipaldi drank orange juice instead of milk. It was not the savviest of decisions because once they realized what happened, Indianapolis fans began booing Fittipaldi for ignoring the tradition.

Team owner Roger Penske gave Fittipaldi some firm advice: Take a swig of milk. He did so, but it was too late. His gesture was not seen on television. The stigma of refusing to follow the tradition with milk and seeming to promote OJ for personal gain stuck to Fittipaldi. Fans all around the circuit in the U.S., not only in Indianapolis began booing him.

For a time Fittipaldi became known as the guy who refused to drink the milk.

1994

It was Al Jr.'s year. Al Unser Jr. took the pole at 228.011 mph and then took the race by out-speeding the other front-row racers Raul Boesel and Emerson Fittipaldi. During the race he out-distanced second-place finisher Jacques Villeneuve, too.

Villeneuve was rookie of the year, a Canadian racer whose debut on speedy machines could be traced back to speeding along on snowmobiles in winter.

Owner Roger Penske's bunch, which included the winner, showed up at the Indianapolis Motor Speedway with new Mercedes-Benz engines that caught competitors off-guard.

There were numerous comings and goings by prominent racers. While Villeneuve marked his debut at Indy, Al Unser Sr. and Johnny Rutherford retired in May at Indianapolis. This was Mario Andretti's last

Indianapolis 500, his twenty-ninth year in the race. He retired at the end of the 1994 season.

On May 1, just as Indianapolis was revving up for the traditional festive month of activity leading up to the Indy 500, three-time Brazilian Formula 1 champion Ayrton Senna was killed in the San Marino Grand Prix. Emerson Fittipaldi, Raul Boesel, and Mauricio Gugelmin, an Indy rookie, who qualified and placed eleventh, flew to Brazil for the funeral and all served as pallbearers before returning to Indiana.

By 1994, Jim Nabors was as much a fixture at the Speedway on Memorial Day as the checkered flag was for the winner. It would not have been surprising, however, if Nabors was absent this year. Showing the same resilience of many of the competitors who drive hurt, Nabors stood up to sing "Back Home Again in Indiana" only months after a liver transplant .

The beloved Jim Nabors became an icon at the Motor Speedway for singing "*Back Home Again in Indiana*" from 1972 to 2014 with only a couple of absences.

Mario Andretti's nephew John because the first driver to make the attempt to race in the Indianapolis 500 during the day and then fly to Charlotte to enter the NASCAR Coca-Cola 600 at night. The daunting challenge has been attempted by several drivers since. The two races call for 1,100 miles of driving in one day in two states hundreds of miles apart.

John Andretti finished tenth at Indianapolis, completing 196 laps by the time the race ended. Andretti did not do quite as well in Charlotte, finishing 36th because of mechanical problems.

The first hints that the new Penske cars were fast occurred when Fittipaldi turned a lap in 226.512 mph nearly a week before pole day.

Although Speedway officials had tried to slow things down a little bit – and definitely did not want to see speeds continue to rise into the 240 mph area – Raul Boesel topped 230 mph in practice. It was the first time in three seasons a car went that fast.

Weather turned the pole qualifying attempts into a hassle. It alternately rained and turned sunny. Whenever the weather was lousy the track shut down. When the sun came out cars hit the track. That stretched attempts out for hours. Al Jr. emerged from the comings and goings as the pole winner.

It was actually perfectly wonderful out on race day with the sky clear and blue and temperatures in the seventies, not too hot or too cold. Jinxed to the end as a reminder of how many times he had driven a promising car, but had it fall apart on him, Mario Andretti's last Indy 500 ended after twenty-three laps because of a faulty fuel system.

Al Jr. and Fittipaldi set the pace from the beginning. When Unser stalled leaving the pits and lost time Fittipaldi took over, stretching his lead to 24.6 seconds. They were the only ones on the lead lap for a while.

Accidents popped up at times, one nearly taking out Unser, although he eluded it. Not so lucky was Nigel Mansell. Dennis Vitolo was going too fast in traffic and hit John Andretti from the rear. Vitolo's car went airborne and landed on top of Mansell's car. Both were knocked out of the race. Mansell was furious and this was his second and last Indy 500.

Fittipaldi seemed to have the superior car, leading seventy-five of the first one hundred laps, and after 175 laps he was ahead of Unser by forty seconds. Fittipaldi planned one quick fuel stop and then was poised to ride it out. He had lapped the whole field. But on lap 185, as Unser had picked up speed, Fittipaldi made a mistake, going too low and driving over the rumble strips. His car slid and a Fittipaldi back wheel hit the wall in turn four. Fittipaldi's car stopped and Unser took the lead.

Now Unser was the man. Villeneuve closed to within 8.6 seconds to place second and was the only other driver to complete the two hundred laps. Bobby Rahal was third. Fourteen other cars passed Fittipaldi and he finished a disappointing seventeenth. That was after leading 145 laps. Unser led forty-eight laps.

With Little Al's second championship that made for nine Indianapolis 500 victories by drivers whose last name was Unser. Big Al shared the record with four and Uncle Bobby had three. Including 1995, when his car did not make qualifying, Al Jr. was in Indianapolis for twenty runnings of the 500, the last in 2007. After 1994, however, when he was at the peak of his game, Unser failed to contend again, with just one more top ten finish.

In early 2007, Unser was arrested for driving under the influence (not at the track). Ironically, one of his penalties was losing his driver's license for ninety days. A few months later, around race time, Unser gave his first interview discussing his personal fight against alcoholism. In May of 2007 when Unser went public with his problem he was forty-five.

"I've been fighting alcoholism for a long time," he said, "and I really feel that by telling a little about my story and my struggles and my knowledge of the disease that I can help people learn about it."

Unser said he did not drink that much when he was younger, but drank more the more he was successful as a racer.

"When you won the race, they gave you champagne," he said. "But…the disease is progressive. So it progressed on me and ended up taking over my life and I didn't even know it. I kind of looked back on the fact that any time I got in trouble, it was alcohol-related. So, I put myself into a rehab. Prior to that my wife Gina would say to me that I'm an alcoholic and I would say, 'No way.'"

Unser said he found it difficult being a professional automobile racer who got arrested for driving under the influence on the street.

Being busted for DUI "made me take a long, hard look at my life," Unser said. "It made me admit one hundred percent I'm an alcoholic."

Although he had spoken out to explain his personal problem, and said life was great without being tied to drinking, Unser relapsed. That battle continued for him and in 2011 he was arrested again for driving while intoxicated.

As of 2015, Al Jr. had been sober for four years.

LYN ST. JAMES

The second woman to race in the Indianapolis 500 established some firsts. Lyn St. James was named rookie of the year in the 1992 *500*, a first for a woman. She placed eleventh, a record-high finish for the time. And at forty-five she was the oldest rookie.

Among St. James' other accomplishments were being part of the winning team twice in the 24 Hours of Daytona and once in the 12 Hours of Sebring.

The 1992 race was the first of six Indianapolis 500 races St. James qualified for by 2000 -- and her best finish.

Although more than a decade had passed since Janet Guthrie broke the gender barrier at the Indianapolis Motor Speedway and the country had moved along with more recognition for equality for women in many ways, St. James still experienced some Neanderthal attitudes from people who did not think a woman should be behind the wheel of a race car.

"Culture changes are very hard," St. James said. "Racing is not a nimble culture."

For all of the years driving it took a long time, into middle age, to become an Indianapolis rookie. She was just starting when others were retiring.

"I remember so many times when I felt frustrated or depressed about how things weren't going according to Plan A, B, or C, yet when I got in the race car all that frustration would float away," she said. "My commitment and passion was derived from the pure desire and pleasure of driving the race car."

It took years to go from female driver number one to female driver number two at Indy, and there haven't been crowds of females clamoring to be admitted to the *500 club* in the years since, either.

"I wish there were more knocking on the door," St. James said.

To facilitate that possibility St. James later opened a driving school with the aim of preparing women drivers for the high speeds of auto racing competition. It was called the Lyn St. James Driving Academy.

In the early 2000s, St. James was able to cite statistics that showed girls were getting more involved in the sport, and at much higher participation numbers in contests like the Soap Box Derby, go-karts, and junior dragsters. For some reason very few advanced to the level of international open-wheel racing, but that was also true of boys, as well. And as the cost of fielding an Indianapolis 500 race car grew to one million just for the machine, it was never more difficult to break in.

At the time a St. James came along once a decade and all the stars had to be aligned to even get a shot at qualifying in Indianapolis. Things haven't changed much on that front yet.

What kept St. James going at all times was her feeling for the speed and the car, the same as anyone else with high hopes in racing.

"I love everything about the sport," she said. "The challenge of driving every lap perfectly, the preparation, the dynamics of putting together the technical-mechanical-human-financial resources, the physical exertion and mental concentration required.

"The grass is greener, the sky bluer, and I sleep better after driving the race car."

There is no question driving an Indy car can be a rush. There are only a tiny percentage of people on the planet who possess the will, reflexes, and skill to drive a car so fast and the Indianapolis 500 sorts out the best of the best on one given day a year.

"There is no sound in the world like the scream of a race car," St. James said.

Only a small number of people will ever hear the sound of a car moving at two hundred mph while steering it. Hundreds of thousands hear it up close at the Speedway and millions more on television. At times the cars can look like a fast-moving insect, making the sound of a high-pitched whine. But it is a whine like nothing else, but what a smoothly operating engine makes.

"Even those who don't follow racing can identify the tenor of an Indy car," St. James said, "which is why television uses an audio teaser to promote the network's telecast of the Indy 500. Why show pictures when two seconds of sound will do the trick?"

St. James said she has very often been asked what it is like to be zooming around so fast in an Indy car. It has come up over and over again. Over the years as she made speeches, gave seminars, and met

people on the street. They cannot really relate to the sensations a driver experiences at such high speeds. Even people arrested for speeding in their own car don't come close to matching what goes on at the Speedway.

Indy cars in no way resemble street cars. The manufacturers who research what it takes to build a super-speed car may benefit from the findings when they make their cars for public consumption, but car to car they are not comparable.

"Speed has always fascinated people and the concept of driving a car two hundred miles is something the general populace cannot fathom," St. James said. "Most people over sixteen spend a considerable amount of time driving cars, but that experience doesn't explain the feeling of racing. Instead, it only adds to the mystique. It's difficult to paint the complete picture in words."

St. James' final Indy 500 was in 2000 at age fifty-three and then she retired from racing in 2001.

1995

Between the 1994 and 1995 race, Indianapolis Motor Speedway president, Tony George, made an announcement that ultimately would rock the Indianapolis 500 in ways never foreseen.

George stated that a new Indy Racing League would begin for the 1996 season.

Also, the United States Automobile Club, supervisor of the Indy 500, which was forever tinkering with the rules governing how car engines could be made, altered limits that drastically affected the Penske team's Mercedes-Benz cars. Penske took the change personally. That was the end of the Mercedes-Benz engines at Indy.

When it came to announcements this was a huge year of attention-getting change. Looking to the future, and recognizing the broad popularity of NASCAR and its stock cars, the Indianapolis Motor Speedway welcomed the start-up of the Brickyard 400 at its facility for the 1996 season.

The true impact of the engine ruling became known during qualifying for the 1995 race. None of the Penske cars were fast enough to make the thirty-three car field, stunningly leaving such drivers as Al Unser Jr. and Emerson Fittipaldi on the sidelines on Memorial Day.

Pole day did not even begin until shortly before 5:00 p.m. because of rain delays, but within a half hour Scott Brayton owned the slot by spinning 231.604 mph. Arie Luyendyk took the second slot and Scott Goodyear filled out the first row.

This was a *500* minus A.J. Foyt, Mario Andretti, any of the Unsers, Fittipaldi, or Nigel Mansell. Past winners in the field were Luyendyk, Danny Sullivan and Bobby Rahal. The only Andretti lined up was Michael. Emerson Fittipaldi was eliminated from the thirty-three car group on bump day, but his nephew, Christian Fittipaldi, was in.

The annoying rain kept popping up, it rained at the Speedway the night before the race so the track was wet on the morning of the race. But the super dryers came out and the race went off only five minutes late.

Things looked fine. They did not remain that way very long. When the green flag caught the breeze, Goodyear zipped to the front and he made that move safely. However, Stan Fox, starting eleventh, did not get away quite so smoothly. Fox moved down low and when his car ran over the warning rumble strips, the steering was affected.

Fox bashed into the wall at turn one and the ripple effect of his twirling car took out Eddie Cheever, Lyn St. James, Carlos Guerrero and Gil de Ferran, whose own car lost its suspension running over hunks of debris. De Ferran made it around one lap. The other four saw their race end right there with zero laps credited.

Fox incurred a serious head injury that had a long recovery time, hence this crash ended his auto racing career. Fox stayed with the sport and in May of 2000 he returned to the Speedway where he took a farewell lap waving to fans.

"It's good to do," Fox said of this appearance that he considered his real retirement moment. "To run around the racetrack, wave goodbye to everybody and say goodbye to everybody, it was a great thing to do."

In December of the same year Fox was visiting friends in New Zealand where he was driving a passenger car and died in a head-on collision at forty-eight.

On lap thirty-seven of the 1995 race, the Indianapolis 500 experienced one of the strangest of all reasons for the waving of a yellow caution flag.

Luyendyk was trying to pass Scott Sharp going into turn one, but Sharp fought back. Luyendyk thought Sharp was illegally blocking him. As he passed the other driver Luyendyk shot him the bird, the raised middle finger insult. But in doing so, Luyendyk's hand hit his helmet headrest cushion and knocked it out of the car onto the track.

When the yellow came out and the pace car took the track, Jacques Villeneuve twice passed the safety vehicle. For a strange reason -Villeneuve didn't know he was in the lead and officials were trying to close up the line of cars behind him. His pit stop thereafter wasn't much smoother. He began pulling away from his crew while the fuel hose was still attached, but he was halted. By then race officials had whacked Villeneuve with a two-lap penalty, one lap for each illegal pass of the pace car.

Lap seventy-seven was its own adventure, with Mauricio Gugelmin slowing and Michael Andretti trying to pass him. Andretti damaged his suspension by touching the wall and had to pull out. Sharp crashed on turn four.

Ordinarily, in a different kind of race, being hit with the two-lap stinger would have cost Villeneuve any chance of victory. But he steadily made up ground and finally regained a spot on the lead lap.

Several cars were in the hunt for the trophy by lap 190 and were moving around the oval under caution. Goodyear was in the lead, trolling behind the pace car. But he shot forward before the pace car exited and the cars trailing him nearly knocked the pace car off the track. It was announced that Goodyear was receiving a stop-and-go penalty, but he declared on his radio that he had a green light and the pace car was going too slow. His team told him to keep racing and they would protest later, so he did not stop.

The angry USAC responded by no longer scoring Goodyear after lap 195 because he had not responded to the penalty. That meant Villeneuve was officially in the lead, whether he knew it or not, and he crossed the finish-line first.

When he got out of his car Goodyear was furious.

"Disbelief is the best word to describe how I feel," he said. "I feel like I won this race."

Goodyear said again he saw the green light flashing to go to full speed, but a film replay showed the light was yellow. When that type of evidence was reviewed, Goodyear's team elected not to protest. Villeneuve's win stood. Christian Fittipaldi took second and Bobby Rahal stormed from twenty-first to take third.

As abnormal a race as this was, this was the last Indianapolis 500 to be run under "normal" conditions for a long time. Tony George's decision to start the Indy Racing League in 1996 as a rival to CART produced a firestorm that disrupted open-wheel racing for years and greatly altered the composition of the *500* fields.

The Indy Racing League adopted its own schedule – with the prestigious Indianapolis 500 as its centerpiece. If you were a CART racer, you were out of luck at Indy.

1996

The war was underway. The Indianapolis 500 was conducted under the auspices of the new Indy Racing League. Drivers who stuck with the older, established CART did not show up for the famed race in 1996.

Bickering between the two groups went on for months before the race, creating a media frenzy of the wrong kind of publicity. The Indy Racing League was recognized by the USAC and those officials sanctioned the first race sponsored by the IRL in January of 1996 in Orlando, Florida.

Meanwhile, the CART group formed its own race to be held on Memorial Day. It was called the U.S. 500 and was conducted at the Michigan International Speedway. CART holdovers accused Indianapolis Motor Speedway president Tony George of attempting to take control of all racing and said they were being locked out of the Indianapolis 500, the most important race. Their answer was to basically stick together and boycott Indy, as painful as that might have been.

To most American auto racing fans, the Indianapolis 500 is the biggest open-wheel racing in the country. It is the one race that even the most casual of fans pay attention to. There is name recognition of the big stars, and just one Indy 500 win made you a star.

There was a generational change in the lineup of the *500* going on at this time as well. Even if nothing changed in the administration of the race, so many big names familiar to any sports fan, not merely a race fan, were retiring. Fresh faces were coming into the sport and becoming prominent through achievements at Indianapolis. Because of this split, there were more new faces than ever.

A hot local racer named Tony Stewart broke in at Indianapolis in 1996, following his lifetime dream of being able to compete in the *500*. Stewart, from nearby Columbus, won the pole with a clocking of 233.718 mph and earned rookie of the year honors. The pre-race performance really won Stewart the award because he placed twenty-fourth and engine failure knocked him out of the race after eighty-two laps. There were fourteen rookies, an unusual number, filling out the field because of the absence of so many veterans and several finished ahead of Stewart. The most notable finish belonged to Richie Hearn in third.

Hearn qualified for six additional *500*s in the 2000s with a next-best finish of sixth.

Stewart went on to a sterling NASCAR career, winning three season points championships and became a team owner. None of the other rookies in the field became nearly as famous as Stewart.

In a twist, *500* officials decided that instead of full-fledged car versus car qualifying, which had always been done, the top twenty-five leaders in the Indy Racing League would be guaranteed spots in the thirty-three car field. The order was still determined by speed.

In addition to the controversy, not even the weather was favorable. It was one of the wettest Mays on record in Indianapolis.

Pole day was a bit crazy. Arie Luyendyk, the only past winner around, set a one-lap record of 234.742 mph and a four-lap record of 233.390 mph to win the pole position. However, his car flunked post-qualifying inspection because it was too light and that washed out his records.

Veteran Scott Brayton, in second, ran 233.851 mph and that became the new one-lap record. His four-lap record of 233.718 mph, which was slower than Luyendyk, set a record too. Brayton had the pole. Stewart had been third fastest, but moved up a position because of Luyendyk's situation.

Luyendyk started all over again the next day and set four straight one-lap records, sitting on 237.498 mph on the fourth time around, and another new four-lap record of 236.986 mph. But he couldn't claim the pole because he was a day late, only a place in the field.

Five days after Luyendyk's fresh run, Brayton returned to the track to test another car. He smashed into the wall coming out of turn two and his car slid six hundred feet. Brayton, unconscious, was rushed to the hospital and died of a fractured skull. Danny Ongais was tabbed to run as a replacement driver, but the circumstances moved Stewart to the pole.

In the midst of controversy and bad feelings in the open-wheel community, Brayton's tragedy took precedence as drivers in both Indiana and Michigan mourned him. Brayton was thirty-seven when he died. Later, a street used in the Michigan Grand Prix in Grand Rapids was named after him.

Mary F. Hulman delivered the starting command for the last time. There was a lady in the field, too, in Lyn St. James, who started eighteenth and finished fourteenth, going out of the race after 153 laps.

Stewart led the first thirty-one laps, but on a pit stop later the fuel nozzle broke, turning his stop into a virtual parking pause. Luyendyk, who had been so fast in practice, suffered car damage in a pit crash on lap ninety-four and that took him out of the race.

Roberto Guerrero, who had shown considerable speed at Indy over the years, but also the victim of considerable bad luck, was near the front as the race entered its final forty laps, going against Buddy Lazier and Davy Jones. After pit stops, Jones had the lead. Lazier waited another seven laps to fill the tank and change four tires under yellow. He was carrying enough gas to go the distance. At about the same time Guerrero was seeking to top off his tank, but his car caught on fire in the pit. He fell a lap behind and also lost use of his radio. It was just another bad day at the office for Roberto.

Italian, Alessandro Zampedri inserted himself into the mix, along with Jones and Lazier up front. Then Zampedri lost his handling smoothness and Jones went to the lead on lap 190. Jones' car began slowing and Lazier took the lead with eight laps remaining. On-track incidents put the race under yellow, but it went green again for the 199th lap. Jones made a run, but Lazier prevailed.

As the top cars finished, there was still another major accident behind them that caught up Guerrero, Zampedri, and Eliseo Salazar. Zampedri's car left the track and soared into the catch fence above the wall. Zampedri, who had raced at Indy the year before, came back in 1997, then spent the rest of his career racing in Europe. Chilean Salazar had been fourth in 1995 and finished sixth in 1996 and became a regular at Indy although he was primarily a Formula 1 racer.

It was a chaotic ending in one of the most confused Indianapolis 500 periods of all.

The racer who best coped with the messy spring and emerged with the best reputation was Lazier. He was in the middle of making twenty-four appearances at the Indy 500 (although he did not qualify a handful of times) and his championship kicked off the prime stretch of his career at the Speedway. Lazier announced he was intending to compete for a spot in the thirty-three car field in a twenty-fifth Speedway appearance in 2016.

"The Indianapolis Motor Speedway has no equals in terms of other tracks around the world," Lazier once said. "The facilities are absolutely the best. I remember as a rookie everyone spoke of the 'year of May,' and I never quite understood it. As a competitor, it is an emotional roller coaster. One day everything can be perfect and you think you have a handle on the track and your race car. The next day you could be totally lost. With so many emotional ups and downs during the month of May, I now understand how it seems to turn into a year."

Rather remarkably, one of the great traditions of the Indianapolis Motor Speedway and championship drivers was not begun in the Indianapolis 500.

Later in the summer of 1996, with the Speedway doors opened to the new Brickyard 400 NASCAR race, a new champion and his crew thought of a different way to celebrate victory.

Dale Jarrett won the Brickyard that year and his crew chief Todd Parrott was so excited that he and Jarrett walked out onto the track, knelt down and kissed the remaining small section of bricks preserved from the early track construction. Then the entire Jarrett crew did likewise.

The idea immediately caught on and Indy 500 and Brickyard 400 winners began following suit. It is a tradition that appealed more to some than drinking milk. It also crossed the lines between stock-car racing and open-wheel racing. This time the stock-car boys added to the lore of the Speedway.

1997

There no longer seemed such a thing as normal for the Indianapolis 500. Whether it was rain, controversy or the continuing dispute between the Indy Racing League and CART something abnormal was always going on.

This was the second year that the Indy Racing League had its tie-in with the Indianapolis 500 and with CART racers on the outs. There was no second U.S. 500 being held in Michigan on Memorial Day.

It rained so often in 1997 that it took three days to finish the race. The 81st Indy 500 began on May 25 and did not finish until May 27.

The scheduled start date of May 25, the Sunday, was rained out completely. Racing resumed on Monday and the drivers made it through fifteen laps. It was Tuesday by the time the rest of the race finished.

Occasioning much comment and interest were the efforts of Robby Gordon. Gordon had been a full-time CART racer through 1996, but switched to NASCAR full-time in 1997. Through careful planning and creative sponsorship, Gordon was able to attempt the two-race Coca Cola 600 and the Indianapolis 500 double. Of course, the rain interfered with the one-day attempt.

Past winner Arie Luyendyk captured the pole with a speed of 218.263 mph. For the second year in a row *500* officials guaranteed twenty-five spots in the thirty-three car field to the top point getters in the Indy Racing League. Twenty-three of those teams entered.

It became clear as qualifying went along that the twenty-five car rule, which was extremely unpopular, might prevent the thirty-three fastest cars from being entered. Rain interfered at the end of qualifying, muddying things even more. Three cars that were bumped were faster than eight cars that had been locked in because of points.

Meetings produced a compromise. Two of the bumped cars, belonging to drivers Lyn St. James and Johnny Unser, son of Jerry Unser and Al Jr.'s cousin, were reinstated. That put two extra cars in the field. So this year only thirty-five cars would start. After this convoluted scenario unfolded officials no longer used the program locking in twenty-five cars because of points and returned to regular qualifying procedures.

On race day rain kept the cars from departing at the scheduled 11 a.m. start time. Forty-five minutes late they lined up, but it started raining again. None of the usual pre-race ceremonies were conducted. Gordon flew to Charlotte, competed in the 600, but crashed after 186 laps and placed 41st.

The next day the Purdue Band played the National Anthem, but Jim Nabors went home the night before. A recording of him singing "Back Home Again in Indiana" was used. Mari Hulman George took over the "start-your-engines" command from her mother. The drivers only made it through fifteen laps before rain took over again, washing out the rest of the day.

On the third day, the race resumed on lap sixteen. Tony Stewart took the early lead. Robby Gordon, back from North Carolina, stopped suddenly on the track after swerving because his car was on fire. So was Gordon. He rolled around on the grass to put out the fire and that was the end of his Indy 500.

Tony Stewart was running strongest in the early going and led through the first hundred miles. He ended up leading sixty-four laps.

On lap 142, rookie Jeff Ward took the lead. Ward was born in Glasgow, Scotland, but was an American citizen. Ward was a superior motorcycle racer switching to open-wheel racing. He won seven motocross national championships and ran well at Indianapolis in eight races spread over ten years. He finished in the top five three times and in the top ten, four times.

After 189 laps Ward was ahead, but he knew he didn't have enough fuel to finish in front without a pit stop. A crash brought out the yellow and Ward slid into the pits to fuel up. The lead was ceded to Luyendyk, chased by Scott Goodyear. Stewart hit the wall with the leaders on lap 198 and that brought out the yellow again for three laps.

Confusion followed. Stewart righted the car and continued. The pace car did not come onto the track under the yellow. Luyendyk and Goodyear took it upon themselves to slow down the race as if there had been a pace car in front of them. The race was nearing its end and officials flew both the green flag and the white flag, but yellow warning lights were still on around the track. The drivers did not know exactly what to do. Luyendyk took off, but Goodyear did not.

"I saw the green and white flags wave and I thought, 'Hell, they better know what they're doing,'" Luyendyk said.

Goodyear was Luyendyk's teammate, so he was happy the team won, but was not pleased with how things played out at the end. He finished .7 seconds behind.

"(I was) disappointed that I didn't win," he said.

Ward took third and was rookie of the year. Buddy Lazier was fourth and Stewart was fifth.

1998

The split between CART and the Indy Racing League remained firmly in place. Cars were back to qualifying for the thirty-three car field purely on the merit of their speed at the Indianapolis Motor Speedway.

One interesting change was adopted. For the first time, cars were allowed to be wheeled to their garages on Gasoline Alley for repairs and then permitted to re-enter the race. Previously, all fix-it jobs had to take place on pit road and if they could not be accomplished the driver was out of luck.

Billy Boat took the pole at 223.503 mph and Jim Nabors was back to sing again. The weather was much better in 1998 than it had been in 1997. But it was hardly perfect, either. It rained on race morning and put back the start by thirty-five minutes.

Veteran, Eddie Cheever was nearly KO'd on the first lap and made minor contact with J.J. Yeley. Yeley stalled out and fell a lap behind, but Cheever righted his car. Cheever had another close call on lap forty-nine when five cars were eliminated in a crash. Cheever successfully slipped past the debris.

After that Cheever's car grew stronger and stronger and by the 160th time around there were only three cars on the lead lap. Cheever, Buddy Lazier and rookie Steve Knapp were at the front. It was a two car race by lap 191 with Cheever and Lazier going head-to-head. Cheever out-ran Lazier by 3.19 seconds for the win and Knapp was rookie of the year. Cheever led for seventy-six laps.

This was the highlight victory in Cheevers' long and varied racing career and even more satisfying, he was his own team's owner.

"From the moment the team won the Indianapolis 500 in 1998, I felt I had a responsibility to represent the Indianapolis Motor Speedway -- and the greatest American spectacle -- all over the United States, and I did so very happily," Cheevers said.

1999

There was no end in sight to the schism between CART and the Indy Racing League and so not all of the best drivers vied for the coveted Indianapolis 500 crown in 1999.

Tony Stewart, of whom it was often said that he could drive anything, was making the shift full-time to NASCAR, but this year he went after the Memorial Day double. Stewart raced in the Indy 500, finishing ninth while completing 196 laps, flew to Charlotte and did complete the six hundred miles of the Coca Cola race. Stewart finished fourth. Afterwards he said he was very, very tired and dehydrated. But following the John Andretti and Robby Gordon attempts, Stewart was the first driver able to pull off the feat of doing both in the same day.

Arie Luyendyk took the pole at Indy with a speed of 225.179 mph. Robby McGehee was rookie of the year, but the race champion was Kenny Brack. Brack was a Swedish driver who won the Indy Racing League's points title in 1998. He was driving for team owner A.J. Foyt at the Speedway in 1999 and the victory gave Foyt a fifth *500* championship in all, four as a driver and his first as an owner.

Practice and qualifying times were condensed into a shorter period. The track did not open until mid-month, instead of opening during the first few days of May. There were still plenty of crashes, Billy Boat alone crashed three times by the end of pole day. For the tribulations

Boat qualified third, starting from the front row. Brack started in the middle of the third row.

Luyendyk led for sixty-three laps in pursuit of his third Indy win. Greg Ray led for thirty-two laps. But both of their cars were out by the 121st lap. Ray did compete in eight Indy 500s with a top finish of eighth in 2003 and started his own team in 2007.

Brack had a history of competing, he was sixth at Indy the year before and had an extensive racing background. In 2009, four years after retiring from the Indy Racing League, Brack was coaxed back into competition for ESPN X Games 15 – and he won.

A NEW ERA OF PEACE

2000-2009

Eventually, the Indy Racing League ruled supreme and after some disruption the finest drivers were all able to qualify for the Indy 500 once more.

A refreshing face added more color to the festivities when Brazilian, Helio Castroneves won in 2001 and 2002 and again in 2009.

In a huge safety breakthrough, the Speedway added the SAFER barrier, a more absorbable wall around the perimeter of the track to lessen the impact of crashes and deaths during the race virtually ceased.

Crowds had suffered during the administrative feud, but began to beef up somewhat again when the 100th anniversary of the opening of the Speedway was celebrated in 2009.

2000

For the first time, two women were entered in the Indianapolis 500 in the same year. Veteran Lyn St. James was joined by Sarah Fisher.

Fisher was from Columbus, Ohio, and carried a woman's role at Indianapolis and in the Indy Car series beyond pioneers like Janet Guthrie and St. James.

She was only nineteen years old for her first Indy start in 2000, Fisher established a number of personal records and firsts for women in Indy car racing. She recorded the highest finish to that point with a third at the Kentucky Speedway, then improved on that with a second, entered nine Indianapolis 500 races, was the first woman to race in the complete Indy Car series, and the first to capture the pole position. A three-time winner of the most popular driver award, in 2008 Fisher became the first woman to establish her own Indy Car race team.

In later years of her Indianapolis 500 driving career, Fisher told stories about how parents wrote letters and postcards to her saying they named their little girls after her because they were inspired by her achievements. Then one day she actually met one of the girls.

"Oh, man, it was awesome," Fisher said. "I was almost speechless. It's just a reminder, something that gives you more motivation to support your character."

In 2000, Greg Ray took the pole at 223.471 mph, but it was a May that belonged to a fresh face, Juan Pablo Montoya from Colombia. He grew up in kart racing, but by 2000 he was an established figure in select forms of racing even though he was a newcomer to the Indy Car circuit.

Two-time champion Al Unser Jr. was back in the field after being away for four years. The only other past winners were recent champs Eddie Cheever and Buddy Lazier. Another notable rookie alongside Montoya was Sam Hornish Jr. Team owner, Chip Ganassi bridged the gap between CART and the Indy Racing League and he brought Montoya and Jimmy Vasser to the Speedway. The connection was viewed as a thaw between the two organizations.

The race began three hours late because of rain, but it did take place on the scheduled May 28. It did not take long to establish that the fastest car belonged to Montoya. In one of the great dominating performances of all time Montoya led for 167 laps. Just twenty-four years old, Montoya was both rookie of the year and the race titlist, and his career was really just getting started.

Lazier finished second, Eliseo Salazar third, Jeff Ward fourth and Cheever fifth. Robby Gordon and Jimmy Vasser followed.

2001

Juan Pablo Montoya's feat of being rookie of the year and champion in the same race was duplicated by Brazilian, Helio Castroneves the next year. Castroneves had been racing in the CART series.

The reconciliation between CART and the Indy Racing League was in the works. Castroneves was racing for Roger Penske, who had been as strongly estranged from Indianapolis as any owner, but where he was so closely identified with excellence. This represented Penske's eleventh win as an owner at the Indianapolis Motor Speedway.

The Indy Racing League was gaining strength and CART was losing the war, though a white flag had not yet flown denoting peace. The battle was quite costly. As NASCAR was ascendant, interest in open-wheel racing in the United States plummeted everywhere but Indianapolis (and even there support was shaky). Television ratings for open-wheel racing dropped precipitously. CART gave up trying to schedule other races on Memorial Day weekend and pretty soon CART would go away altogether, due to bankruptcy in 2003.

However, attendance was still strong at the Indianapolis Motor Speedway, Scott Sharp won the pole at the Speedway in 2001 at 226.037 mph. After two years away, Arie Luyendyk was back trying to win a third Indianapolis 500.

Race day brought cool temperatures and early crashes. Sharp didn't complete a lap and Sarah Fisher and Scott Goodyear went out after seven laps. Goodyear broke his back, an injury severe enough to push him into retirement. This was the last of his eleven Indianapolis 500s. Al Unser Jr. only made it through sixteen laps, proving for the infinite time, the track did not discriminate in what cars were demolished.

Castroneves, who became a regular at Indianapolis, was the new star on the block. When he won the race, Castroneves leapt out of his car, exulted, ran to the wall and began climbing the fencing separating fans from the track. In what famously became known as his Spider-man climb, for a moment it looked as if Castroneves might hurl himself over the fence and allow himself to be body surfed by fans. Instead, he kept pumping his arm and fist from on high. Then his entire pit crew climbed the fence with him. The fans loved the uninhibited display of joy.

Teammate Gil de Ferran, another Penske racer, took second. Michael Andretti finished third with Vasser behind him. Castroneves led for fifty-two laps, but others took some lengthy turns at the front until their cars flaked out on them. Greg Ray led forty laps, Mark Dismore twenty-nine, de Ferran twenty-seven, and Robby Gordon twenty-two laps.

Not all of them made it to the finish line, but the race did despite two rain delays.

2002

Helio did it again. Practically viewed as a rock star following his exuberant victory celebration in 2001, Helio Castroneves repeated his Indianapolis 500 victory in 2002.

Bruno Junqueira from Brazil won the pole at a blistering 231.342 mph, but rookie South African Tomas Scheckter's eighty-five laps led were the most of the day. He ended up crashing on the 173rd lap and finishing 26th.

It is the end of this race that is best-remembered. Castroneves was leading, but on the 199th lap Paul Tracy made a move for the lead and was passing.

"Yeah, baby!" Tracy shouted into his radio.

Crew members responded, "There's a problem."

Elsewhere on the track there was a crash and the yellow caution flag came out because of that incident. That meant Tracy was not allowed to pass Castroneves. Tracy believed he made the pass before the yellow. The officials ruled he did not. When the race ended the hundreds of thousands of fans at the Speedway were not sure who had won. Neither were broadcasters. Chief official Brian Barnhart immediately declared, "Yellow, yellow, yellow, three is your leader," which was Castroneves. Barnhart's assistant Mel Harder repeated that over the race radio frequency. At this stage of sophistication at Indianapolis, not only the caution flag was waved, but yellow lights flashed alongside the track and there was a dashboard system in the cars telling drivers the race was under yellow.

TV, radio, and track historian Donald Davidson all had the right call, but not for the right reason. They reported that the scoring reverted to the previous lap. But that was an old rule. Nobody said Tracy won it. Television was able to show that the crash did occur before Tracy passed Castroneves, even if no tape evidence showed the timing of the yellow.

Tracy's team filed a protest, but it was denied about five weeks later in early July.

So Castroneves, growing in popularity in Indianapolis, was the winner.

There was also a new aspect of the Speedway in use for the first time in 2002. At a race track that was almost as closely identified with the tragedy of many deaths as it was with speed, a monumental change revolved around the installation of the SAFER barrier.

The first test of the new so called "soft wall" occurred on the first day of practice at the Speedway when Robby McGehee smashed into the wall at about 220 mph backwards, but was not seriously hurt.

This was only the beginning of the new revolutionary racing barrier that transformed the Speedway and other tracks.

"I guess I'm the first driver to test the new soft-wall system," McGehee said after his crash, "which is a distinction I'd rather not have. I can tell you it's not soft. I hit hard. But I can also assure you I am very glad it was there."

SAFER BARRIER

From the time the Indianapolis Motor Speedway opened in 1909 and the first Indianapolis 500 was held in 1911, the sub-plot of any race was death.

The risk of death.

The reality of death.

For more than ninety years deaths at the Indy 500 were so commonplace that officials were noticeably relieved any time a race ended without a fatality amongst a driver, track worker, pit crew member, or fan. People came for a good time, but somebody always seemed to leave headed to a funeral home.

So often the culprit in an accident was the unforgiving track outer wall. If a driver hit it at high speed often he or she was killed on the spot. Sometimes their car bounced backward into oncoming traffic, collecting more cars in the crash. Sometimes pieces of his car flew into the stands and killed spectators.

In the late 1990s, Speedway president Tony George began investing in research that would provide an antidote to the deadly walls. Eventually, he spent one million dollars helping Dr. Dean Sicking at the Midwest Roadside Safety Facility at the University of Nebraska invent a new kind of gentler wall.

The result was the SAFER Barrier. The letters stand for Steel and Foam Energy Reduction Barrier. The barrier is made from steel tubes connected to foam. The barriers were installed right alongside the concrete track walls. At Indianapolis there were thirty inches between the walls. The way the barrier was constructed when a driver hit the new wall the force was diffused and spread out more than it had been by hitting the old concrete.

The Speedway was the first to install the SAFER barrier and it was so successful that every major track in the United States had installed it by 2005.

This development immediately followed the highest profile death in the history of auto racing. In 2001, Dale Earnhardt, a seven-time NASCAR champion, was killed by hitting the wall at the Daytona 500. This was front-page news across America. Earnhardt's death culminated an awful streak of violent deaths linked to crashes in NASCAR within a fourteen month period. Horrified fans and officials were on the same page and agreed that driver safety was an urgent issue.

Earnhardt's death was also linked to his not wearing the new HANS Safety Device which offered added protection to the head and neck. At the time of Earnhardt's death the device was available, but optional to drivers. Many more drivers began wearing the Head and Neck Support system after that and many racing governing bodies made wearing some version of the device mandatory for their drivers.

Overnight, racing fatalities went from being common occurrences to extreme rarities. The last time a driver died at Indianapolis was when Tony Renna crashed during a private tire test in 2003. In 2004, a safety patrol employee died of a heart attack at the track during the Brickyard 400. And in 2010, a thirteen year old was killed during the Red Bull Indianapolis Grand Prix when run over by a motorcycle.

That is a totally different history than the annual litany of death and survivor notes from practice, pole qualifying, and the Indianapolis 500 race for drivers.

Early segments of SAFER Barrier walls are now on display at the Indianapolis Motor Speedway Hall of Fame Museum.

"Tony George's pioneering of the soft wall was humongous," said driver Scott Sharp.

2003

There was still fallout from the CART and Indy Car wars affecting the Indianapolis 500. The rise in popularity of NASCAR and the highly publicized divisiveness between the two Indy Car authorities, combined with the retirement of several top drivers in recent years changed the public perception of the race.

While the Indianapolis Motor Speedway never announced the exact attendance for the *500*, it was always a sellout and for ages there had been huge crowds spilling over into the infield for estimated attendance turnouts of 300,000 to 400,000 people. In 2003, the race was not sold out, a rare occurrence.

The usual fanfare surrounded the race. That did not change. Former presidents George H.W. Bush and President Bill Clinton both attended – it was a first for two presidents to attend the same race. A.J. Foyt IV was only nineteen when he became the youngest Indy driver ever. Michael Andretti said this would be his final Indy 500 because he was moving into team ownership. Father Mario climbed in an Indy car for the first time in nine years and ran 223 mph at sixty-three while testing. But his car hit some debris on the track and he crashed.

Helio Castroneves, chasing his third straight win, captured the pole at 231.725 mph. Only twice had the race had an overflow field with more than thirty-three cars, but as time was running out on qualifying, there were just thirty-one qualified cars. Still, the field did fill out.

The race began on time at 11 a.m., although the starting time was going to be changed in future years. Castroneves led for the first sixteen laps. Michael Andretti's last race ended badly. He led for twenty-eight laps, but went out of the race during a lap ninety-eight pit stop because of mechanical failure.

After 150 laps, Castroneves and teammate Gil de Ferran were first and second. They retained their front-running spots for the last quarter of the race and went head-to-head at the end. De Ferran prevailed by 0.2290 seconds over Castroneves. Castroneves had hoped to become the first Indy 500 driver to notch three straight wins. Afterwards, he cajoled De Ferran into climbing the fence, mimicking Castroneves' own celebration style.

There were nine cars running on the lead lap, completing two hundred laps. Tony Kanaan, who would endear himself to Indy fans with his style, finished third. Tomas Scheckter, who had done so well the previous year, took fourth. Rookie of the year, Tora Takaga, was fifth and Al Unser Jr. was ninth while A.J. Foyt IV finished eighteenth.

This was de Ferran's fourth and last Indy. He retired after the race as champion.

De Ferran walked away on top after finishing second once before in the *500*. Winning it was special, as it always is, for whoever grabs the title in any given year.

"I always dreamed of winning this race," de Ferran said. "Certainly, I have won championships and all that, but this is one of the most prestigious prizes in international racing. To cross the checkered flag, I am like, 'It is really happening.' Because you don't, I don't allow myself to get carried away."

2004

Rain shortened the *500* to 450 miles in 2004 and a new face got the win. Buddy Rice who competed for Rahal-Letterman Racing, operated by team owners Bobby Rahal, the former driver, and David Letterman, the comic talk show host, won the pole and took the race.

Rice ran 222.024 mph in qualifying and outmaneuvered the raindrops, as well as the thirty-two other drivers. Once again Indianapolis Motor Speedway officials reduced the power of engines and decreased the amount of fuel that could be carried on board to thirty gallons. Speeds had been inching up to 230 mph again and they feared the possibility of a return to the era of more wrecks.

"When the car's going well, I purr like a kitten," Rice said.

This was the second of seven Indianapolis 500s for Rice, who also was part of the winning team in the 24 Hours of Daytona in 2009.

While Rice took the pole, the other two spots in the front row went to drivers who would make a bigger impact at Indianapolis in the coming years, Dan Wheldon and Dario Franchitti.

The race started more than two hours late because of rain. Then rain forced a re-start after another delay of almost two hours. A crash further delayed things under yellow. But as the end of the first 250 miles approached, Wheldon was in the lead with Helio Castroneves second.

After 150 laps Bruno Junqueira led Rice and Tony Kanaan. There was more shuffling and then more rain, beginning on lap 174. A thunderstorm stopped the race after 180 laps, Rice in charge.

Rain poured down, accumulating 3.80 inches that day, a record rainfall for Indianapolis. A tornado flared up across town. Yet fourteen riders completed 180 laps and were still going, with twenty-two cars in all still running when the rain disrupted things the last time.

"I don't think you'll understand the true repercussions of what the *500* does for you until years down the road," Rice said.

2005

Tony Kanaan won the pole at 227.566 mph, Dan Wheldon won the race, and Danica Patrick won fans' hearts.

It was an Indianapolis 500 that agreed with the majority of fans. From the time Brazilian Kanaan first appeared at the Indianapolis Motor Speedway spectators liked his style. They could tell he always gave it his all, that he burned to win, but that he could be gracious in defeat. And Kanaan had his share of defeats because things often went wrong.

Wheldon was the first British winner since Graham Hill in 1996. He was handsome, dashing, had an aura of charm, and was good-humored.

The diminutive Patrick was the latest woman to burst onto the Indy scene, but the first in some time and also the first whose attractiveness also seemed to make a difference in her attaining sponsorships. The 5-foot-2, one hundred pound Patrick added to the excitement surrounding the race. She got people talking – for better or worse – and was so much in the news and became better known than more experienced, top drivers that some sportswriters referred to the phenomenon as "Danica Mania."

After the CART-Indy Car split helped drive down attention, Patrick's hot driving gave the Indy 500 a higher national television profile than it had enjoyed in a decade.

The race and track underwent a certain amount of retooling between 2004 and 2005. The Speedway was repaved and the track surface spruced up. Also, the start time was moved from the usual 11 a.m. to noon.

As soon as practice started Patrick proved she belonged, turning a lap in 222.741 mph. Patrick went faster from there. By the end of the first week of practice Patrick had floated around the track at 227.860 mph. Patrick earned the fourth place on the starting grid, on the inside of the second row. Defending champ Buddy Rice crashed and was hospitalized with a concussion. He had to withdraw and his replacement driver was Kenny Brack, the 1999 Indy champ.

Kanaan started well, but Sam Hornish Jr. overtook him en route to leading a race-high seventy-seven laps. That didn't get him much because Hornish crashed after 146 laps and finished twenty-third. On lap 155, Patrick, sitting in eighth, saw her car spin half-way around and hit another driver. The nose of her car was ruined, but frantic repairs got her back on the track.

After 170 laps Wheldon led. Patrick, who grabbed the front on lap fifty-six, became the first woman to lead the Indianapolis 500. She also got to the front again on lap 172. Patrick, who led nineteen laps in all, was ahead by less than one second and Wheldon passed her on lap 186.

Patrick came back after 190 laps to pass Wheldon, but he worked his way back in front once more and then Vitor Moira and Bryan Herta passed Patrick. There was a crash behind them, and as Wheldon accelerated away, the yellow flag came out. Wheldon won under caution. Patrick placed fourth, finishing well ahead of Janet Guthrie's previous best finish by a woman in ninth.

Patrick's showing gained her an avalanche of publicity. She promptly wrote a book, appearing on the cover in an evening gown while holding a racing helmet.

"Racing in the 2005 Indianapolis 500 would be a life-altering experience for me and record-setting race for the IRL," Patrick said. "This was the event in which I would prove that behind the wheel everything is equal for a man and a woman. My car has no idea if I am male or female."

A few drivers on the circuit who couldn't believe the amount of attention she earned began strutting around in parody T-shirts. Wheldon wore one that read, "Actually won the Indy 500."

Wheldon worked to get that lead back at the end.

"That sequence of laps where I was able to get by Vitor, then get by (Ryan) Briscoe, by Bryan and then Danica, was pretty special," Wheldon said. "It was sheer determination."

2006

Sam Hornish Jr. looked dangerous all of May. He won the pole with a clocking of 228.985 mph, but until the last five hundred feet of the five hundred miles nobody thought he was going to win the race.

Not terribly unusual for Indianapolis in May, the *500* preparations were plagued by rain. In one change going into the race, defending champ Dan Wheldon changed teams so that he was racing for Chip Ganassi. Wheldon turned a lap at 228.663 mph, so it didn't seem as if he was missing any horsepower.

That put Wheldon on the outside of row one, with Hornish inside and Helio Castroneves in the middle.

There was an interesting cast of characters involved in the pre-race action. Bicycle champion, Lance Armstrong drove the pace car and world champion boxer, Sugar Ray Leonard, waved the green flag. Indiana was on Daylight Savings Time, so the race actually began after 1 p.m. instead of just after noon in the east.

Wheldon was in the lead before the first 2.5 mile lap concluded. Wheldon led for 148 laps and it definitely looked like his day for most of the day. By sixty-five laps Wheldon had lapped twenty-five of the other thirty-two cars in the race. Crashes and yellow flags occasionally tightened things up. The scariest accident involved Tomas Scheckter on lap sixty-seven. Pieces of his car shot into the grandstand. Five spectators were injured.

Castroneves knocked himself out of the race, ending his streak of finishing each Indy he began, when he hit Buddy Rice from behind. Both former champs exited the field after that contact.

A newcomer in the Indy 500 was another Andretti, Marco, Mario's grandson. And he was driving like an Andretti, up front. Wheldon and Andretti were looking like the survivors for a last run after 190 laps. Michael Andretti, who had previously retired, returned to the race and after 193 laps took the lead. For a bit, Michael was first and Marco, his son, was second. Fans were going crazy in anticipation of the possibility of such a finish.

Then they reversed roles, Marco dashing to the lead. Realizing Marco probably had the faster car Michael sought to block other contenders.

Hornish avoided that attempt and moved into second. Hornish closed on Marco and tried to pass, but couldn't get around this Andretti.

With one lap remaining and the white flag flying, Marco led by one second. Hornish kept pushing and as they roared down the straightaway to the finish one last-gasp acceleration by Hornish thrust him in front within the last 450 feet and he won by 0.0635 seconds, the third closest margin ever. This was also the first time in history a driver passed a contender for the lead on the final lap to win. Wheldon finished fourth.

"I figured I came all this way, I ought to give myself one more shot at it," Hornish said. "I kind of looked at it as I was going to drive over him if I had to."

Marco Andretti acquitted himself brilliantly in winning rookie of the year, but well aware of his family history at the track he knew there was no time like the present to take a chance to win.

"I do not want to wait until next year," the younger Andretti said. "I have to take advantage of everything because second's nothing."

Indeed, despite five additional top six finishes, ten years later Andretti was still looking for his first Indianapolis 500 victory.

2007

It was beginning to look like another fence-climbing year for Helio Castroneves after he won the pole with a clocking of 225.817 mph, but a new winner broke through after Indianapolis Colts star quarterback Peyton Manning served as honorary starter. Jim Nabors was ill and could not be present to sing "Back Home Again in Indiana." Officials had the Purdue Band play the song and fans sang it instead.

Castroneves' company on the front row was Tony Kanaan and Dario Franchitti.

Their biggest worry during the day was the incessant rain. It rained overnight, but the track was dried. It rained in the middle and the race was delayed.

Scheduled for two hundred laps, the Indianapolis 500 becomes official each year when the drivers pass beyond one hundred laps. On May 27, 2007 the race was halted after 113 laps with Kanaan in front, Marco Andretti in second and Danica Patrick in third. As the drivers and their pit crews twiddled their thumbs for three hours, the race paused. Officials could have called it and sent it into the books as official, but instead resumed after 6 p.m.

Kanaan continued running strong and Patrick passed Andretti for second place. Driver Marty Roth had an accident on lap 151 and the race went yellow. As some leaders made pit stops, others, fearful that it was going to rain again and the order would be frozen and perhaps even declared final, stayed out.

Franchitti moved ahead and indeed, when another deluge struck, the race ended after 166 laps with him in front. It was so wet at the Speedway that the winner's ceremony was moved indoors instead of being held in the traditional winner's circle. Scott Dixon was second, 0.3610 seconds behind Franchitti, with Castroneves third. Kanaan led eighty-three laps and finished twelfth.

A native of Scotland, Franchitti was emerging as one of the finest Indy 500 racers of the era. This first victory was a big step for him and the points earned contributed to the first of four Indy Car series season championships for him.

At the time Franchitti was married to actress Ashley Judd, who attended the races and drew her own fair amount of attention at the Speedway. The couple later divorced in 2013.

After the race Franchitti explained that he had to make a pit stop earlier "for safety" in changing a tire and that helped put him in the lead later when other cars stopped for fuel. He told reporters that he had a room in his house in Scotland dedicated to racing legend Jimmy Clark.

"I think he's the hero of any Scottish driver and one of the best drivers in the world ever," Franchitti said.

2008

Jim Nabors was back in the house and singing as well as ever. The National Anthem was sung by Julianne Hough. During the off-season Helio Castroneves was invited to participate on the TV show "Dancing With The Stars." Hough was his partner and they won the title. Former U.S. figure skating Olympic Kristi Yamaguchi was the honorary starter who waved the green flag.

She sent Scott Dixon off to victory. Dixon was born in Australia to parents from New Zealand. Over the years he has emerged as one of the finest Indy Car racers, winning four season championships. However he never had a better month than May 2008.

Dixon won the pole for Chip Ganassi Racing at 226.366 mph ahead of Dan Wheldon and Ryan Briscoe, his other front-row companions. The second row consisted of Castroneves, Danica Patrick, and Tony Kanaan. Dixon and Wheldon were teammates.

Sarah Fisher, whose car did not start properly when the cars took off, stayed on the track during the first caution when other cars pitted and moved into third place. Then she spun out and lost three laps. Indianapolis giveth and Indianapolis taketh away.

During the first half of the race Dixon and Wheldon exchanged the lead most of the time, but Kanaan got ahead of them by lap ninety-four. When Kanaan moved into the lead he established a record of being the first driver to lead at some point during seven straight races. Rick Mears had the old record of leading in six consecutive races.

The handling on Wheldon's car began to fade and Kanaan crashed and was out. By lap 159 Vitor Meira was in the lead, just ahead of Dixon and Marco Andretti. Six other drivers were farther back, but still potential threats.

Ryan Briscoe and Danica Patrick lost their cars when they touched on pit road. Patrick looked angry enough to start a fight with Briscoe and began marching to his team pit before being headed off by a security guard. Briscoe had nicked Patrick and sent her car into a spin and Briscoe hit the wall. In a bit of rather zealous policing, the drivers were summoned to meet with officials after the race and fined $100,000 and put on probation for the season.

Dixon just outran everyone else from lap 175 on with Meira second by 1.7498 seconds. Dixon led 115 laps of the race.

"For me, when I won in 2008, it was almost a massive amount of weight lifted off your shoulders to say you've put your stamp on it," Dixon said, "and you're on a short list of sixty-four or sixty-five people that have ever won this race in the world."

2009

Helio Castroneves did it. He won the third Indy 500 of his career after winning two in a row in 2001 and 2002. Castroneves' victory made him the first foreign-born driver to win the *500* three times. The Brazilian won from the pole, clocking in at 224.864 mph in qualifying.

The 93rd running of the Indianapolis 500 kicked off a multi-year celebration that took note of several milestones in the history of the track and the race. It was the 100th anniversary of the opening of the Indianapolis

Hélio Castroneves, speaking at a press conference, has won three Indianapolis 500s.
Photo Courtesy of Lew Freedman

Motor Speedway. The 2011 race would be the 100th anniversary of the first *500* and the 2016 race would be the 100th running of the race.

Castroneves' triumph was also a triumph for Roger Penske's team. As an owner this was Penske's fifteenth win at Indy.

Ryan Briscoe and Dario Franchitti filled out the front row next to Castroneves.

Castroneves actually messed up the original start, driving out of formation just as the green flag was coming out. The cars lined up again and started a second time.

As had happened so many times, there was a first-lap accident, this one driving Mario Moraes out of the race and taking Marco Andretti with him. Andretti touched the wall, spouted off angrily at Moraes, blaming him for the incident, but then getting back into the race for fifty-six laps.

Scott Dixon, Castroneves and Franchitti were the front-runners over the first 250 miles. A frightening collision between Vitor Meira and Raphael Matos ended their day. Meira was hospitalized with a broken back.

By lap 185 Castroneves had control of the race with Dan Wheldon, Danica Patrick, and Townsend Bell futilely chasing him.

It had been seven years since Castroneves' last victory, but he repeated his popular fence climbing routine, once again pleasing the fans.

"This is incredible," Castroneves said after his third Indy win. "I think my tears speak for everything. What a day. This place is magical. Wow. Three. I can't believe it."

This was the last race that Tony George presided over as president of the Indianapolis Motor Speedway. He resigned from the job on June 30. Joie Chitwood and Jeff Belskus followed him, and by 2013 Doug Boles was the new president of the Speedway.

NEW FAN FAVORITES TAKE OVER

2010-2016

Scotsman Dario Franchitti won his first Indy championship in 2007, but added two more titles in 2010 and 2012. Injuries forced him to retire before he could add a fourth.

Dan Wheldon was a popular champion, winning in 2005 and 2011, but spectators were crushed when the Englishman was killed in a race at another venue later in 2011.

Because the Indianapolis 500 went on hiatus during World War I and World War II, the 100th anniversary of the first race in 2011 was not the 100th race. That was scheduled for 2016.

As this first century of racing came to an end, the Indianapolis 500 remained the most prestigious auto race in the world with the largest attendance of any event in any sport.

2010

Coming off his special 2009 Indianapolis 500 victory, Helio Castroneves seemed poised to go for four. He won the pole, qualifying with a speed of 227.970 mph and the Brazilian driver seemed as hungry as ever for a win at the Indianapolis Motor Speedway.

Pole qualifying was altered – which historically was never popular – with race officials adopting what they called a shootout style for choosing the thirty-three car field. The plan was adapted from the Indy Car Series and after the first twenty-four cars took a shot the first three cars advanced to the shootout. Winning the pole usually carried a $100,000 payoff. Under this approach the payout was increased to $175,000. The second-fastest driver earned $75,000 and the third qualifier, filling out the front row, received $50,000.

Castroneves took first, Will Power grabbed second and Dario Franchitti was third.

Various celebrities helped kick off the festivities. Sports television personality Robin Roberts drove the pace car. Behind her was an unusual two-seater car driven by Michael Andretti that carried actor Mark Wahlberg. Actor, Jack Nicholson waved the green flag to start the race.

It took almost no time for a problem to emerge. Davey Hamilton's race ended without a lap driven when Tomas Scheckter squeezed by him on a pass. Hamilton called Scheckter "an idiot." Hamilton was out, Scheckter continued and completed 199 laps, finishing fifteenth.

It also took no time for Franchitti to take the lead and he led the race almost all day long. Franchitti led 155 laps and won his second Indy 500. Dan Wheldon finished second without ever leading a lap. Mike Conway was the next busiest leader, ahead on fifteen laps.

A messy accident occurred when Ryan Hunter-Reay and his car was slowing to a stop and Mike Conway hit him from behind. Conway's car turned over and took to the air, hitting the protective wall and completely destroying his car. Ana Beatriz spun out seeking to avoid the cars. Conway was taken to the hospital with a broken leg, fractured vertebrae in his neck, and a compression fracture in his back, while two spectators suffered minor injuries.

Franchitti didn't even bother with a pit stop over the last thirty-six laps and in celebrating his victory said of drinking from the bottle of milk, "This tastes just as good the second time."

2011

The capriciousness of life at the Indianapolis 500 was never clearer than in the 2011 race. JR Hildebrand had the race won on the last lap, but Dan Wheldon actually won it.

Hildebrand was poised to become the rare driver to capture the rookie of the year award and the race title itself in the same year when it took an extraordinary amount of luck for him to finish at all.

Alex Tagliani was the hot driver early, taking the pole position with a spin of 227.472 mph. "Tags," as he is nicknamed, is a Canadian driver who was coming off eleventh and tenth place finishes in his first two Indy 500 runs.

Tagiliani stole much of the pre-race thunder at the Indy race that commemorated the 100th anniversary of the first *500* at the Indianapolis Motor Speedway in 1911. As part of the festivities there was a Celebration of Automobiles that highlighted race cars and other special cars connected to Indianapolis from 1911 to 1961.

Leading up to the events the Speedway announced that millionaire real estate mogul, Donald Trump would drive the pace car commemorating the 100th anniversary. While this was long before Trump pursued the Republican nomination for president for 2016, the public outcry led to him withdrawing and being replaced by A.J. Foyt, whom many felt should have been chosen in the first place as probably the greatest driver in race history.

Foyt was seventy-six at the time, still a towering figure at the Speedway as a team owner, as well as a four-time driving champion. When Foyt was growing up in Houston he listened to the Indy 500 on the radio and he dreamed not of racing in it or winning it, but merely of traveling to Indiana once to see it. The 2011 event was the 53rd consecutive year Foyt was at the Speedway for Memorial Day.

"Then, when I did see it, I was hoping someday I'd be fortunate enough to be able to try to race in a car," he said. "I'm glad to be named amongst a bunch of the great, great race drivers. I don't feel I'm no better than any of the other ones at their time. I look back at history, back at this place. You couldn't hog-tie me in some of those cars they run over a hundred miles an hour in."

Foyt did not brag about his four wins in 1961, 1964, 1967 and 1977, plus taking the pole four times and racing for thirty-five years in a row. But track president Jeff Belskus said what most people believe. He called Foyt, "the greatest race car driver in the history of the Indianapolis 500, maybe the history of the world."

Indy 500 officials were determined to make the 100th anniversary one giant party and one way they succeeded was by allowing children under twelve free entry if accompanied by an adult. Star drivers, past winners, were all over the race track signing autographs in events leading up to the start.

"It's a milestone," said Mario Andretti. "A hundred years of anything is something you only experience once, I think."

He did not expect to be present for the 200th anniversary.

Tagliani was good enough to lead for twenty laps on May 29, and finished 28th in the field. Helio Castronves did 199 laps, but finished seventeenth in his quest for a fourth Indy crown. Dario Franchitti, who led for fifty-one laps, completed all 200, but placed twelfth. Danica Patrick took tenth. Scott Dixon led for seventy-three laps, but placed fifth.

JR Hildebrand from California, was twenty-three at the time and raced twice in Indy Car in 2010. He led seven laps and seemed a sure bet to make it eight as the race finish and the checkered flag loomed about a thousand feet ahead of him.

That was after Graham Rahal, Bobby's son, took the lead in the late going for six laps. Tony Kanaan, who was seeking his first win, was positioned as high as second, but couldn't grab the lead. Dixon and Franchitti seemed likely to slug it out, but had to pit and Bernard Baguette, a comparative unknown from Belgium, stayed out, taking the risk he could out-run his dwindling fuel. He could not, finally pitting with three laps left.

When Baguette surrendered, Hildebrand inherited the lead. Going into the last turn on the last lap he drove high to avoid the slowing car of Charlie Kimball. Only Hildebrand went too high, hit the wall, and wrecked his car. The force of the impact robbed Hildebrand of his steering and tore off one tire. With no control Hildebrand's car went into a long skid.

Wheldon, who had not led a single lap in the race – something which had not happened before – zoomed past Hildebrand and shot across the finish line first. In 1912, winner Joe Dawson took the checkered flag after leading just two laps. In this race there were twenty-three lead changes.

Hildebrand's car kept skidding right across the finish line, giving him second place.

"It's a helpless feeling," Hildebrand said of the crazy way he lost control of the most famous race in the world. The only thing Hildebrand was able to keep doing was accelerating to the end. "I was flat on the gas, man," he said.

There had never been a finish quite like it in a century of Indianapolis 500 racing. The crowd of about 300,000 went wild with disbelief. Wheldon's winning average speed of 170.265 mph reflected a mostly clean race.

"It's just an incredible day," an emotional Wheldon said afterwards.

Despite being a past winner he did not even have a full-time ride for the season. His contract with Brian Herta Autosport actually expired at midnight at the end of the day of the race.

Wheldon scooted past Hildebrand by staying wide of the other car.

"I just carried on by," Wheldon said. "At that point I knew it was mine."

Without a full-time commitment for the rest of the summer, Wheldon said he would soon be hanging out on the beach in Florida with his wife and two young sons, sometimes changing diapers. He said his victory could be called "a Cinderella story."

Wheldon also recalled for those with less-clear memories that in 2006 he had the race won, but suffered a flat tire. So he could identify a bit with Hildebrand.

"It's unfortunate, but it's Indianapolis," Wheldon said.

DAN WHELDON

The death of two-time Indianapolis 500 winner Dan Wheldon was one of the most shocking occurrences in open-wheel racing in a decade.

After safety advances at the Indianapolis Motor Speedway and in equipment the world had changed for auto racers even though they still sped around tracks at 200 mph. From an every-year occurrence, racers simply did not die in crashes anymore at Indy.

Wheldon, then only thirty-three, did not perish in a car at Indianapolis, where only months earlier he had claimed his second *500* title. He died in an open-wheel race in Las Vegas a few months later on October 16, 2011.

The likeable Englishman who had made friends all over the racing world, was competing in the IZOD Indy Car World Championship at the Las Vegas Motor Speedway. There was a surreal, fifteen car accident that Wheldon was caught up in. His car went airborne head-first into a catch fence after flying about 325 feet. Wheldon's head struck a pole on the perimeter of the track before his car landed back inside the track.

"Dan was always a very happy guy," said racer Oriol Servia. "He was always smiling. He was a funny, great person that touched a lot of people."

Wheldon was dead on arrival at the hospital, and unlike Indianapolis, where the show always went on despite heavy hearts, drivers voted

to stop racing. An autopsy concluded that Wheldon twice hit his head and the second impact killed him.

"It's a black day for the sport," said driver James Hinchcliffe.

Many drivers expressed similar sentiments.

"What a tremendously sad day," said JR Hildebrand.

Las Vegas was a season-ending championship for Indy Car, but after the calamity the circuit announced it would no longer race at that Speedway.

Only months before Wheldon, who was not at that moment affiliated full-time with a team, won the Indy 500 while driving a borrowed car. The odds were so high against Wheldon winning the 2011 Indy 500 he broke into tears when he triumphed. He dedicated the win to his mother Sue, who was suffering from Alzheimer's disease. Handsome, with blond hair slicked back, Wheldon won $2.5 million in that race. Wheldon was married with two young children, age two, and an infant.

Wheldon was from Emberton, England, although he was living in St. Petersburg, Florida at the time of his death. That's where his funeral was held with fellow drivers Dario Franchitti, Tony Kanaan, and Scott Dixon among the pallbearers. The man who shed tears only months earlier at Indy made so many others cry with his passing.

When he raced, Weldon wore a racing helmet that on the back had a painted picture of Richard the Lionhearted. That helmet failed to save him.

At Indianapolis Wheldon had two firsts, two seconds, a third, and a fourth in his nine starts.

"A little bit of everybody in Indy Car racing died today," said team owner Chip Ganassi, who was Wheldon's former boss.

A few months after his death, a charity race was held in Wheldon's name roughly ten miles from where he was born. An Indiana track named its prize for a certain race the Dan Wheldon Trophy. A street in St. Petersburg was named Dan Wheldon Way.

Dan Wheldon died in a race car at a time when drivers no longer died in their race cars. That probably tripled the stunning impact of his death. Deaths at places like the Indianapolis 500 and the other big tracks were no longer taken for granted, were no longer the cost of doing business. They were flukes.

That is how Dan Wheldon died, in a fluke manner, at the wheel of his race car, at a speed of something more than two hundred mph. It was a reminder to the racing world that despite the adjustments and protections added to the mix, this is still a dangerous sport.

2012

As astounding as the 2011 race was, the 2012 race nearly eclipsed it for thrills and chills, though not for a bizarre finish. However, there were a record thirty-four lead changes on the two hundred laps and the driver who emerged as king for a year was Dario Franchitti, now a three-time champion.

Rules changes, equipment trends, and Indianapolis Motor Speedway policies resulted in all thirty-three cars driving turbocharged engines and employing new chassis. That should have made for a more or less equal race and the drivers drove as if that was true.

There was no defending champion because of the death of Dan Wheldon in the Las Vegas race the preceding October. The last time that had occurred was 1947.

Although the Speedway safety record had improved considerably in the 2000s, officials decided that one way to further tighten up was to make all cars line up single-file for a re-start following yellow flags. That diminished the chances of cars swerving into one another.

Jim Nabors was too ill to travel to Indianapolis to sing "Back Home Again in Indiana," so Indiana flew to him. Nabors resides in Hawaii and a film crew went to his home to tape him singing the song and the tape was shown at the Speedway on May 27.

The pole winner was Ryan Briscoe at 226.484 mph, with James Hinchcliffe second and Ryan Hunter-Reay completing the first row. Marco Andretti, Will Power, and Helio Castroneves filled the second row. Castroneves was hungry to take his fourth win and tie the record. During the early going Castroneves had trouble in the pits twice and that set him back.

The usual car attrition helped thin the herd as the race went on with Simona de Silvestro and Jean Alesi the first ones out after ten and nine laps, respectively, because their cars were going too slowly. Twenty-two cars completed at least 199 laps, with few knocked out because of accidents. The most notable victim of a crash was Japanese driver Takuma Sato, who led thirty-one laps and was challenging Franchitti for the lead near the end when he hit the wall.

Marco Andretti led the most laps with fifty-nine, but he crashed on lap 187. Scott Dixon, the runner-up, led fifty-three laps. Tony Kanaan kept plugging away near the front of the pack, but could not grab an Indy victory. He placed third. The top three finishers had been pallbearers at Wheldon's funeral.

Franchitti won the *500* for the third time and he dedicated his victory to his close friend Dan Wheldon, whose nickname to him was D-dub, as in DW.

"Everybody up there was a friend of Dan's and that about sums it up," Franchitti said. "Everybody loved him. What a race! What a race! I think D-dub would have been proud of it."

Dixon and his family relocated to St. Petersburg to help Wheldon's wife Susie with her children.

Kanaan said, "His three best friends in the top three."

2013

While Tony Kanaan has many friends and fans in Indianapolis, likely not one in a hundred of them could easily recall his complete name. The Brazilian star was born Antoine Rizkallah Kanaan Filho of Lebanese heritage.

At the end of the 2013 race the many thousands of rooters at the Indianapolis Motor Speedway were chanting just a simple, "Tony!" Kanaan's long-time dream of winning the Indianapolis 500 came true.

Kanaan had won many races and many honors, but the top of the podium at the Indy 500 had always eluded him. He had finished in the top five four times and led at other times, but everything clicked for him in 2013.

That year, Ed Carpenter won the pole with a ride of 228.762 mph. Rookie, Carlos Munoz was second on the starting grid and Marco Andretti was on the outside of the front row. Kanaan started twelfth, on the outside of the fourth row.

Kanaan was one of several drivers who shared the lead during the first one hundred laps, including Andretti, Ryan Hunter-Reay, and A.J. Allmendinger. Allmendinger is primarily a NASCAR racer, but he took a detour for the Indy race in 2013 and qualified fifth. He also led for twenty-three laps while finishing a solid seventh as a rookie.

"It was probably the coolest feeling in my life to take the lead at Indy and to lead the Indy 500," the stock-car racer said. "That's a feeling I'll never forget."

Although he was not a factor, former champ Buddy Lazier, who made his first start at Indy in 1989, was back for his first ride since 2009. He finished 31st.

Yellow caution flags, rather than the green flag dominated the last laps of the race. Kanaan took the lead by passing Hunter-Reay as things got funky. Graham Rahal crashed with seven laps to go and Franchitti crashed with three laps to go. Clean-up crews could not clear the track in time for the race to resume green. That allowed Kanaan to coast home the last few laps without being challenged.

"This is it, man," Kanaan said when his first Indy triumph was official. "Finally, they're going to put my ugly face on this trophy."

Hardly anyone was ever so happy to have his visage engraved on the Borg-Warner Trophy, no matter what kind of job the artists did. It took Kanaan twelve tries to win the Indy 500 and supersede all of his other top performances and close calls.

Until the end of the race there weren't nearly as many accidents or yellow flag problems as usual and the winning average time was the fastest-ever at 187.433 mph. The race was over in two hours, forty minutes, 3.4181 seconds, which was about four hours and two minutes faster than Ray Harroun completed the event in 1911.

The previous record was thirty-four lead changes, but there were sixty-eight lead changes in 2013. The old record for the most drivers leading at least a lap was twelve. There were fourteen different drivers who led in this race, four of them for just one lap.

"I think this race, for the fans, was unbelievable," Kanaan said.

Kanaan may never drink milk again, but the gulp of the milk in Victory Lane was probably the most thirst-quenching beverage he ever savored.

2014

Tony Kanaan was back to defend his title, but Ed Carpenter won the pole for the second year in a row with a clocking of 231.067 mph. Another NASCAR specialist, Kurt Busch, turned up to give it a try in the Indianapolis 500. Busch was attempting the Indianapolis-Charlotte double for Memorial Day.

Busch placed sixth at Indy and won rookie of the year, but a blown engine finished him in North Carolina.

Jacques Villeneuve, the 1995 champion who had not raced since, came back. Not in the field was a former champ who wanted to be there. Three-time winner, Dario Franchitti was seriously injured in a crash in October of 2013 during a race in Houston. Besides other broken bones, Franchitti incurred a concussion that led to memory loss. Doctors advised that he retire and he did so a month later. Franchitti was invited to drive the pace car in 2014.

Also in 2014, Franchitti was awarded the honor of Member of the Order of the British Empire.

This was Jim Nabors' swan song, singing the traditional "Back Home Again in Indiana" song. Nabors said he was no longer strong enough to plan regular travel trips to Indiana from his Hawaii home after this.

Another former champion in the field was Juan Pablo Montoya. The Colombian won the race in 2000, but subsequently took a long hiatus, switching to NASCAR. He had recently returned to open-wheel racing as his major focus. Montoya qualified second at more than 231 mph and finished a strong fifth despite his long absence from Indy.

The race produced a new winner in Ryan Hunter-Reay. Hunter-Reay was thirty-five, but looked more boyish. Originally from Dallas, he had been knocking on the door at Indy since 2008. In-between, Hunter-Reay won the Indy Car Series championship in 2012. Before his victory he had finished sixth at Indy in 2008 and third in 2013.

Hunter-Reay, whose mother died of cancer, drove the number twenty-eight car in his racing career to symbolize twenty-eight million people in the United States suffering from cancer.

The race began so smoothly that no yellow caution flag waved for 149 laps. While probably an all-time record, nobody knew since before 1976 officials did not keep track of the places where caution flags first appeared in a given race.

The problem on the 149th lap was a Charlie Kimball crash. Scott Dixon crashed a bit later and dropped out after 167 laps. Dixon had completed 1,733 laps in a row at the Speedway, going back to starting the 2006 race.

Pole sitter Carpenter went out after 175 laps and returning champ Kanaan went out after 177. Twenty-five of the thirty-three cars completed at least 190 laps and the first twenty finished all two hundred laps.

Castroneves was running near the front on lap 195 when he soared into the lead, seemingly ready to capture his fourth Indy 500 title. Over the final laps, there was fierce racing involving Castroneves, Hunter-Reay, who regained the lead, and Marco Andretti.

Andretti dropped back slightly with two laps to go and Castroneves once again passed Hunter-Reay for the lead. Hunter-Reay made a slingshot pass on the final lap and although he challenged down the homestretch, Castroneves could not inch into first. Hunter-Reay won by 0.600 seconds, the second closest finish in history to 1992.

"The race was ridiculously close and competitive," Hunter-Reay said. "Just glad I picked the right time to go."

2015

Gratification came to Juan Pablo Montoya slowly, gradually, and then in a rush. Fifteen years after he won the Indianapolis 500 as a young man, the Colombian racer won it again as a thirty-nine year old, bounce-back racer in Indy Car competition.

"I was screaming," Montoya said of his closing rush on the Indianapolis Motor Speedway track on May 24 when he realized he was once again the champion of the *500*. "I was so happy." As the final mileage clicked away, he said he thought, "Oh, my god. I've got this."

Montoya had defected from open-wheel racing to cast his fortune with stock cars for years. But he switched back and his reward was this title.

The 2015 start of the greatest spectacle in racing.

This was the 99th running of the Indianapolis 500, the first of which was held in 1911, but was interrupted by two world wars. Thoughts were already turning to 2016 when the 100th running was scheduled, but the early part of May was quite gloomy. Not only did rain interrupt the proceedings, but there was a near-death of a driver at the track during practice.

James Hincliffe, a Canadian competitor, was involved in a major crash with serious injuries and was impaled through the left upper thigh by a piece of his broken suspension and it caused massive bleeding. Medical help was prompt in aiding Hinchcliffe and staunching the bleeding. In some quarters, medics were credited with saving his life. Hinchcliffe was rushed to the hospital, underwent surgery and stayed in-house for nine days. His already-qualified car was raced by Ryan Briscoe.

"He got unlucky," JR Hildebrand said of Hinchcliffe. "It's not like that can't happen again. Again, that's racing. We always have these types of deals. All of these drivers know that's a possibility when you get in the race car. Wrecking race cars is normal. You're never going to get away from wrecking race cars ."

Briscoe finished twelfth as the Hinchcliffe fill-in.

"I just want to thank everyone for the opportunity to jump in the car at the last minute," Briscoe said. "We're all thinking of Hinch and I was thinking of him during the race, as well."

As the days passed before Hinchcliffe was released, it became known that he had arrived at the hospital in critical condition. Friend and fellow driver, Ryan Hunter-Reay, said things were "touch and go at times" for Hinchcliffe, who came that close to becoming the first driver fatality at Indy in years. Hinchcliffe called the track medical personnel, and those helpers at the hospital, "my heroes." He returned to driving before the end of the year.

Veteran Scott Dixon took the pole at 226.760 mph and Gabby Chaves, who finished sixteenth, was rookie of the year.

After Dixon, the rest of the two front rows consisted of Will Power, Simon Pagenaud, Tony Kanaan, Helio Castroneves and Justin Wilson. Montoya qualified fifteenth.

Two cars never finished a lap, but after that the field hung together through sixty-one laps before any other dropped out. Twenty cars finished the two hundred laps. The car belonging to Justin Wilson toured 199 laps by the time the race ended. In late August, Wilson, a British racer, was killed at age thirty-seven in a race at Pocono Raceway in Pennsylvania.

Much of the drama was packed into the last fifty laps. Kanaan crashed on lap 153. Montoya was hit from behind by Simona de Silvestro on lap seven and needed repair work. Although it was early it was feared his race chances were gone. However, he fought his way back to near the front.

"She didn't do it on purpose," Montoya said after the race was over. "If you're going to make a mistake, make it early. That's what happens when you qualify bad. You find yourself with the wrong crowd."

A series of yellows from various crashes saw Dixon, Power and Montoya in control after lap 184, with the three drivers trading the lead. After 196 laps Montoya powered past Power and the two cars battled over the final stretch. Power could not overtake Montoya and it was on the last lap that he went through those emotional feelings about becoming an Indy 500 winner again after such a long wait.

Dixon had actually led eighty-four laps, Power led twenty-three, Charlie Kimball, who placed third led for ten, and Montoya nine laps. Earlier, Pagenaud led for thirty-five laps.

"Anywhere else, I'd be happy with second," Power said. "There was some great battling out there."

The top two finishers were both driving for Roger Penske, who earned his sixteenth title at the Brickyard as an owner. Helio Castroneves, who was still fighting for a fourth championship, finished seventh. He was also running for Penske. Castroneves had walked away from a frightening practice crash earlier in May.

"It's the 500," Castroneves said. "You're going to do everything you can to win. You're going to go all in, but you've always got to make sure you finish. You've got to have a chance to be battling."

Montoya said he was a much more mature driver than he was when he won the *500* for the first time and he did not panic when briefly sidelined by the early mishap, reminding himself that this is a long race.

"In 2000, I was really young," he said. "It was just the start of my career. You're wiser. You know where races are lost. You've got to figure out how to make your move. There's one hundred ways to throw this away. With eight laps to go I had no idea if I had a shot at winning. We were all so equal."

Roger Penske extended his level of dominance at the Indy 500 after the showing of his cars, and there was no doubt why his nickname was "The Captain." He is the captain of the team that has won more in the Indianapolis 500 than any other.

The sixteenth win came a few months after a Penske-owned car driven by Joey Logano won the Daytona 500 in NASCAR and that isn't even Penske's specialty.

Penske cannot go on forever. He was seventy-eight for his 2015 Indianapolis victory. But he sounded as if he might like to do so.

"At ninety-two I might have a (sponsor) sticker on the car and I'll be a member of the Oldtimers Club," Penske said.

2016 AND BEYOND

The Indianapolis 500 of 2016 was planned as the biggest party in the United States outside of New Year's Eve in Times Square.

The Indianapolis Motor Speedway is the biggest sporting arena in the world, but it cannot hold one million people.

Preparations and thoughts turned to the 2016 Indianapolis 500 seemingly minutes after the 2015 race ended.

The 2016 Indy 500, scheduled for May 29 was a big-time party being planned for the Indianapolis Motor Speedway and race officials hoped the celebratory shindig would send the event into a second century of racing on a good note.

Every driver participating in the 2015 race wanted to qualify for the 2016 race. Perhaps as much as any other year they sought to be part of a major event that is likely to be remembered as a milestone Indy 500 for a long time. And just being on the starting grid for the command to rev up the engines, wasn't going to be enough for some.

"This is the Super Bowl, the Olympics, the World Cup, so if you're going to win one race, this is the one," said driver Helio Castroneves.

The Brazilian fan favorite had been chasing a fourth Indianapolis victory for some years. He dreamed of matching A.J. Foyt, Rick Mears, and Al Unser Sr. and he could think of nothing better than tying the mark

A happy Juan Pablo Montoya after his 2015 *500* victory.
Photo Courtesy of Lew Freedman.

for individual driver victories on a special occasion. Four time winner were the sweetest words that could ever be written in front of his name

For the 100th running of the Indianapolis 500, the Speedway was continuing its policy of allowing free admission to children twelve years and younger accompanied by an adult. The idea was to make memories for the youngsters at a young age and make them *500* fans for life.

There was every reason to believe that one of the biggest race crowds in years would show up. Anyone who attended an Indy 500 in the past would want to be on the grounds for the 100th race. And anyone who attended regularly was a sure bet to show.

Prices started at forty dollars for general admission tickets and fifty dollars and up in the grandstand with the hopes of filling the 257,000 seating area and with the grand hope of topping the 300,000 mark for the special anniversary once more.

At the start of the anniversary weekend, the Speedway was featuring a concert by the rock band Journey. Fans were coming for fun and to say that had gone to the Indianapolis 500. Drivers wanted to be able to tell children and grandchildren they were not only there at the Speedway, but part of the race.

As the 2015 race loomed drivers reflected on what the Indianapolis 500 meant to their careers and how much they were looking forward to qualifying for the 2016 race. They all wanted to be part of the celebration surrounding the 100th running of the world's best-known auto race.

As much of an icon as he has been at the Indianapolis 500, first as a driver for thirty-five straight years with four victories, and subsequently as a long-time team owner, A.J. Foyt, often opinionated, frequently blunt, always tough, has not boasted much about his accomplishments on the track.

Foyt always said that he felt lucky to ever qualify for the race and just to get a chance to race at the Indianapolis Motor Speedway in the great race was a big thrill.

"And then being lucky enough to win it, that was great!" he said.

There is no mistaking the feeling that the drivers have for Indianapolis, the Speedway, and the *500*. They love winning anywhere they compete, but they all know that Indy 500 is more special than all of those other places and that if they win the *500* they not only put a notch in their belt, they make history.

Scott Dixon has won the Indy Car points championship four times with thirty-seven Indy Car wins, including the 2008 Indy 500. But one win at the Speedway makes you want more and winning in Indy means more than all of Dixon's other wins.

"You know, this is the big one," Dixon said. "I would probably eliminate thirty of my wins for three of these. Would you rather win three championships or three Indy 500 races? I know what that would be. It's the biggest race in the world, so you would trade a lot of things for this. A lot of people would."

Dixon most assuredly would like to win one more Indy 500 before he retires.

"It's the sense of accomplishment," he said. "I think as you follow and look at the history of the race, a lot of people have had the chance to win this race, but a lot smaller list of people have won it multiple times."

Mario Andretti won the Indianapolis 500 in 1969 and as great a career as he had as a driver for the many years he competed, he could not win it again. His son Michael had a terrific driving career and did not win Indy. His nephew John never won the Indy 500, either. The Andretti in the mix these days is Marco. The same fire to win Indianapolis, to follow in the footsteps of his grandfather, burns inside him.

"You can't let it frustrate you," Marco said of coming close to winning by finishing second, third three times, and fourth. "But I think it's a good thing that we're here every year. You know I want to win more than ever. I get more and more anxious. After the checkered flag I can't wait another 365 days to do it again. The reason I'm here at Indy is that it's my favorite day of the year."

Not Christmas, New Year's or any other holiday, but Indianapolis 500 Day, that's Marco Andretti's favorite day on the calendar. It is no surprise how important it is for him to win the *500* given the blood that courses through his veins.

"It's just this place," he said. "The magnitude of what this event brings. It's waking up in the morning and seeing all of the people funneling into the Speedway. It's what we live for. It's the biggest race in the world."

Andretti is not the only driver to call the Indianapolis 500 race day his favorite day though, "That's pretty much it exactly," said Josef Newgarden, a young driver from Tennessee. "It is, you know, the most important race of the year, a big day. You'd be a liar if you said it wasn't an important day. It's a big deal. If you show up, you'd better be ready to do battle all day long."

When Ryan Hunter-Reay won the Indy 500 in 2014 it was the first time an American had won since 2006.

"It is a race that transcends sports," Hunter-Reay said. "It's an American tradition and you can really feel that once you've won. I remember after the race, going around the Speedway waving to the fans hearing 'USA' chants. That was one of my favorite parts about it. Winning on home turf like that does have an impact."

Some have labeled the Andretti clan's squadron of great racers with just than one Indy 500 victory on the family resume to be a curse. But, Marco Andretti has a chance to lift any curse that exists and go down in history as the winner of the 100th *500* race. That would be awesome for the Andretti family, but it is likely that any driver who wins in 2016 will be even more closely identified with the race than usual.

"It's going to be crazy," driver Ed Carpenter said of the 100th running hoopla. "There are lot of other race tracks I enjoy going to and love racing at, but nothing compares to Indianapolis. What I like most is just the tradition and how huge the event is. It's still the largest, single sporting event in the world."

The tradition includes the patriotic theme of the day, the singing of "Back Home Again in Indiana," the winner drinking the milk, and kissing the bricks.

"Getting ready you have a little bit of nervous energy," said Will Power. "Then you hear the fans and you're standing on the grid when the National Anthem is being sung and the Navy bombers are flying overhead. The stakes are quite high for us. It's just an exciting day."

Powers believes fans give equal import to this race as the drivers do. "Hands down this is still the one race that the most people know about. I don't think there is a single person anywhere that doesn't know about the Indianapolis 500. Even if you go abroad and tell people you race cars they'll ask about the Indianapolis 500. It definitely has that kind of reach. For sure."

Power loves being in the midst of the pre-race traditions and wants to become part of the post-victory traditions.

"That's a part of it that I think is really cool," he said. "Why Indianapolis retains that kind of aura is because of the fact that they've done such a good job of repeating those traditions."

Nowhere does drinking milk taste as good as in Victory Lane at the Indianapolis Motor Speedway.

When the Indianapolis 500 community gathered in May of 2016 for the start of the 100th running of this special event, Juan Pablo Montoya was the defending champion. He has raced in NASCAR and raced in other kinds of cars, but the Indy 500 is the best of them all in his mind.

"It's one of the best shows," Montoya said, "and what makes the show so special is the people and the tradition and the history behind it. People have been coming here since 1960, 1970, and they say, 'It's my 40th race, my 50th race.' Those kind of people is what makes Indy, Indy."

Indy , capping off one hundred years of racing – and beginning one hundred more.

Those kind of people love the Indianapolis 500 and millions more who have either made it to the Speedway for one race as part of their bucket list, or those who have never traveled east of the Rocky Mountains on Memorial Day and study it each year on television, recognize the things that have made Indy Indy for a century.

The Indianapolis 500 is bigger and better than the other auto races, has been part of American society longer than the others, means more to the fans and the participants than any other.

Indy is worthy of worthy of a massive birthday bash. The cake should be wearing 100 candles for 100 years of racing. And yes, one more to grow on to acknowledge the kick-off of a second century of speed.

A century ago it was a challenge for race people to contemplate tires spinning at 100 mph. A century from now there just may be cars running at 300 mph.

The Celebration of 100 years of the Indianapolis 500.

Names mentioned left to right.
Front Row: Bruce Walkup, Mike Hiss, Jim McElreath, Joe Leonard, Donnie Allison, Paul Goldsmith, Chip Ganassi, Scott Dixon, Dan Wheldon, Buddy Rice, Gil de Ferran, Kenny Bräck, Mario Andretti, Arie Luyendyk, Dario Franchitti, Helio Castroneves, Bobby Unser, Al Unser, A.J. Foyt, Rick Mears, Johnny Rutherford, Emerson Fittipaldi, Parnelli Jones, Tom Sneva, Bobby Rahal, Al Unser Jr., Buddy Lazier, Pancho Carter, Ed Pimm, Jack Hewitt, Donniw Beechler, Buzz Calkins, Vern Schuppan, Bob Harkey, Van Krisiloff, Mari Hulman George, Kathy George Conforti, Olivia Conforti.
Second Row: Billy Vukovich, Cory Witherall, Janet Guthrie, Jon Herb, Stefan Johansson, Jimmy Vasser, Robbie Groff, Brian Bonner, Sarah Fisher, Billy Boat, Steve Chassey, Shigeaki Hattori, Tero Palmroth, Lyn St. James, Jeff MacPherson, Eliseo Salazar, Ted Prappas, Scott Harrington, Eric Bachelart, Scott Pruett, Brian Till, Herm Johnson, Dan Gurney, Dominic Dobson, John Martin, Max Papis, Hiro Matsushita, Johnny Unser, Bill Whittington, Teo Fabi, Lee Kunzman, Bill Alsup, Chuck Hulse, Michael Changler, Pete Halsmer, Joe Saldana, Tom Bigelow, Phil Krueger, Denny Zimmerman.
Third Row: Gary Bettenhausen, Bill Puterbaugh, Patrick Bedard, PJ Chesson, Jeff Andretti, Jim Guthrie, Phil Giebler, Ana Beatriz, Andre Ribiero, Roger Yasukawa, P.J. Jones, Roberto Moreno, Vincenzo Sospiri, Raul Boesel, Didier THeys, Eldon Rasmussen, Sebastian Saavedra, Roberto Guerrero, Steve Knapp, Tom Bagley, Don Edmunds, Roger Mears, George Snider, John Jones, Stephan Gregoire, Mel Kenyon, Mike Groff, Spike Gehlhausen, Billy Roe, Dennis Firestone, John Hollansworth Jr., Arie Luyendyk Jr., Robby McGehee, Tyce Carlson, Bobby Johns, Nancy George, Josie George, Jarrod Krisiloff, Daxton Krisiloff, Kyle Krisiloff.
Fourth Row: Justin Wilson, Ryan Hunter-Reay, Simona De Silvestro, Graham Rahal, Charlie Kimball, Marco Andretti, Jay Howard, Bertrand Baguette, Jerry Sneva, Hector Rebaque, Bill Simpson, John Mahler, John Andretti, Greg Leffler, Davey Hamilton, Danica Patrick, Bryan Herta, Robbie Buhl, Jack Miller, Andy Hillenburg, Art Malone, Rocky Moran.
Fifth Row: Townsend Bell, Ed Carpenter, Will Power, Ryan Briscoe, E.J. Viso, Oriol Servia, Tony Kanaan, James Hinchcliffe, Vitor Meira, Larry Foyt, Takuma Sato, J.R. Hildebrand, Alex Tagliani, Pippa Mann, Alex Lloyd, Paul Tracy, Mark Dismore, Willy T. Ribbs, Wym Eyckmans, Jeff Simmons, Randy Lewis, Johnny Parsons, Howdy Holmes, Jeret Schroeder, Paul Durant, Jimmy Kite, Claude Bourbonnais, Billy Engelhart, Bob Lazier, Wally Dallenbach, Steve Krisiloff.

Winners of the Indianapolis 500

Year	Winner	Team	Engine	Tire	Chassis
1911	Ray Harroun	Nordyle & Marmon Company	Marmon	Firestone	Marmon
1912	Joe Dawson	National Motor Vehicle Company	National	Michelin	National
1913	Jules Goux	Peugeot	Peugeot	Firestone	Peugeot
1914	René Thomas	Louis Delâge Company	Delage	Palmer Cord Tyres	Delage
1915	Ralph DePalma	E.C. Patterson	Mercedes	Goodrich Corporation	Mercedes
1916	Dario Resta	Peugeot Auto Racing Company	Peugeot	Goodrich Corporation	Peugeot
1919	Howdy Wilcox	I.M.S Corporation	Premier	Goodyear	Premier
1920	Gaston Chevrolet	William Small Company	Frontenac	Firestone	Frontenac
1921	Tommy Milton	Louis Chevrolet	Frontenac	Firestone	Frontenac
1922	Jimmy Murphy	Jimmy Murphy	Miller	Firestone	Duesenberg
1923	Tommy Milton	H.C.S. Motor Company	Miller	Firestone	Miller
1924	Lora L. Corum/Joe Boyer	Duesenberg	Duesenberg	Firestone	Duesenberg
1925	Peter DePaolo	Duesenberg	Duesenberg	Firestone	Duesenberg
1926	Frank Lockhart	Peter Kreis	Miller	Firestone	Miller
1927	George Souders	William S. White	Duesenberg	Firestone	Duesenberg
1928	Louis Meyer	Alden Sampson, II	Miller	Firestone	Miller
1929	Ray Keech	M. A. Yagle	Miller	Firestone	Miller
1930	Billy Arnold	Harry Hartz	Miller	Firestone	Summers
1931	Louis Schneider	B. L. Schneider	Miller	Firestone	Stevens
1932	Fred Frame	Harry Hartz	Miller	Firestone	Wetteroth
1933	Louis Meyer	Louis Meyer	Miller	Firestone	Miller
1934	Bill Cummings	H. C. Henning	Miller	Firestone	Miller
1935	Kelly Petillo	Kelly Petillo	Offenhauser	Firestone	Wetteroth
1936	Louis Meyer	Louis Meyer	Miller	Firestone	Stevens
1937	Wilbur Shaw	Wilbur Shaw	Offenhauser	Firestone	Shaw
1938	Floyd Roberts	Lou Moore	Miller	Firestone	Wetteroth

Year	Winner	Team	Engine	Tire	Chassis
1939	Wilbur Shaw	Boyle Racing Headquarters	Maserati	Firestone	Maserati
1940	Wilbur Shaw	Boyle Racing Headquarters	Maserati	Firestone	Maserati
1941	Floyd Davis/Mauri Rose	Lou Moore	Offenhauser	Firestone	Wetteroth
1946	George Robson	Thorne Engineering	Sparks	Firestone	Adams
1947	Mauri Rose	Lou Moore	Offenhauser	Firestone	Deidt
1948	Mauri Rose	Lou Moore	Offenhauser	Firestone	Deidt
1949	Bill Holland	Lou Moore	Offenhauser	Firestone	Deidt
1950	Johnnie Parsons	Kurtis Kraft	Offenhauser	Firestone	Kurtis Kraft
1951	Lee Wallard	Murrell Belanger	Offenhauser	Firestone	Kurtis Kraft
1952	Troy Ruttman	J. C. Agajanian	Offenhauser	Firestone	Kuzma
1953	Bill Vukovich	Howard B. Keck	Offenhauser	Firestone	Kurtis Kraft
1954	Bill Vukovich	Howard B. Keck	Offenhauser	Firestone	Kurtis Kraft
1955	Bob Sweikert	John Zink	Offenhauser	Firestone	Kurtis Kraft
1956	Pat Flaherty	John Zink	Offenhauser	Firestone	Watson
1957	Sam Hanks	George Salih	Offenhauser	Firestone	Salih
1958	Jimmy Bryan	George Salih	Offenhauser	Firestone	Salih
1959	Rodger Ward	Leader Cards	Offenhauser	Firestone	Watson
1960	Jim Rathmann	Ken-Paul	Offenhauser	Firestone	Watson
1961	A.J. Foyt	Bignotti-Bowes Racing	Offenhauser	Firestone	Trevis
1962	Rodger Ward	Leader Cards	Offenhauser	Firestone	Watson
1963	Parnelli Jones	J.C. Agajanian	Offenhauser	Firestone	Watson
1964	A.J. Foyt	Ansted-Thompson Racing	Offenhauser	Firestone	Watson
1965	Jim Clark	Team Lotus	Ford	Firestone	Lotus
1966	Graham Hill	Mecom Racing Team	Ford	Firestone	Lola
1967	A.J. Foyt	Ansted-Thompson Racing	Ford	Goodyear	Coyote
1968	Bobby Unser	Leader Cards	Offenhauser	Goodyear	Eagle

Year	Winner	Team	Engine	Tire	Chassis
1969	Mario Andretti	STP Corporation	Ford	Firestone	Hawk
1970	Al Unser	Vel's Parnelli Jones Ford	Ford	Firestone	Colt
1971	Al Unser	Vel's Parnelli Jones Ford	Ford	Firestone	Colt
1972	Mark Donohue	Roger Penske Enterprises	Offenhauser	Goodyear	McLaren
1973	Gordon Johncock	Patrick Racing Team	Offenhauser	Goodyear	Eagle
1974	Johnny Rutherford	Bruce McLaren Motor Racing	Offenhauser	Goodyear	McLaren
1975	Bobby Unser	All American Racers	Offenhauser	Goodyear	Eagle
1976	Johnny Rutherford	Bruce McLaren Motor Racing	Offenhauser	Goodyear	McLaren
1977	A.J. Foyt	A.J. Foyt Enterprises	Foyt	Goodyear	Coyote
1978	Al Unser	Chaparral Racing	Cosworth	Goodyear	Lola
1979	Rick Mears	Penske Racing	Cosworth	Goodyear	Penske
1980	Johnny Rutherford	Chaparral Racing	Cosworth	Goodyear	Chaparral
1981	Bobby Unser	Penske Racing	Cosworth	Goodyear	Penske
1982	Gordon Johncock	STP Patrick Racing Team	Cosworth	Goodyear	Wildcat
1983	Tom Sneva	Bignotti-Cotter	Cosworth	Goodyear	March
1984	Rick Mears	Penske Cars	Cosworth	Goodyear	March
1985	Danny Sullivan	Penske Cars	Cosworth	Goodyear	March
1986	Bobby Rahal	Truesports	Cosworth	Goodyear	March
1987	Al Unser	Penske Racing, Incorporated	Cosworth	Goodyear	March
1988	Rick Mears	Penske Racing, Incorporated	Chevrolet	Goodyear	Penske
1989	Emerson Fittipaldi	Penske Racing, Incorporated	Chevrolet	Goodyear	Penske
1990	Arie Luyendyk	Doug Shierson Racing	Chevrolet	Goodyear	Lola
1991	Rick Mears	Penske Racing, Incorporated	Chevrolet	Goodyear	Penske
1992	Al Unser, Jr	Galles-Kraco Racing	Chevrolet	Goodyear	Galmer
1993	Emerson Fittipald	Penske Racing, Incorporated	Chevrolet	Goodyear	Penske
1994	Al Unser, Jr	Penske Racing, Incorporated	Mercedes-Benz	Goodyear	Penske

Year	Winner	Team	Engine	Tire	Chassis
1995	Jacques Villeneuve	Team Green	Ford Cosworth	Goodyear	Reynard
1996	Buddy Lazier	Hemelgarn Racing	Ford Cosworth	Firestone	Reynard
1997	Arie Luyendyk	Treadway Racing	Oldsmobile	Firestone	G Force
1998	Eddie Cheever, Jr.	Team Cheever	Oldsmobile	Goodyear	Dallara
1999	Kenny Bräck	A.J. Foyt Enterprises	Oldsmobile	Goodyear	Dallara
2000	Juan Pablo Montoya	Chip Ganassi Racing	Oldsmobile	Firestone	G Force
2001	Hélio Castroneves	Marlboro Team Penske	Oldsmobile	Firestone	Dallara
2002	Hélio Castroneves	Marlboro Team Penske	Chevrolet	Firestone	Dallara
2003	Gil de Ferran[	Marlboro Team Penske	Toyota	Firestone	Panoz G Force
2004	Buddy Rice	Rahal Letterman Racing	Honda	Firestone	Panoz G Force
2005	Dan Wheldon	Andretti Green Racing	Honda	Firestone	Dallara
2006	Sam Hornish, Jr.	Marlboro Team Penske	Honda	Firestone	Dallara
2007	Dario Franchitti	Andretti Green Racing	Honda	Firestone	Dallara
2008	Scott Dixon	Chip Ganassi Racing	Honda	Firestone	Dallara
2009	Hélio Castroneves	Marlboro Team Penske	Honda	Firestone	Dallara
2010	Dario Franchitti	Chip Ganassi Racing	Honda	Firestone	Dallara
2011	Dan Wheldon	Bryan Herta Autosport	Honda	Firestone	Dallara
2012	Dario Franchitti	Chip Ganassi Racing	Honda	Firestone	Dallara
2013	Tony Kanaan	KV Racing Technology	Chevrolet	Firestone	Dallara
2014	Ryan Hunter-Reay	Andretti Autosport	Honda	Firestone	Dallara
2015	Juan Pablo Montoya	Team Penske	Chevrolet	Firestone	Dallara

Indianapolis Motor Speedway Owners

1909-1927: Founder and owner, Carl G. Fisher, alongside his three partners, James Allison, Arthur Newby, and Frank Wheeler, built the IMS in 1909 and maintained joint ownership until 1927.

1927-1945: Eddie Rickenbacker bought the Indianapolis Motor Speedway in 1927 for $750,000. He was the owner until 1945. After World War II the track needed so much maintenance Rickenbacker feared it could never be profitable again.

1945-present day: In 1945 Tony Hulman bought the rundown track for $750,000 under the encouragement of renowned driver, Wilbur Shaw. The Speedway still remains in the Hulman-George family under Hulman & Company as Mari Hulman George acts as chairman.